EMBRACING GRATITUDE

A Year of Seeking One Good Thing Daily

Mike G Farrell

Barefoot Kicker   #15

MICHAEL G FARRELL

Requests for information should be addressed to:
www.barefootkicker.com/contact

For more information go to : www.barefootkicker.com

EMBRACING GRATITUDE

INTRODUCTION

Welcome to "Embracing Gratitude," a daily devotional designed to inspire and encourage you on your journey of cultivating gratitude and finding joy in the simplest aspects of life. Over the next year, we will embark on a transformative adventure together, where each day we will focus on seeking one good thing in our lives. By intentionally shifting our perspective and embracing gratitude, we can experience a profound sense of contentment, discover hidden blessings, and foster a deeper connection with ourselves and the world around us.

These devotionals aim to uplift and inspire you through the discovery of natural and simple things in life, while also connecting each theme to relevant scriptures from the Bible. Remember that joy can be found in the most ordinary aspects of life, and through these devotionals, may you be encouraged to see God's hand at work in every detail. May your heart be filled with gratitude, and may you experience the joy that comes from knowing and following Christ's purpose for your life.

DAY 1

AWARENESS

Scripture: "This is the day the Lord has made; let us rejoice and be glad in it." - Psalm 118:24 (NIV)

Devotional: Today, let us begin our journey of seeking one good thing each day. Take a moment to pause, breathe, and become aware of your surroundings. What do you notice that brings you joy or peace? It could be a gentle breeze, a ray of sunlight, or the sweet sound of birds singing. Open your heart and allow gratitude to fill your soul as you appreciate the beauty that surrounds you. Embrace this awareness and carry it with you throughout your day.

Reflection: In your journal, write down the one good thing you discovered today and reflect on how it made you feel. How can you cultivate this sense of awareness and gratitude in other areas of your life?

Prayer: Dear Lord, thank You for the gift of today. Help me to open my eyes and heart to the goodness that surrounds me. May I cultivate a spirit of gratitude and find joy in the simple pleasures of life. In Jesus' name, I pray. Amen.

DAY 2

RELATIONSHIPS

Scripture: "Two are better than one because they have a good return for their labor." - Ecclesiastes 4:9 (NIV)

Devotional: Today, let us focus on the relationships that bless our lives. Take a moment to appreciate the people who bring joy, love, and support into your journey. It could be a family member, a friend, or a mentor. Reach out to someone today and express your gratitude for their presence in your life. Cherish the connections you have and let the warmth of these relationships fill your heart.

Reflection: In your journal, write down the name of a person you are grateful for and why they are significant to you. How can you nurture and strengthen this relationship? Consider ways you can show your appreciation today.

Prayer: Heavenly Father, thank You for the gift of relationships. I am grateful for the people You have placed in my life. Help me to cherish and nurture these connections. May I be a source of love and support to others as well. In Jesus' name, I pray. Amen.

DAY 3

ABUNDANCE

Scripture: "And God is able to bless you abundantly, so that in all things at all times, having all that you need, you will abound in every good work." - 2 Corinthians 9:8 (NIV)

Devotional: Today, let us focus on the abundance that surrounds us. Take a moment to reflect on the blessings in your life—both big and small. Consider the gifts of love, health, opportunities, and the provision that you have received. Embrace an attitude of gratitude and recognize that you have all that you need to live a fulfilling life. Let gratitude fill your heart as you realize the abundance of blessings bestowed upon you.

Reflection: In your journal, make a list of five things you are grateful for in your life. How can you share your abundance with others? Consider ways you can give back and make a positive impact in the lives of those around you.

Prayer: Gracious God, thank You for the abundance You have showered upon me. Help me to appreciate the blessings in my life and to be a channel of abundance to others. May my gratitude overflow into acts of generosity and kindness. In Jesus' name, I pray. Amen.

DAY 4

SIMPLE PLEASURES

Scripture: "Every good and perfect gift is from above, coming down from the Father of the heavenly lights, who does not change like shifting shadows." - James 1:17 (NIV)

Devotional: Today, let us find joy in the simple pleasures that bring a smile to our faces. Pause for a moment and appreciate the little things that often go unnoticed—a warm cup of coffee, the sound of laughter, a beautiful sunset, or a cozy blanket. Take pleasure in these small moments and let them fill your heart with gratitude. Remember, it's often the simplest joys that have the power to uplift our spirits.

Reflection: In your journal, write down three simple pleasures that brought you joy today. How can you incorporate more of these moments into your daily life? Consider ways to savor the simple pleasures and find gratitude in them.

Prayer: Loving Father, thank You for the gift of simple pleasures. Help me to slow down and appreciate the beauty in the small things. May I find joy and gratitude in the moments that bring a smile to my face. In Jesus' name, I pray. Amen.

DAY 5

STRENGTH IN ADVERSITY

Scripture: "But he said to me, 'My grace is sufficient for you, for my power is made perfect in weakness.' Therefore I will boast all the more gladly about my weaknesses, so that Christ's power may rest on me." - 2 Corinthians 12:9 (NIV)

Devotional: Today, let us focus on finding strength in the face of adversity. Life's challenges may sometimes feel overwhelming, but remember that you are not alone. Reflect on the difficult times you have faced and the lessons you have learned. In moments of struggle, there is an opportunity for growth and resilience. Embrace gratitude for the strength that has carried you through hardships and trust that God's grace will sustain you.

Reflection: In your journal, write about a challenging experience that has shaped you into the person you are today. How can you find gratitude in the lessons learned from adversity? Consider ways you can encourage and support others who are facing difficulties.

Prayer: Dear Lord, thank You for being my source of strength in times of adversity. Help me to find gratitude in the challenges I face and to trust in Your provision. May my experiences be a testimony of Your faithfulness and grace. In Jesus' name, I pray. Amen.

DAY 6

WONDER OF CREATION

Scripture: "The heavens declare the glory of God; the skies proclaim the work of his hands." - Psalm 19:1 (NIV)

Devotional: Today, let us marvel at the wonder of God's creation. Step outside and take a moment to observe the world around you. Look up at the vast sky, notice the intricate details of a flower, or listen to the soothing sounds of nature. As you immerse yourself in the beauty of creation, let gratitude well up within you. Recognize the divine artistry and wisdom displayed in every aspect of the natural world.

Reflection: In your journal, describe a specific element of nature that fills you with wonder. How can you cultivate a deeper connection with nature in your daily life? Consider ways to be a steward of the environment and appreciate God's creation.

Prayer: Creator God, thank You for the breathtaking beauty of Your creation. Help me to be in awe of Your handiwork and to be a responsible caretaker of the earth. May I find solace and inspiration in the wonders of nature. In Jesus' name, I pray. Amen.

DAY 7

ACTS OF KINDNESS

Scripture: "Be kind and compassionate to one another, forgiving each other, just as in Christ God forgave you." - Ephesians 4:32 (NIV)

Devotional: Today, let us focus on acts of kindness and compassion. Take a moment to reflect on the times when someone extended love and grace to you. Now, consider how you can pay it forward and be a source of kindness to others. Whether it's a smile, a helping hand, or a kind word, even the smallest acts of kindness can have a profound impact. Embrace gratitude for the opportunity to make a positive difference in someone's life.

Reflection: In your journal, write about an act of kindness you performed or witnessed today. How did it make you feel? How can you incorporate more acts of kindness into your daily routine?

Prayer: Gracious Lord, thank You for the gift of kindness. Help me to be compassionate and loving towards others, just as You have been towards me. May my actions bring joy and comfort to those around me. In Jesus' name, I pray. Amen.

DAY 8

GRATITUDE FOR GROWTH

Scripture: "But grow in the grace and knowledge of our Lord and Savior Jesus Christ. To him be glory both now and forever! Amen." - 2 Peter 3:18 (NIV)

Devotional: Today, let us reflect on our personal growth and transformation. Consider the challenges you have faced and how they have shaped you into a stronger, wiser individual. Embrace gratitude for the lessons learned along the way and the person you are becoming. Recognize that growth is a continuous process, and each step forward is a reason for gratitude.

Reflection: In your journal, write about an area of personal growth you have experienced recently. How has it positively impacted your life? How can you continue to nurture your growth journey?

Prayer: Heavenly Father, I am grateful for the growth and transformation You have brought into my life. Help me to continue growing in Your grace and knowledge. May I always strive to become the person You have created me to be. In Jesus' name, I pray. Amen.

DAY 9

GRATITUDE FOR FRIENDSHIP

Scripture: "A friend loves at all times, and a brother is born for a time of adversity." - Proverbs 17:17 (NIV)

Devotional: Today, let us focus on the gift of friendship. Take a moment to think about the friends who have walked alongside you through different seasons of life. Appreciate the support, love, and laughter they have brought into your journey. Reach out to a friend today, express your gratitude, and let them know how much they mean to you. Cherish the bonds of friendship and celebrate the joy of companionship.

Reflection: In your journal, write down the names of three friends you are grateful for and the qualities you appreciate in them. How can you nurture and strengthen these friendships? Consider ways to deepen your connection with your friends.

Prayer: Loving God, thank You for the gift of friendship. I am grateful for the friends You have placed in my life. Help me to be a faithful and supportive friend in return. May our friendships bring glory to You. In Jesus' name, I pray. Amen.

DAY 10

FINDING JOY IN CHILDHOOD MEMORIES

Scripture: "He called a little child to him, and placed the child among them. And he said: 'Truly I tell you, unless you change and become like little children, you will never enter the kingdom of heaven.'" - Matthew 18:2-3 (NIV)

Devotional: Today, let's focus on finding joy in childhood memories. Take time to reminisce about the simple pleasures of your childhood, whether it's playing games, exploring nature, or spending time with family. Embrace the innocence and wonder of childhood and allow these memories to bring joy and a sense of nostalgia to your heart.

Reflection: In your journal, write about the childhood memories that bring you joy. How can you incorporate the spirit of childlike wonder and simplicity into your adult life? How can you share these joyful memories with others, especially children in your life? How can embracing childlike faith deepen your connection with God?

Prayer: Heavenly Father, I thank You for the joy found in childhood memories. As I reminisce about the simple pleasures of my youth, help me to embrace the spirit of childlike wonder and innocence. May these memories remind me of the joy found in the simple things and deepen my faith in You. In Jesus' name, I pray. Amen.

DAY 11

GRATITUDE FOR HEALTH

Scripture: "Do you not know that your bodies are temples of the Holy Spirit, who is in you, whom you have received from God? You are not your own; you were bought at a price. Therefore honor God with your bodies." - 1 Corinthians 6:19-20 (NIV)

Devotional: Today, let us focus on the gift of health. Take a moment to appreciate the remarkable abilities of your body and the vitality it provides. Reflect on the times your health has allowed you to experience joy, pursue dreams, and serve others. Embrace gratitude for the well-being of your body and commit to caring for it as a sacred temple. Treasure the blessing of health and make choices that honor and nourish your body.

Reflection: In your journal, write down three aspects of your health that you are grateful for. How can you cultivate a healthier lifestyle and take care of your body? Consider ways to prioritize your well-being and express gratitude for the gift of health.

Prayer: Heavenly Father, I am grateful for the gift of health and the abilities You have given me. Help me to honor You by taking care of my body. Give me the strength and wisdom to make choices that promote well-being and vitality. In Jesus' name, I pray. Amen.

DAY 12

GRATITUDE FOR CONTENTMENT

Scripture: "I have learned to be content whatever the circumstances." - Philippians 4:11 (NIV)

Devotional: Today, let us reflect on the beauty of contentment. Take a moment to appreciate the present moment and find satisfaction in what you have rather than yearning for what you lack. Embrace gratitude for the simple joys and the blessings that surround you right now. Cultivate a heart of contentment and let it bring peace and fulfillment into your life.

Reflection: In your journal, write down three things you are content with in your life. How can you practice contentment in areas where you struggle? Consider ways to cultivate a mindset of gratitude and contentment.

Prayer: Gracious God, teach me the secret of contentment. Help me to appreciate the blessings in my life and find satisfaction in the present moment. May I live with a grateful heart, trusting Your provision and embracing contentment in all circumstances. In Jesus' name, I pray. Amen.

DAY 13

GRATITUDE FOR FREEDOM

Scripture: "So if the Son sets you free, you will be free indeed." - John 8:36 (NIV)

Devotional: Today, let us reflect on the freedom we have in Christ. Consider the liberation from sin, guilt, and shame that comes through His sacrifice. Embrace gratitude for the transformative power of God's love and the freedom we experience in Him. Take a moment to appreciate the liberties we enjoy in our lives and the opportunities they provide. Let gratitude fill your heart as you recognize the immense freedom found in Christ.

Reflection: In your journal, write about a specific area of freedom you have experienced in your life. How has it impacted your journey? How can you use your freedom to bring hope and liberation to others?

Prayer: Heavenly Father, I am grateful for the freedom I have in Christ. Thank You for liberating me from sin and offering me a life of abundant freedom. Help me to live in the fullness of this freedom and to extend it to others. In Jesus' name, I pray. Amen.

DAY 14

GRATITUDE FOR FORGIVNESS

Scripture: "Be kind and compassionate to one another, forgiving each other, just as in Christ God forgave you." - Ephesians 4:32 (NIV)

Devotional: Today, let us focus on the power of forgiveness. Reflect on the times when you have been forgiven and the freedom it brought to your heart. Embrace gratitude for the forgiveness extended to you by God and others. Take a moment to release any lingering resentment or bitterness and choose to forgive those who have wronged you. Let gratitude and forgiveness intertwine, bringing healing and restoration to your relationships.

Reflection: In your journal, write down a situation where you extended forgiveness or received forgiveness. How did it impact you? How can you cultivate a heart of forgiveness in your daily life?

Prayer: Loving Father, thank You for the gift of forgiveness. Help me to extend grace and forgiveness to others, just as You have forgiven me. May forgiveness bring healing and reconciliation to my relationships. In Jesus' name, I pray. Amen.

Day 15

GRATITUDE FOR CREATIVITY

Scripture: "So God created mankind in his own image, in the image of God he created them; male and female he created them." - Genesis 1:27 (NIV)

Devotional: Today, let us reflect on the gift of creativity. Consider the ways in which you express your creativity, whether through art, music, writing, or other forms. Embrace gratitude for the ability to imagine, innovate, and bring beauty into the world. Take a moment to engage in a creative activity, allowing your heart to overflow with gratitude for the gift of creativity.

Reflection: In your journal, write about a creative pursuit or project that brings you joy. How can you further nurture and develop your creative gifts? Consider ways to incorporate creativity into your daily life.

Prayer: Creator God, I am grateful for the gift of creativity. Thank You for imparting Your creative spirit within me. Help me to use my creative gifts to bring beauty, inspiration, and joy to others. May my creativity be a reflection of Your goodness and glory. In Jesus' name, I pray. Amen.

DAY 16

GRATITUDE FOR REST

Scripture: "Come to me, all you who are weary and burdened, and I will give you rest." - Matthew 11:28 (NIV)

Devotional: Today, let us focus on the gift of rest. In our busy lives, it is essential to take intentional moments to pause, rejuvenate, and find rest for our souls. Embrace gratitude for the restful moments you have experienced and the peace that comes from being still. Take time today to rest, whether through a nap, reading a book, or simply being in nature. Let gratitude for rest and rejuvenation fill your heart.

Reflection: In your journal, write about a specific restful experience you have had recently. How did it refresh and rejuvenate you? How can you prioritize rest in your daily life?

Prayer: Heavenly Father, I am grateful for the gift of rest. Thank You for inviting me to find rest in Your presence. Help me to prioritize rest and rejuvenation in my life, that I may be refreshed and ready to fulfill Your purposes. In Jesus' name, I pray. Amen.

DAY 17

GRATITUDE FOR LAUGHTER

Scripture: "A cheerful heart is good medicine, but a crushed spirit dries up the bones." - Proverbs 17:22 (NIV)

Devotional: Today, let us reflect on the joy of laughter. Laughter has the power to uplift our spirits, bring healing, and strengthen our relationships. Embrace gratitude for the moments of laughter you have experienced and the joy it brings to your life. Take time today to engage in activities that bring laughter—watch a comedy, share funny stories with a friend, or simply find reasons to laugh. Let gratitude for the gift of laughter fill your heart.

Reflection: In your journal, write down a recent moment that made you laugh. How did it impact your mood and well-being? How can you cultivate more laughter in your daily life?

Prayer: Loving God, thank You for the gift of laughter. I am grateful for the joy it brings and the bonds it strengthens. Help me to embrace laughter, to find reasons to smile, and to spread laughter to those around me. In Jesus' name, I pray. Amen.

DAY 18

GRATITUDE FOR OPPORTUNITIES

Scripture: "And whatever you do, whether in word or deed, do it all in the name of the Lord Jesus, giving thanks to God the Father through him." - Colossians 3:17 (NIV)

Devotional: Today, let us focus on the abundance of opportunities that come our way. Embrace gratitude for the doors that open, the chances to learn and grow, and the possibilities that lie ahead. Reflect on the opportunities you have been given and the ways in which they have shaped your life. Take a moment to appreciate the diverse paths available to you and commit to making the most of each opportunity.

Reflection: In your journal, write down three opportunities you are grateful for in your life. How can you embrace and maximize these opportunities? Consider ways to pursue new avenues and step out of your comfort zone.

Prayer: Gracious Father, I am grateful for the opportunities You have placed in my life. Help me to recognize and seize these opportunities, using them to glorify You and bless others. Guide me as I navigate the paths before me. In Jesus' name, I pray. Amen.

Day 19

Gratitude for Simplicity

Scripture: "But godliness with contentment is great gain." - 1 Timothy 6:6 (NIV)

Devotional: Today, let us reflect on the beauty of simplicity. In a world filled with complexity and constant busyness, simplicity provides a respite for our souls. Embrace gratitude for the simple pleasures, the moments of stillness, and the unhurried pace of life. Reflect on the times when simplicity has brought you peace, clarity, and a sense of contentment. Let gratitude for the gift of simplicity fill your heart.

Reflection: In your journal, write about a specific way in which simplicity has brought you joy or contentment. How can you incorporate more simplicity into your daily life? Consider ways to declutter your schedule and embrace the beauty of simplicity.

Prayer: Heavenly Father, I am grateful for the gift of simplicity. Help me to appreciate the beauty in the uncomplicated moments of life. May simplicity bring peace, contentment, and a renewed focus on what truly matters. In Jesus' name, I pray. Amen.

DAY 20

GRATITUDE FOR GUIDANCE

Scripture: "Trust in the LORD with all your heart and lean not on your own understanding; in all your ways submit to him, and he will make your paths straight." - Proverbs 3:5-6 (NIV)

Devotional: Today, let us focus on gratitude for the guidance we receive from God. Reflect on the times when He has provided wisdom, direction, and discernment in your life. Embrace gratitude for the ways in which He leads you along the right path. Take a moment to seek His guidance in a specific area of your life and trust that He will provide the clarity and direction you need.

Reflection: In your journal, write about a recent experience where you felt guided by God. How did His guidance impact your decisions and outcomes? How can you cultivate a greater reliance on His guidance in your daily life?

Prayer: Gracious God, I am grateful for Your guidance in my life. Thank You for leading me on the right path and providing wisdom when I need it. Help me to trust in Your guidance and to seek Your will in all I do. In Jesus' name, I pray. Amen.

DAY 21

GRATITUDE FOR NEW BEGINNINGS

Scripture: "Therefore, if anyone is in Christ, the new creation has come: The old has gone, the new is here!" - 2 Corinthians 5:17 (NIV)

Devotional: Today, let us reflect on the gift of new beginnings. Embrace gratitude for the fresh starts, the second chances, and the opportunities to begin anew. Reflect on the times when God has brought restoration and renewal into your life. Take a moment to let go of past mistakes or regrets and embrace the hope and possibility of new beginnings. Let gratitude for the gift of a fresh start fill your heart.

Reflection: In your journal, write about an area of your life where you are seeking a new beginning. How can you embrace the opportunities for growth and transformation? Consider ways to release the past and step into a brighter future.

Prayer: Loving Father, I am grateful for the gift of new beginnings. Thank You for the opportunities to grow, change, and start afresh. Guide me as I embark on new journeys and help me to surrender the past to Your grace. In Jesus' name, I pray. Amen.

DAY 22

GRATITUDE FOR GUIDANCE

Scripture: "Your word is a lamp for my feet, a light on my path." - Psalm 119:105 (NIV)

Devotional: Today, let us focus on gratitude for the guidance we receive from God's Word. Reflect on the times when His Word has provided wisdom, comfort, and direction in your life. Embrace gratitude for the light it sheds on your path. Take a moment to read a scripture passage and meditate on its meaning for your life. Let gratitude for the gift of divine guidance through His Word fill your heart.

Reflection: In your journal, write down a scripture verse that has been particularly meaningful to you recently. How has it impacted your perspective or decisions? How can you incorporate more regular scripture reading and reflection into your daily life?

Prayer: Heavenly Father, I am grateful for the guidance Your Word provides. Thank You for the wisdom and encouragement found within its pages. Help me to seek guidance from Your Word and to apply its teachings to my life. In Jesus' name, I pray. Amen.

DAY 23

GRATITUDE FOR STRENGTH

Scripture: "I can do all this through him who gives me strength." - Philippians 4:13 (NIV)

Devotional: Today, let us reflect on gratitude for the strength that God provides. Reflect on the times when His strength has sustained you through challenges and empowered you to overcome obstacles. Embrace gratitude for the inner resilience and courage that comes from Him. Take a moment to pray and ask for His strength to fill you today, enabling you to face whatever lies ahead. Let gratitude for His unwavering strength in your life fill your heart.

Reflection: In your journal, write down a recent experience where you felt God's strength carrying you through a difficult situation. How did His strength impact your response and outcome? How can you lean on His strength in your daily life?

Prayer: Mighty God, I am grateful for the strength You provide. Thank You for empowering me to face challenges and for carrying me through difficult times. Fill me with Your strength today and help me to rely on You in all circumstances. In Jesus' name, I pray. Amen.

Day 24

Gratitude for Provision

Scripture: "And my God will meet all your needs according to the riches of his glory in Christ Jesus." - Philippians 4:19 (NIV)

Devotional: Today, let us focus on gratitude for God's provision in our lives. Reflect on the times when He has provided for your needs, both big and small. Embrace gratitude for His faithfulness and trustworthiness in meeting your needs. Take a moment to recount His provisions and offer a prayer of thanksgiving for His abundant care. Let gratitude for His provision fill your heart.

Reflection: In your journal, write down three ways in which God has provided for you recently. How have His provisions impacted your life? How can you cultivate a deeper trust in His provision?

Prayer: Loving Father, I am grateful for Your provision in my life. Thank You for meeting my needs and for Your faithfulness. Help me to trust in Your provision and to be a faithful steward of the resources You have given me. In Jesus' name, I pray. Amen.

DAY 25

GRATITUDE FOR SILENCE

Scripture: "Be still, and know that I am God; I will be exalted among the nations, I will be exalted in the earth." - Psalm 46:10 (NIV)

Devotional: Today, let us reflect on the gift of silence. In the midst of a noisy and busy world, silence provides an opportunity for stillness, reflection, and connection with God. Embrace gratitude for the moments of quietness in your life, where you can listen to His voice and experience His presence. Take a moment to find a peaceful place, close your eyes, and engage in silent prayer. Let gratitude for the gift of silence fill your heart.

Reflection: In your journal, write about a recent experience where you found solace and connection with God in moments of silence. How did it impact your spiritual journey? How can you incorporate more intentional periods of silence into your daily life?

Prayer: Heavenly Father, I am grateful for the gift of silence. Thank You for the stillness that allows me to hear Your voice and experience Your presence. Help me to create moments of silence in my daily life, where I can connect with You on a deeper level. In Jesus' name, I pray. Amen.

DAY 26

GRATITUDE FOR GOD'S HOLINESS

Scripture: "Exalt the LORD our God and worship at his holy mountain, for the LORD our God is holy." - Psalm 99:9 (NIV)

Devotional: Today, let us reflect on gratitude for God's holiness. Embrace gratitude for His absolute purity and moral perfection. Reflect on the times when His holiness has inspired awe and reverence within you. Take a moment to pray and worship Him for His holiness, acknowledging His greatness and uniqueness. Let gratitude for the gift of His holiness fill your heart.

Reflection: In your journal, write about a specific moment where you experienced the majesty of God's holiness. How did it deepen your worship and surrender? How can you cultivate a greater reverence for His holiness in your daily life?

Prayer: Holy God, I am grateful for Your perfect holiness. Thank You for Your purity and moral perfection. Help me to worship and adore You with reverence, acknowledging Your greatness and uniqueness. In Jesus' name, I pray. Amen.

DAY 27

GRATITUDE FOR NATURE

Scripture: "The heavens declare the glory of God; the skies proclaim the work of his hands." - Psalm 19:1 (NIV)

Devotional: Today, let us reflect on the beauty of nature and embrace gratitude for God's creation. Take a moment to observe the wonders of the natural world around you—the vibrant colors of flowers, the majesty of mountains, the soothing sounds of a flowing river. Embrace gratitude for the gift of nature and the opportunity to experience its beauty. Reflect on the ways in which nature points to the Creator and offers a glimpse of His glory. Let gratitude for the wonders of nature fill your heart.

Reflection: In your journal, write about a specific element of nature that fills you with awe and appreciation. How can you cultivate a deeper connection with nature in your daily life? Consider ways to be a responsible steward of the environment and to spend more time outdoors.

Prayer: Creator God, I am grateful for the breathtaking beauty of Your creation. Thank You for the wonders of nature that reflect Your glory. Help me to appreciate and care for the environment, and to find peace and inspiration in the natural world. In Jesus' name, I pray. Amen.

Day 28

Gratitude for Peace

Scripture: "Peace I leave with you; my peace I give you. I do not give to you as the world gives. Do not let your hearts be troubled and do not be afraid." - John 14:27 (NIV)

Devotional: Today, let us focus on gratitude for the gift of peace. Reflect on the times when God's peace has enveloped your heart, calming fears and anxieties. Embrace gratitude for the inner tranquility that comes from knowing His presence. Take a moment to pause, breathe deeply, and invite His peace to fill you today. Let gratitude for the gift of His peace fill your heart.

Reflection: In your journal, write about a recent experience where you felt a deep sense of peace from God. How did it impact your perspective or actions? How can you cultivate an atmosphere of peace in your daily life?

Prayer: Prince of Peace, I am grateful for the gift of Your peace. Thank You for calming my fears and anxieties, and for offering me a deep sense of tranquility. Help me to rely on Your peace in all circumstances and to be an instrument of peace in the world. In Jesus' name, I pray. Amen.

DAY 29

GRATITUDE FOR PURPOSE

Scripture: "For we are God's handiwork, created in Christ Jesus to do good works, which God prepared in advance for us to do." - Ephesians 2:10 (NIV)

Devotional: Today, let us reflect on gratitude for the purpose God has given us. Embrace gratitude for the unique gifts, talents, and passions He has placed within you. Reflect on the opportunities to make a positive difference in the world and to contribute to His kingdom. Take a moment to pray and seek His guidance in aligning your life with His purpose. Let gratitude for the gift of purpose fill your heart.

Reflection: In your journal, write down the ways in which you feel called to fulfill God's purpose in your life. How can you align your actions and decisions with His plan? Consider ways to make a meaningful impact in the lives of others.

Prayer: Heavenly Father, I am grateful for the purpose You have given me. Thank You for the unique gifts and talents You have entrusted to me. Guide me as I seek to fulfill Your purpose in my life. May my actions and decisions bring glory to Your name and bless others. In Jesus' name, I pray. Amen.

DAY 30

GRATITUDE FOR LOVE

Scripture: "And now these three remain: faith, hope and love. But the greatest of these is love." - 1 Corinthians 13:13 (NIV)

Devotional: Today, let us focus on gratitude for the greatest gift of all—love. Reflect on the depth of God's love for you and the love He calls you to share with others. Embrace gratitude for the love that fills your heart and sustains your relationships. Take a moment to express your love to those around you, whether through kind words, acts of service, or simply being present. Let gratitude for the gift of love fill your heart.

Reflection: In your journal, write down the ways in which you have experienced and witnessed love recently. How has love impacted your life? How can you cultivate a greater love for others?

Prayer: Loving God, I am grateful for the gift of love. Thank You for pouring out Your love upon me and teaching me how to love others. Help me to be a vessel of Your love, spreading kindness, compassion, and grace. May love be the guiding force in my life. In Jesus' name, I pray. Amen.

DAY 31

GRATITUDE FOR TRANSFORMATION

Scripture: "Therefore, if anyone is in Christ, the new creation has come: The old has gone, the new is here!" - 2 Corinthians 5:17 (NIV)

Devotional: Today, let us reflect on gratitude for the transformative power of God's love. Reflect on the ways in which He has brought about transformation in your life—redeeming brokenness, healing wounds, and renewing your spirit. Embrace gratitude for the newness and wholeness found in Him. Take a moment to pray and surrender any areas of your life that need transformation, trusting that He is faithful to complete the work He has begun in you. Let gratitude for the gift of transformation fill your heart.

Reflection: In your journal, write about a specific area of your life where you have experienced transformation through God's love. How has it impacted your journey? How can you continue to surrender to His transformative power?

Prayer: Gracious Father, I am grateful for the transformative power of Your love. Thank You for making me a new creation in Christ. Continue to transform my heart, mind, and life according to Your perfect plan. May Your love be evident in all that I say and do. In Jesus' name, I pray. Amen.

DAY 32

GRATITUDE FOR WISDOM

Scripture: "For the LORD gives wisdom; from his mouth come knowledge and understanding." - Proverbs 2:6 (NIV)

Devotional: Today, let us focus on gratitude for the wisdom that comes from God. Reflect on the times when He has provided insight, discernment, and guidance in your life. Embrace gratitude for His infinite wisdom and His willingness to bestow it upon you. Take a moment to seek His wisdom in a specific area of your life, praying for clarity and understanding. Let gratitude for the gift of wisdom fill your heart.

Reflection: In your journal, write about a recent experience where you felt God's wisdom leading you. How did it impact your decisions and outcomes? How can you continue to seek His wisdom in your daily life?

Prayer: Wise God, I am grateful for the wisdom You provide. Thank You for guiding me and bestowing Your understanding upon me. Help me to seek Your wisdom in all areas of my life, trusting Your guidance above all else. In Jesus' name, I pray. Amen.

DAY 33

GRATITUDE FOR COMPASSION

Scripture: "Finally, all of you, be like-minded, be sympathetic, love one another, be compassionate and humble." - 1 Peter 3:8 (NIV)

Devotional: Today, let us reflect on gratitude for the gift of compassion. Embrace gratitude for the times when others have shown compassion to you, offering understanding, empathy, and support. Reflect on the ways in which you can extend compassion to those around you, seeking to alleviate their burdens and share in their joys. Take a moment to pray and ask God to deepen your capacity for compassion. Let gratitude for the gift of compassion fill your heart.

Reflection: In your journal, write down a recent experience where someone showed you compassion. How did it impact you? How can you cultivate a heart of compassion in your daily life?

Prayer: Compassionate God, I am grateful for the gift of compassion. Thank You for the times when others have shown me kindness and understanding. Help me to extend compassion to those around me, reflecting Your love and grace. May my actions bring comfort and healing to others. In Jesus' name, I pray. Amen.

DAY 34

GRATITUDE FOR STRENGTH IN WEAKNESS

Scripture: "But he said to me, 'My grace is sufficient for you, for my power is made perfect in weakness.' Therefore I will boast all the more gladly about my weaknesses, so that Christ's power may rest on me." - 2 Corinthians 12:9 (NIV)

Devotional: Today, let us focus on gratitude for the strength that God provides in our weaknesses. Reflect on the times when you have felt inadequate or overwhelmed, and how God's strength sustained you. Embrace gratitude for His grace that empowers you to persevere and overcome. Take a moment to surrender your weaknesses to Him, acknowledging your need for His strength. Let gratitude for the gift of strength in weakness fill your heart.

Reflection: In your journal, write about a specific area of weakness where you have experienced God's strength. How did His strength impact your journey? How can you lean on His strength in your daily life?

Prayer: Mighty God, I am grateful for the strength You provide in my weaknesses. Thank You for empowering me to face challenges and for carrying me through difficult times. Fill me with Your strength today and help me to rely on You in all circumstances. In Jesus' name, I pray. Amen.

DAY 35

GRATITUDE FOR GRACE

Scripture: "For it is by grace you have been saved, through faith—and this is not from yourselves, it is the gift of God." - Ephesians 2:8 (NIV)

Devotional: Today, let us reflect on gratitude for the gift of grace. Reflect on the unmerited favor and forgiveness that God offers through His grace. Embrace gratitude for His love that knows no bounds and His mercy that is new every morning. Take a moment to offer a prayer of thanksgiving for the grace that has saved you and transformed your life. Let gratitude for the gift of grace fill your heart.

Reflection: In your journal, write down a recent experience where you witnessed God's grace in your life. How did it impact your perspective or actions? How can you extend His grace to others?

Prayer: Gracious God, I am grateful for the gift of Your grace. Thank You for your unending love, forgiveness, and mercy. Help me to embrace and extend Your grace to others, reflecting Your character in all I do. In Jesus' name, I pray. Amen.

DAY 36

GRATITUDE FOR PATIENCE

Scripture: "But if we hope for what we do not yet have, we wait for it patiently." - Romans 8:25 (NIV)

Devotional: Today, let us focus on gratitude for the virtue of patience. Reflect on the times when God has called you to wait and trust in His timing. Embrace gratitude for the lessons learned in seasons of waiting and the growth that comes from practicing patience. Take a moment to surrender any areas of impatience or frustration to God, asking Him to cultivate patience in your heart. Let gratitude for the gift of patience fill your heart.

Reflection: In your journal, write about a specific situation where you have experienced God's faithfulness and provision through practicing patience. How did it strengthen your faith? How can you cultivate a patient spirit in your daily life?

Prayer: Patient God, I am grateful for the virtue of patience. Thank You for the lessons learned in waiting and for Your faithfulness during seasons of delay. Help me to trust in Your perfect timing and to practice patience in all areas of my life. In Jesus' name, I pray. Amen.

DAY 37

GRATITUDE FOR DIVERSITY

Scripture: "After this I looked, and there before me was a great multitude that no one could count, from every nation, tribe, people and language, standing before the throne and before the Lamb." - Revelation 7:9 (NIV)

Devotional: Today, let us reflect on gratitude for the beauty of diversity. Embrace gratitude for the rich tapestry of cultures, backgrounds, and perspectives that exist in our world. Reflect on the ways in which diversity enriches our lives and brings us closer to understanding the vastness of God's creation. Take a moment to appreciate the uniqueness of each individual you encounter, celebrating the diversity that unites us. Let gratitude for the gift of diversity fill your heart.

Reflection: In your journal, write down three aspects of diversity that you appreciate and find value in. How can you actively embrace and promote diversity in your daily life? Consider ways to build bridges of understanding and inclusivity.

Prayer: Creator God, I am grateful for the gift of diversity. Thank You for the richness that comes from the various cultures, backgrounds, and perspectives in our world. Help me to appreciate and celebrate diversity, treating every individual with respect and love. In Jesus' name, I pray. Amen.

DAY 38

GRATITUDE FOR SOLITUDE

Scripture: "But Jesus often withdrew to lonely places and prayed." - Luke 5:16 (NIV)

Devotional: Today, let us focus on gratitude for the gift of solitude. Reflect on the times when Jesus Himself sought solace and communion with God in quiet places. Embrace gratitude for the moments of stillness and reflection that solitude offers. Take a moment to find a peaceful spot, disconnect from distractions, and engage in prayer or meditation. Let gratitude for the gift of solitude fill your heart.

Reflection: In your journal, write about a recent experience where you found solace and connection with God in moments of solitude. How did it refresh and rejuvenate you? How can you incorporate more intentional periods of solitude into your daily life?

Prayer: Heavenly Father, I am grateful for the gift of solitude. Thank You for the stillness that allows me to hear Your voice and experience Your presence. Help me to create moments of solitude in my daily life, where I can connect with You on a deeper level. In Jesus' name, I pray. Amen.

DAY 39

GRATITUDE FOR OPPORTUNITIES TO SERVE

Scripture: "For even the Son of Man did not come to be served, but to serve, and to give his life as a ransom for many." - Mark 10:45 (NIV)

Devotional: Today, let us reflect on gratitude for the opportunities to serve others. Embrace gratitude for the privilege of making a difference in someone's life and the joy that comes from selflessly giving. Reflect on the times when you have experienced the transformative power of service, both for the recipient and for yourself. Take a moment to pray and ask God to open your eyes to the needs around you and to guide you in acts of service. Let gratitude for the gift of serving fill your heart.

Reflection: In your journal, write down three ways in which you can serve others in your community or circle of influence. How can you cultivate a servant's heart and make a positive impact on those around you? Consider tangible ways to extend kindness and support.

Prayer: Loving God, I am grateful for the opportunities to serve others. Thank You for the joy and fulfillment that comes from selflessly giving. Open my eyes to the needs around me, and guide me in acts of service that reflect Your love and grace. In Jesus' name, I pray. Amen.

Day 40

Gratitude for Miracles

Scripture: "Jesus looked at them and said, 'With man this is impossible, but with God all things are possible.'" - Matthew 19:26 (NIV)

Devotional: Today, let us focus on gratitude for the miracles that God performs in our lives. Reflect on the times when you have witnessed His power, provision, and intervention in impossible situations. Embrace gratitude for the wonders and signs that point to His faithfulness and sovereignty. Take a moment to recall a specific miracle that has impacted you, and offer a prayer of thanksgiving for His supernatural work. Let gratitude for the gift of miracles fill your heart.

Reflection: In your journal, write about a specific miracle that you have experienced or witnessed. How did it deepen your faith? How can you cultivate a greater expectation for God's miraculous work in your daily life?

Prayer: Mighty God, I am grateful for the miracles You perform in my life. Thank You for displaying Your power, provision, and faithfulness. Help me to trust in Your ability to do the impossible, and to anticipate Your miraculous work with faith and expectancy. In Jesus' name, I pray. Amen.

DAY 41

GRATITUDE FOR CONTENTMENT

Scripture: "I know what it is to be in need, and I know what it is to have plenty. I have learned the secret of being content in any and every situation, whether well fed or hungry, whether living in plenty or in want." - Philippians 4:12 (NIV)

Devotional: Today, let us reflect on gratitude for the virtue of contentment. Embrace gratitude for the ability to find satisfaction and peace regardless of external circumstances. Reflect on the times when God has taught you the valuable lesson of contentment and provided for your needs. Take a moment to pray and ask Him to cultivate a spirit of contentment within you, freeing you from the pursuit of worldly desires. Let gratitude for the gift of contentment fill your heart.

Reflection: In your journal, write about a recent experience where you found contentment despite challenging circumstances. How did it change your perspective? How can you cultivate a spirit of contentment in your daily life?

Prayer: Gracious God, I am grateful for the virtue of contentment. Thank You for teaching me the importance of finding satisfaction in You alone. Help me to release the grip of worldly desires and to embrace contentment in all circumstances. In Jesus' name, I pray. Amen.

DAY 42

GRATITUDE FOR THE HOLY SPIRIT

Scripture: "But the Advocate, the Holy Spirit, whom the Father will send in my name, will teach you all things and will remind you of everything I have said to you." - John 14:26 (NIV)

Devotional: Today, let us focus on gratitude for the presence and work of the Holy Spirit in our lives. Reflect on the times when the Spirit has guided, comforted, and empowered you. Embrace gratitude for His role as your Advocate, Teacher, and Helper. Take a moment to invite the Holy Spirit to fill you afresh, asking Him to empower you for the day ahead. Let gratitude for the gift of the Holy Spirit fill your heart.

Reflection: In your journal, write about a recent experience where you felt the guidance or comfort of the Holy Spirit. How did it impact your journey? How can you cultivate a greater sensitivity to His leading in your daily life?

Prayer: Heavenly Father, I am grateful for the presence of the Holy Spirit in my life. Thank You for His guidance, comfort, and empowerment. Fill me afresh with the Holy Spirit today, that I may walk in step with His leading and be empowered to fulfill Your purposes. In Jesus' name, I pray. Amen.

DAY 43

GRATITUDE FOR REDEMPTION

Scripture: "In him we have redemption through his blood, the forgiveness of sins, in accordance with the riches of God's grace." - Ephesians 1:7 (NIV)

Devotional: Today, let us reflect on gratitude for the gift of redemption through Jesus Christ. Embrace gratitude for the forgiveness of sins and the restoration of relationship with God. Reflect on the times when His grace has transformed your life and set you free from the bondage of sin. Take a moment to offer a prayer of thanksgiving for the redemptive work of Jesus on the cross. Let gratitude for the gift of redemption fill your heart.

Reflection: In your journal, write down a specific area of your life where you have experienced God's redemptive power. How has it impacted your spiritual journey? How can you live in light of His redemption?

Prayer: Gracious God, I am grateful for the gift of redemption through Jesus Christ. Thank You for the forgiveness of sins and the restoration of relationship with You. Help me to live in the freedom of Your grace, embracing the new life I have in Christ. In Jesus' name, I pray. Amen.

DAY 44

GRATITUDE FOR THE GIFT OF SALVATION

Scripture: "For God so loved the world that he gave his one and only Son, that whoever believes in him shall not perish but have eternal life." - John 3:16 (NIV)

Devotional: Today, let us focus on gratitude for the gift of salvation through Jesus Christ. Reflect on the immense love of God, who sent His Son to redeem us and offer eternal life. Embrace gratitude for the assurance of salvation and the hope we have in Christ. Take a moment to express your gratitude to God for the gift of salvation and the transformation it brings to your life. Let gratitude for the gift of salvation fill your heart.

Reflection: In your journal, write about a specific moment when you experienced the reality of salvation in your life. How has it shaped your perspective and choices? How can you share the gift of salvation with others?

Prayer: Loving Father, I am grateful for the gift of salvation through Jesus Christ. Thank You for the sacrifice of Your Son and the hope we have in Him. Help me to live out my salvation daily, sharing Your love and grace with others. In Jesus' name, I pray. Amen.

DAY 45

GRATITUDE FOR THE FAMILY OF GOD

Scripture: "So in Christ we, though many, form one body, and each member belongs to all the others." - Romans 12:5 (NIV)

Devotional: Today, let us reflect on gratitude for the family of God. Embrace gratitude for the community of believers that supports, encourages, and uplifts one another. Reflect on the times when you have experienced the love and fellowship of the family of God. Take a moment to pray for your brothers and sisters in Christ, expressing gratitude for their presence in your life. Let gratitude for the gift of the family of God fill your heart.

Reflection: In your journal, write down the names of three individuals in your church or spiritual community who have made a positive impact on your life. How can you cultivate deeper connections and support one another? Consider ways to actively contribute to the family of God.

Prayer: Heavenly Father, I am grateful for the family of God. Thank You for the community of believers that surrounds and supports me. Help me to cultivate deep and meaningful relationships within the family of God, serving and loving one another as You have commanded. In Jesus' name, I pray. Amen.

DAY 46

GRATITUDE FOR GOD'S UNCHANGING NATURE

Scripture: "Jesus Christ is the same yesterday and today and forever." - Hebrews 13:8 (NIV)

Devotional: Today, let us focus on gratitude for God's unchanging nature. Embrace gratitude for His constancy and faithfulness in every season. Reflect on the times when His unchanging nature has brought stability and assurance to your life. Take a moment to pray and thank God for His unwavering character, which you can always rely on. Let gratitude for the gift of His unchanging nature fill your heart.

Reflection: In your journal, write down three attributes of God's character that remain constant in your life. How does His unchanging nature bring you security and peace? How can you reflect His constancy in your relationships and commitments?

Prayer: Faithful God, I am grateful for Your unchanging nature. Thank You for being constant and reliable in every season. Help me to trust in Your faithfulness and to reflect Your constancy in my relationships and commitments. In Jesus' name, I pray. Amen.

DAY 47

GRATITUDE FOR GOD'S REDEMPTION

Scripture: "In him we have redemption through his blood, the forgiveness of sins, in accordance with the riches of God's grace." - Ephesians 1:7 (NIV)

Devotional: Today, let us reflect on gratitude for God's redemption. Embrace gratitude for the salvation and forgiveness of sins that comes through Jesus Christ. Reflect on the times when His redemption has brought new life and restored your relationship with Him. Take a moment to offer a prayer of thanksgiving for His redemptive work and to live in the freedom He has given you. Let gratitude for the gift of His redemption fill your heart.

Reflection: In your journal, write about a specific experience where you witnessed God's redemption in your life. How did it transform your identity and purpose? How can you embrace and share His redemptive love with others?

Prayer: Redeeming God, I am grateful for Your work of redemption in my life. Thank You for the forgiveness of sins and the new life I have in Christ. Help me to walk in the freedom of Your redemption and to share Your redemptive love with others. In Jesus' name, I pray. Amen.

DAY 48

GRATITUDE FOR GOD'S SOVEREIGNTY

Scripture: "I know that you can do all things; no purpose of yours can be thwarted." - Job 42:2 (NIV)

Devotional: Today, let us focus on gratitude for God's sovereignty. Embrace gratitude for His absolute rule and authority over all things. Reflect on the times when His sovereignty has brought comfort and assurance in the midst of uncertainty. Take a moment to pray and acknowledge His sovereignty in your life, surrendering your plans and desires to His perfect will. Let gratitude for the gift of His sovereignty fill your heart.

Reflection: In your journal, write about a specific moment where you experienced the reality of God's sovereignty. How did it bring you peace and trust? How can you submit to His sovereignty in your current circumstances?

Prayer: Sovereign God, I am grateful for Your absolute rule and authority. Thank You for being in control of all things. Help me to trust in Your sovereignty and to surrender my plans and desires to Your perfect will. In Jesus' name, I pray. Amen.

DAY 49

GRATITUDE FOR FORGIVENESS

Scripture: "If we confess our sins, he is faithful and just and will forgive us our sins and purify us from all unrighteousness." - 1 John 1:9 (NIV)

Devotional: Today, let us reflect on gratitude for the gift of forgiveness. Embrace gratitude for the mercy and grace of God, who offers forgiveness for our sins through Jesus Christ. Reflect on the times when His forgiveness has brought healing and restoration to your life. Take a moment to confess any sins or mistakes to God, knowing that He is faithful to forgive. Let gratitude for the gift of forgiveness fill your heart.

Reflection: In your journal, write about a specific moment when you experienced God's forgiveness and the freedom it brought. How has His forgiveness impacted your relationship with Him and others? How can you extend forgiveness to those who have wronged you?

Prayer: Gracious God, I am grateful for the gift of forgiveness through Jesus Christ. Thank You for Your mercy and grace that washes away my sins. Help me to forgive others as You have forgiven me and to walk in the freedom of Your forgiveness. In Jesus' name, I pray. Amen.

DAY 50

GRATITUDE FOR HOPE

Scripture: "May the God of hope fill you with all joy and peace as you trust in him, so that you may overflow with hope by the power of the Holy Spirit." - Romans 15:13 (NIV)

Devotional: Today, let us focus on gratitude for the gift of hope. Reflect on the confident expectation and assurance we have in God's promises. Embrace gratitude for the hope that anchors our souls and sustains us through trials. Take a moment to pray and ask God to fill you with His hope, allowing it to overflow into every aspect of your life. Let gratitude for the gift of hope fill your heart.

Reflection: In your journal, write down a specific promise or hope from God's Word that you are holding onto. How does it bring you comfort and confidence? How can you share the hope of Christ with others?

Prayer: Faithful God, I am grateful for the gift of hope that You provide. Thank You for the assurance and confidence I have in Your promises. Fill me with Your hope today, that I may overflow with joy, peace, and a steadfast spirit. In Jesus' name, I pray. Amen.

DAY 51

GRATITUDE FOR GRACE IN DIFFICULTIES

Scripture: "But he said to me, 'My grace is sufficient for you, for my power is made perfect in weakness.' Therefore I will boast all the more gladly about my weaknesses, so that Christ's power may rest on me." - 2 Corinthians 12:9 (NIV)

Devotional: Today, let us reflect on gratitude for the grace of God that sustains us in difficult times. Embrace gratitude for His sufficient grace that carries us through weakness and trials. Reflect on the times when His grace has been evident in your life, providing comfort, strength, and perseverance. Take a moment to offer a prayer of thanksgiving for His grace that is always available to you. Let gratitude for the gift of grace in difficulties fill your heart.

Reflection: In your journal, write about a specific experience where you witnessed God's grace carrying you through a challenging season. How did it strengthen your faith? How can you rely on His grace in your current circumstances?

Prayer: Gracious God, I am grateful for Your grace that sustains me in difficult times. Thank You for Your strength, comfort, and provision. Help me to trust in Your sufficient grace and to lean on You in every circumstance. In Jesus' name, I pray. Amen.

DAY 52

GRATITUDE FOR GOD'S UNFAILING LOVE

Scripture: "Give thanks to the LORD, for he is good; his love endures forever." - 1 Chronicles 16:34 (NIV)

Devotional: Today, let us focus on gratitude for the unfailing love of God. Reflect on the depth and constancy of His love, which never wavers or diminishes. Embrace gratitude for His relentless pursuit of your heart and His faithfulness in every season. Take a moment to offer a prayer of thanksgiving for God's enduring love that knows no bounds. Let gratitude for the gift of His unfailing love fill your heart.

Reflection: In your journal, write down three specific ways in which you have experienced God's unfailing love in your life. How has His love impacted your journey? How can you extend His love to those around you?

Prayer: Loving Father, I am grateful for Your unfailing love. Thank You for loving me relentlessly and faithfully. Help me to receive Your love fully and to share it with others, that they may know of Your great love. In Jesus' name, I pray. Amen.

DAY 53

GRATITUDE FOR RENEWAL

Scripture: "Create in me a pure heart, O God, and renew a steadfast spirit within me." - Psalm 51:10 (NIV)

Devotional: Today, let us reflect on gratitude for the renewal that comes from God. Embrace gratitude for His transformative power that restores and refreshes our hearts and minds. Reflect on the times when He has brought renewal to your life, redeeming brokenness and infusing you with hope. Take a moment to pray and ask God to renew your spirit and fill you with His presence. Let gratitude for the gift of renewal fill your heart.

Reflection: In your journal, write about a specific area of your life where you have experienced renewal through God's work. How has it impacted your journey? How can you invite His renewal into other areas of your life?

Prayer: Heavenly Father, I am grateful for the gift of renewal through Your power. Thank You for restoring and refreshing my heart and mind. Continue to renew me, creating in me a pure heart and a steadfast spirit. In Jesus' name, I pray. Amen.

Day 54

Gratitude for Healing

Scripture: "He heals the brokenhearted and binds up their wounds." - Psalm 147:3 (NIV)

Devotional: Today, let us focus on gratitude for the healing power of God. Reflect on the times when He has brought healing to your body, mind, or spirit. Embrace gratitude for His compassion and care that mends our brokenness. Take a moment to pray for healing in any areas of your life that need restoration, trusting in His faithfulness. Let gratitude for the gift of healing fill your heart.

Reflection: In your journal, write down a recent experience where you witnessed God's healing in your life or in the lives of others. How did it strengthen your faith? How can you extend His healing touch to those around you?

Prayer: Healing God, I am grateful for Your power to heal and restore. Thank You for Your compassion and care. Bring healing to the areas of brokenness in my life, and use me as an instrument of Your healing touch to others. In Jesus' name, I pray. Amen.

DAY 55

GRATITUDE FOR THE GIFT OF FRIENDSHIP

Scripture: "A friend loves at all times, and a brother is born for a time of adversity." - Proverbs 17:17 (NIV)

Devotional: Today, let us reflect on gratitude for the gift of friendship. Embrace gratitude for the companionship, support, and encouragement that friends provide. Reflect on the times when friendships have brought joy and strength to your life. Take a moment to reach out to a friend, expressing gratitude for their presence in your life. Let gratitude for the gift of friendship fill your heart.

Reflection: In your journal, write down the names of three friends who have made a positive impact on your life. How have they contributed to your well-being? How can you nurture and invest in your friendships?

Prayer: Loving God, I am grateful for the gift of friendship. Thank You for the friends who have journeyed with me and brought joy to my life. Help me to be a faithful and supportive friend, reflecting Your love in my relationships. In Jesus' name, I pray. Amen.

DAY 56

GRATITUDE FOR REST

Scripture: "Come to me, all you who are weary and burdened, and I will give you rest." - Matthew 11:28 (NIV)

Devotional: Today, let us focus on gratitude for the gift of rest. Reflect on the times when God has provided rest for your weary soul and rejuvenated your spirit. Embrace gratitude for the invitation to find rest in Him, setting aside the demands and pressures of life. Take a moment to intentionally rest, engaging in a peaceful activity that brings you joy and refreshment. Let gratitude for the gift of rest fill your heart.

Reflection: In your journal, write about a specific time when you experienced deep rest and renewal in God's presence. How did it restore your energy and perspective? How can you prioritize rest in your daily life?

Prayer: Gracious Father, I am grateful for the gift of rest that You offer. Thank You for the rejuvenation and peace that comes from resting in Your presence. Help me to prioritize rest and find moments of refreshment in the midst of busyness. In Jesus' name, I pray. Amen.

DAY 57

GRATITUDE FOR THE BEAUTY OF CREATION

Scripture: "The heavens declare the glory of God; the skies proclaim the work of his hands." - Psalm 19:1 (NIV)

Devotional: Today, let us reflect on gratitude for the beauty of God's creation. Embrace gratitude for the wonders of nature, the intricacies of the world around us, and the breathtaking displays of His creativity. Reflect on the times when you have been awestruck by the beauty of creation. Take a moment to step outside and immerse yourself in the beauty of nature, offering a prayer of thanksgiving for the gift of creation. Let gratitude for the beauty of God's creation fill your heart.

Reflection: In your journal, write down three aspects of nature or creation that you find particularly beautiful and awe-inspiring. How does the beauty of creation point you to the greatness of God? How can you steward and protect the environment as an expression of gratitude?

Prayer: Creator God, I am grateful for the beauty of Your creation. Thank You for the wonders of nature that surround me. Help me to appreciate and care for the environment, recognizing it as a gift from You. In Jesus' name, I pray. Amen.

DAY 58

GRATITUDE FOR UNITY

Scripture: "Make every effort to keep the unity of the Spirit through the bond of peace." - Ephesians 4:3 (NIV)

Devotional: Today, let us focus on gratitude for the unity we share as brothers and sisters in Christ. Embrace gratitude for the bond of peace that unites us despite our differences. Reflect on the times when unity has brought strength and harmony to your relationships and communities. Take a moment to pray for unity within the body of Christ, asking God to guide your actions and attitudes towards fostering unity. Let gratitude for the gift of unity fill your heart.

Reflection: In your journal, write about a specific experience where you witnessed the power of unity in a group or community. How did it impact your sense of belonging and purpose? How can you actively promote unity in your relationships and spheres of influence?

Prayer: Loving God, I am grateful for the unity we share as Your children. Thank You for the bond of peace that unites us. Help me to actively pursue and promote unity within the body of Christ and in all areas of my life. In Jesus' name, I pray. Amen.

DAY 59

GRATITUDE FOR TRANSFORMATION

Scripture: "Therefore, if anyone is in Christ, the new creation has come: The old has gone, the new is here!" - 2 Corinthians 5:17 (NIV)

Devotional: Today, let us reflect on gratitude for the transformative power of God. Embrace gratitude for the new life and identity we have in Christ. Reflect on the times when God has brought about transformation in your character, attitudes, or circumstances. Take a moment to pray and ask Him to continue His transformative work in your life, conforming you to the image of Christ. Let gratitude for the gift of transformation fill your heart.

Reflection: In your journal, write down three areas of your life where you have experienced significant transformation through God's work. How has it shaped your perspective and actions? How can you embrace ongoing transformation in your daily life?

Prayer: Heavenly Father, I am grateful for the transformative power of Your love and grace. Thank You for the new life I have in Christ. Continue to transform me from the inside out, conforming me to the image of Your Son. In Jesus' name, I pray. Amen.

DAY 60

GRATITUDE FOR ETERNAL PERSPECTIVE

Scripture: "So we fix our eyes not on what is seen, but on what is unseen, since what is seen is temporary, but what is unseen is eternal." - 2 Corinthians 4:18 (NIV)

Devotional: Today, let us focus on gratitude for the eternal perspective that God gives us. Embrace gratitude for the assurance that this life is not all there is, and that we have a glorious eternity awaiting us. Reflect on the times when an eternal perspective has brought hope and meaning to your present circumstances. Take a moment to fix your eyes on the unseen, setting your heart and mind on the eternal promises of God. Let gratitude for the gift of an eternal perspective fill your heart.

Reflection: In your journal, write about a specific situation where an eternal perspective has shifted your focus and brought peace and hope. How does it impact your daily choices and priorities? How can you cultivate a greater awareness of eternity in your life?

Prayer: Eternal God, I am grateful for the perspective You give me that extends beyond this temporary life. Thank You for the hope and assurance of eternity with You. Help me to fix my eyes on the unseen, living with a heavenly perspective in all I do. In Jesus' name, I pray. Amen.

DAY 61

GRATITUDE FOR GOD'S GUIDANCE

Scripture: "Your word is a lamp for my feet, a light on my path." - Psalm 119:105 (NIV)

Devotional: Today, let us reflect on gratitude for God's guidance in our lives. Embrace gratitude for His Word, which illuminates our path and directs our steps. Reflect on the times when His guidance has brought clarity and wisdom to your decisions. Take a moment to pray and ask God to continue guiding you in all areas of your life. Let gratitude for the gift of His guidance fill your heart.

Reflection: In your journal, write down a specific situation where you sought God's guidance and experienced His leading. How did it impact your choices and outcomes? How can you cultivate a deeper reliance on His guidance in your daily life?

Prayer: Heavenly Father, I am grateful for Your guidance in my life. Thank You for Your Word that illuminates my path. Help me to seek Your guidance in all areas of my life, trusting in Your wisdom and direction. In Jesus' name, I pray. Amen.

DAY 62

GRATITUDE FOR GOD'S PROTECTION

Scripture: "The LORD will keep you from all harm—he will watch over your life." - Psalm 121:7 (NIV)

Devotional: Today, let us focus on gratitude for God's protection. Embrace gratitude for His watchful care over your life. Reflect on the times when His protection shielded you from harm and danger. Take a moment to offer a prayer of thanksgiving for His unfailing protection and ask Him to continue guarding and guiding you. Let gratitude for the gift of His protection fill your heart.

Reflection: In your journal, write down three specific instances where you experienced God's protection in your life. How did His protection bring you peace and assurance? How can you trust in His protection in times of uncertainty?

Prayer: Loving Father, I am grateful for Your divine protection over my life. Thank You for keeping me safe from harm. Help me to trust in Your protection, knowing that You are my fortress and refuge. In Jesus' name, I pray. Amen.

DAY 63

GRATITUDE FOR GOD'S COMFORT

Scripture: "Praise be to the God and Father of our Lord Jesus Christ, the Father of compassion and the God of all comfort." - 2 Corinthians 1:3 (NIV)

Devotional: Today, let us reflect on gratitude for God's comfort in times of need. Embrace gratitude for His compassion and the solace He provides. Reflect on the times when His comfort has carried you through grief, pain, or hardship. Take a moment to pray and ask God to wrap you in His comforting embrace and to comfort those who are hurting. Let gratitude for the gift of His comfort fill your heart.

Reflection: In your journal, write about a specific experience where you felt God's comfort in a difficult season. How did His comfort bring you strength and peace? How can you extend His comfort to others who are hurting?

Prayer: Comforting God, I am grateful for Your compassion and the comfort You provide. Thank You for being with me in times of sorrow and pain. Wrap me in Your comforting embrace, and help me to share Your comfort with others. In Jesus' name, I pray. Amen.

DAY 64

GRATITUDE FOR GOD'S PROVISION IN TIMES OF NEED

Scripture: "And my God will meet all your needs according to the riches of his glory in Christ Jesus." - Philippians 4:19 (NIV)

Devotional: Today, let us focus on gratitude for God's provision in times of need. Embrace gratitude for His faithfulness to supply all your needs according to His abundant riches. Reflect on the times when His provision came at the right time and in unexpected ways. Take a moment to offer a prayer of thanksgiving for His unwavering provision and to trust Him for your present and future needs. Let gratitude for the gift of His provision fill your heart.

Reflection: In your journal, write down three instances where you witnessed God's provision in times of need. How did His provision strengthen your faith and dependence on Him? How can you steward His provision wisely and generously?

Prayer: Provider God, I am grateful for Your faithful provision in my life. Thank You for meeting my needs according to Your riches. Help me to trust in Your provision and to use it wisely for Your glory and the well-being of others. In Jesus' name, I pray. Amen.

DAY 65

GRATITUDE FOR GOD'S FAITHFULNESS

Scripture: "Know therefore that the LORD your God is God; he is the faithful God, keeping his covenant of love to a thousand generations of those who love him and keep his commandments." - Deuteronomy 7:9 (NIV)

Devotional: Today, let us reflect on gratitude for God's faithfulness. Embrace gratitude for His unwavering commitment and love that endures through all circumstances. Reflect on the times when His faithfulness has been evident in your life, even when you faltered. Take a moment to offer a prayer of thanksgiving for His faithfulness and to commit yourself to loving and obeying Him. Let gratitude for the gift of His faithfulness fill your heart.

Reflection: In your journal, write about a specific experience where you witnessed God's faithfulness in your life. How did His faithfulness impact your trust and obedience? How can you reflect His faithfulness in your relationships and commitments?

Prayer: Faithful God, I am grateful for Your steadfast love and faithfulness. Thank You for keeping Your promises and for being faithful to me even when I am unfaithful. Help me to love and obey You wholeheartedly, reflecting Your faithfulness to others. In Jesus' name, I pray. Amen.

DAY 66

GRATITUDE FOR GOD'S WISDOM

Scripture: "If any of you lacks wisdom, you should ask God, who gives generously to all without finding fault, and it will be given to you." - James 1:5 (NIV)

Devotional: Today, let us focus on gratitude for God's wisdom. Embrace gratitude for His divine insight and understanding that surpasses human knowledge. Reflect on the times when His wisdom has guided your decisions and actions. Take a moment to pray and ask God to grant you wisdom in areas where you lack clarity or understanding. Let gratitude for the gift of His wisdom fill your heart.

Reflection: In your journal, write down a specific situation where you sought God's wisdom and experienced His guidance. How did His wisdom bring discernment and peace? How can you cultivate a greater reliance on His wisdom in your daily life?

Prayer: Wise God, I am grateful for Your perfect wisdom. Thank You for granting me wisdom when I seek Your guidance. Help me to rely on Your wisdom in all areas of my life, trusting in Your understanding that surpasses my own. In Jesus' name, I pray. Amen.

DAY 67

GRATITUDE FOR GOD'S PEACE

Scripture: "Peace I leave with you; my peace I give you. I do not give to you as the world gives. Do not let your hearts be troubled and do not be afraid." - John 14:27 (NIV)

Devotional: Today, let us reflect on gratitude for God's peace. Embrace gratitude for the inner calm and serenity that comes from knowing and trusting in Him. Reflect on the times when His peace has guarded your heart amidst chaos and uncertainty. Take a moment to pray and ask God to fill you with His peace, allowing it to reign in your heart and mind. Let gratitude for the gift of His peace fill your heart.

Reflection: In your journal, write about a specific experience where you felt God's peace in a challenging situation. How did His peace sustain and guide you? How can you cultivate a greater sense of His peace in your daily life?

Prayer: Peaceful God, I am grateful for Your peace that surpasses all understanding. Thank You for guarding my heart and mind with Your peace. Fill me afresh with Your peace today, and help me to extend Your peace to those around me. In Jesus' name, I pray. Amen.

DAY 68

GRATITUDE FOR GOD'S STRENGTH

Scripture: "The LORD is my strength and my shield; my heart trusts in him, and he helps me. My heart leaps for joy, and with my song I praise him." - Psalm 28:7 (NIV)

Devotional: Today, let us focus on gratitude for God's strength. Embrace gratitude for His empowering presence that sustains and upholds you. Reflect on the times when His strength has enabled you to persevere and overcome challenges. Take a moment to pray and ask God to fill you with His strength, enabling you to face every obstacle with courage and faith. Let gratitude for the gift of His strength fill your heart.

Reflection: In your journal, write about a specific situation where you experienced God's strength carrying you through a difficult season. How did His strength impact your response and outcome? How can you rely on His strength in your daily life?

Prayer: Mighty God, I am grateful for Your strength that enables me to face challenges. Thank You for empowering me and upholding me. Fill me afresh with Your strength today, that I may walk in courage and faith. In Jesus' name, I pray. Amen.

DAY 69

GRATITUDE FOR GOD'S PATIENCE

Scripture: "But you, Lord, are a compassionate and gracious God, slow to anger, abounding in love and faithfulness." - Psalm 86:15 (NIV)

Devotional: Today, let us reflect on gratitude for God's patience. Embrace gratitude for His long-suffering and forbearance towards our shortcomings and failures. Reflect on the times when His patience has given you space to grow and learn. Take a moment to offer a prayer of thanksgiving for His patient love and to ask Him to cultivate patience within you towards others. Let gratitude for the gift of His patience fill your heart.

Reflection: In your journal, write about a specific instance where you witnessed God's patience in your life. How did His patience impact your relationship with Him and others? How can you extend patience to those around you?

Prayer: Patient God, I am grateful for Your long-suffering and forbearance. Thank You for Your patient love that never gives up on me. Help me to cultivate patience in my relationships, reflecting Your patience and grace. In Jesus' name, I pray. Amen.

DAY 70

GRATITUDE FOR GOD'S JOY

Scripture: "You make known to me the path of life; you will fill me with joy in your presence, with eternal pleasures at your right hand." - Psalm 16:11 (NIV)

Devotional: Today, let us focus on gratitude for God's joy. Embrace gratitude for the deep and abiding joy that comes from knowing Him. Reflect on the times when His joy has lifted your spirits and brought delight to your soul. Take a moment to pray and ask God to fill you with His joy, allowing it to overflow in your life and relationships. Let gratitude for the gift of His joy fill your heart.

Reflection: In your journal, write about a specific experience where you felt God's joy in a season of happiness or amidst challenges. How did His joy strengthen and sustain you? How can you cultivate a greater sense of His joy in your daily life?

Prayer: Joyful God, I am grateful for the joy that comes from knowing You. Thank You for filling me with Your joy. Help me to live with a joyful heart, reflecting Your joy in all I do. In Jesus' name, I pray. Amen.

DAY 71

THE COMFORT OF A WARM HUG

Scripture: "A friend loves at all times, and a brother is born for a time of adversity." - Proverbs 17:17 (NIV)

Devotional: Today, let's find joy in the simplicity of a warm hug. Physical touch, especially from loved ones or friends, has the power to bring comfort and convey love and support. Embrace the joy of offering and receiving warm hugs, knowing that God has created us to express and experience love through physical touch.

Reflection: In your journal, write about the comfort and joy you experience in giving and receiving hugs. How does physical touch positively impact your emotional well-being? How can you intentionally offer hugs to those who may need comfort or encouragement? How can you create a safe and loving environment where hugs are welcomed and celebrated?

Prayer: Loving Father, I thank You for the comfort and joy found in a warm hug. As I embrace and offer physical touch to others, help me to do so with love and compassion. May my hugs be a source of comfort and support to those around me, reflecting Your love and care. In Jesus' name, I pray. Amen.

DAY 72

GRATITUDE FOR GOD'S COMPASSION

Scripture: "The LORD is gracious and compassionate, slow to anger and rich in love." - Psalm 145:8 (NIV)

Devotional: Today, let us focus on gratitude for God's compassion. Embrace gratitude for His tender-heartedness and mercy towards us. Reflect on the times when His compassion has lifted you up in moments of despair or weakness. Take a moment to pray and ask God to deepen your awareness of His compassion and to help you extend compassion to others. Let gratitude for the gift of His compassion fill your heart.

Reflection: In your journal, write down a specific instance where you experienced God's compassion in your life. How did His compassion bring comfort and hope? How can you reflect His compassion in your interactions with others?

Prayer: Compassionate God, I am grateful for Your tender-heartedness and mercy. Thank You for your compassion that never fails. Help me to be aware of Your compassion in my life and to extend it to those around me. In Jesus' name, I pray. Amen.

DAY 73

GRATITUDE FOR GOD'S GRACE

Scripture: "For it is by grace you have been saved, through faith—and this is not from yourselves, it is the gift of God." - Ephesians 2:8 (NIV)

Devotional: Today, let us reflect on gratitude for God's grace. Embrace gratitude for His unmerited favor and the salvation He offers us through Jesus Christ. Reflect on the times when His grace has rescued you from sin and restored your relationship with Him. Take a moment to offer a prayer of thanksgiving for His amazing grace and to extend grace to others. Let gratitude for the gift of His grace fill your heart.

Reflection: In your journal, write about a specific experience where you witnessed God's grace at work in your life. How did His grace transform you? How can you extend grace to those who may not deserve it?

Prayer: Gracious God, I am grateful for Your amazing grace. Thank You for saving me and extending Your unmerited favor towards me. Help me to receive Your grace fully and to extend it to others, just as You have done for me. In Jesus' name, I pray. Amen.

DAY 74

GRATITUDE FOR GOD'S HOLINESS

Scripture: "Exalt the LORD our God and worship at his holy mountain, for the LORD our God is holy." - Psalm 99:9 (NIV)

Devotional: Today, let us reflect on gratitude for God's holiness. Embrace gratitude for His absolute purity and moral perfection. Reflect on the times when His holiness has inspired awe and reverence within you. Take a moment to pray and worship Him for His holiness, acknowledging His greatness and uniqueness. Let gratitude for the gift of His holiness fill your heart.

Reflection: In your journal, write about a specific moment where you experienced the majesty of God's holiness. How did it deepen your worship and surrender? How can you cultivate a greater reverence for His holiness in your daily life?

Prayer: Holy God, I am grateful for Your perfect holiness. Thank You for Your purity and moral perfection. Help me to worship and adore You with reverence, acknowledging Your greatness and uniqueness. In Jesus' name, I pray. Amen.

DAY 75

EMBRACING GOD'S PURPOSE IN TIMES OF WAITING

Scripture: "Wait for the Lord; be strong and take heart and wait for the Lord." - Psalm 27:14 (NIV)

Devotional: Today, let us explore the theme of embracing God's purpose in times of waiting. Waiting can be challenging, but it provides an opportunity for growth and reliance on God. Reflect on the significance of waiting with patience and trust in His plan. Take a moment to pray and ask God to help you wait with strength and hope, knowing that He is with you in the waiting. Let gratitude for His guidance and the joy that comes from waiting on His timing fill your heart.

Reflection: In your journal, write about the impact of embracing God's purpose in times of waiting. How can you intentionally wait for the Lord with strength and hope in His plan? How does the act of embracing God's purpose in times of waiting contribute to your overall sense of perseverance, faith, and spiritual growth? How can you use your patient waiting to reflect God's love and bring joy to others through your humble and steadfast attitude?

Prayer: Gracious God, I thank You for Your guidance in times of waiting and the joy that comes from trusting Your timing. Help me to wait for You with strength and hope in Your plan. Show me how to reflect Your love and bring joy through my humble and steadfast response to waiting. Fill my heart with gratitude for Your presence and the joy that comes from embracing Your purpose in times of waiting. In Jesus' name, I pray. Amen.

DAY 76

Scripture: "For I am the Lord, I do not change." - Malachi 3:6 (NIV)

Devotional: Today, let us focus on embracing God's purpose in times of change. Change can be challenging, but God's character and promises remain constant. Reflect on the significance of finding security and peace in Him amidst life's transitions. Take a moment to pray and ask God to help you trust His unchanging nature and find purpose in times of change. Let gratitude for His steadfastness and the joy that comes from relying on His unchanging love fill your heart.

Reflection: In your journal, write about the impact of embracing God's purpose in times of change. How can you intentionally trust His unchanging nature and find purpose amidst life's transitions? How does the act of embracing God's purpose in times of change contribute to your overall sense of stability, faith, and spiritual resilience? How can you use your experiences of navigating change to reflect God's love and bring joy to others through your humble and steady attitude?

Prayer: Heavenly Father, I thank You for Your unchanging nature and the joy that comes from finding purpose in times of change. Help me to trust in You with all my heart and seek Your guidance in times of doubt. Show me how to reflect Your love and bring joy through my humble and secure response to uncertainty. Fill my heart with gratitude for Your presence and the joy that comes from embracing Your purpose in times of change. In Jesus' name, I pray. Amen.

DAY 77

EMBRACING GOD'S PURPOSE IN TIMES OF UNCERTAINTY

Scripture: "Trust in the Lord with all your heart and lean not on your own understanding; in all your ways submit to him, and he will make your paths straight." - Proverbs 3:5-6 (NIV)

Devotional: Today, let us focus on embracing God's purpose in times of uncertainty. When faced with unknowns, we can trust in the One who knows all things. Reflect on the significance of submitting to God's will and seeking His guidance in times of doubt. Take a moment to pray and ask God to help you find peace and direction, knowing that He will make your paths straight. Let gratitude for His wisdom and the joy that comes from trusting His plan fill your heart.

Reflection: In your journal, write about the impact of embracing God's purpose in times of uncertainty. How can you intentionally trust in the Lord with all your heart and seek His guidance in times of doubt? How does the act of embracing God's purpose in times of uncertainty contribute to your overall sense of peace, confidence, and spiritual assurance? How can you use your experience of trusting God in uncertainty to reflect His love and bring joy to others through your humble and secure attitude?

Prayer: Heavenly Father, I thank You for Your wisdom and the joy that comes from trusting Your plan in times of uncertainty. Help me to trust in You with all my heart and seek Your guidance in times of doubt. Show me how to reflect Your love and bring joy through my humble and secure response to uncertainty. Fill my heart with gratitude for Your presence and the joy that comes from embracing Your purpose in times of uncertainty. In Jesus' name, I pray. Amen.

DAY 78

EMBRACING GOD'S PURPOSE THROUGH SURRENDER

Scripture: "Then Jesus said to his disciples, 'Whoever wants to be my disciple must deny themselves and take up their cross and follow me.'" - Matthew 16:24 (NIV)

Devotional: Today, let us explore the theme of embracing God's purpose through surrender. Surrendering our lives to Christ is an act of trust and devotion. Reflect on the significance of denying ourselves and following His path for us. Take a moment to pray and ask God to help you surrender your will to His, seeking His guidance in every aspect of your life. Let gratitude for His guidance and the joy that comes from walking in His purpose fill your heart.

Reflection: In your journal, write about the impact of embracing God's purpose through surrender. How can you intentionally deny yourself and follow His path for you? How does the act of embracing God's purpose through surrender contribute to your overall sense of faith, obedience, and spiritual transformation? How can you use your surrender to reflect God's love and bring joy to others through your humble and devoted attitude?

Prayer: Gracious God, I thank You for Your guidance and the joy that comes from walking in Your purpose. Help me to deny myself and follow Your path for me. Show me how to reflect Your love and bring joy through my humble and devoted surrender to Your will. Fill my heart with gratitude for Your presence and the joy that comes from embracing Your purpose through surrender. In Jesus' name, I pray. Amen.

Day 79

Embracing God's Purpose in Times of Scarcity

Scripture: "And my God will meet all your needs according to the riches of his glory in Christ Jesus." - Philippians 4:19 (NIV)

Devotional: Today, let us focus on embracing God's purpose in times of scarcity. Even in moments of need, God promises to provide for us according to His riches. Reflect on the significance of trusting His provision and seeking His guidance in times of lack. Take a moment to pray and ask God to help you find contentment and peace, knowing that He is faithful to meet your needs. Let gratitude for His faithfulness and the joy that comes from relying on His abundance fill your heart.

Reflection: In your journal, write about the impact of embracing God's purpose in times of scarcity. How can you intentionally trust His provision and find contentment in times of need? How does the act of embracing God's purpose in times of scarcity contribute to your overall sense of faith, reliance, and spiritual growth? How can you use your experience of depending on God's abundance to reflect His love and bring joy to others through your humble and hopeful attitude?

Prayer: Heavenly Father, I thank You for Your promise to provide for me even in times of scarcity, and the joy that comes from relying on Your abundance. Help me to trust Your provision and find contentment in You. Show me how to reflect Your love and bring joy through my humble and hopeful response to times of need. Fill my heart with gratitude for Your faithfulness and the joy that comes from embracing Your purpose in times of scarcity. In Jesus' name, I pray. Amen.

DAY 80

EMBRACING GOD'S PURPOSE IN TIMES OF ABUNDANCE

Scripture: "Every good and perfect gift is from above, coming down from the Father of the heavenly lights, who does not change like shifting shadows." - James 1:17 (NIV)

Devotional: Today, let us explore the theme of embracing God's purpose in times of abundance. In seasons of plenty, God calls us to use His blessings to bless others and bring glory to His name. Reflect on the significance of stewarding His gifts with gratitude and generosity. Take a moment to pray and ask God to help you be faithful in times of abundance, using what you have to further His kingdom. Let gratitude for His provision and the joy that comes from being His channel of blessings fill your heart.

Reflection: In your journal, write about the impact of embracing God's purpose in times of abundance. How can you intentionally use His blessings to bless others and bring glory to His name? How does the act of embracing God's purpose in times of abundance contribute to your overall sense of stewardship, gratitude, and spiritual impact? How can you use your abundance to reflect God's love and bring joy to others through your humble and generous attitude?

Prayer: Gracious God, I thank You for Your abundant blessings and the joy that comes from being Your channel of blessings. Help me to use what I have to further Your kingdom and bless others. Show me how to reflect Your love and bring joy through my humble and generous stewardship. Fill my heart with gratitude for Your provision and the joy that comes from embracing Your purpose in times of abundance. In Jesus' name, I pray. Amen.

DAY 81

EMBRACING GOD'S PURPOSE IN TIMES OF MOURNING

Scripture: "Blessed are those who mourn, for they will be comforted." - Matthew 5:4 (NIV)

Devotional: Today, let us focus on embracing God's purpose in times of mourning. During moments of grief, God offers His comfort and presence. Reflect on the significance of finding solace in Him and allowing His love to heal your broken heart. Take a moment to pray and ask God to help you find hope and peace in the midst of sorrow. Let gratitude for His faithfulness and the joy that comes from His restoration fill your heart.

Reflection: In your journal, write about the impact of embracing God's purpose in times of mourning. How can you intentionally seek His comfort and find hope in Him during moments of grief? How does the act of embracing God's purpose in times of mourning contribute to your overall sense of healing, trust, and spiritual restoration? How can you use your experience of finding comfort in God to reflect His love and bring joy to others through your humble and compassionate attitude?

Prayer: Heavenly Father, I thank You for Your comfort and the joy that comes from finding hope in You during times of mourning. Help me to seek Your solace and trust Your healing in moments of grief. Show me how to reflect Your love and bring joy through my humble and compassionate response to sorrow. Fill my heart with gratitude for Your presence and the joy that comes from embracing Your purpose in times of mourning. In Jesus' name, I pray. Amen.

DAY 82

EMBRACING GOD'S PURPOSE IN TIMES OF REJOICING

Scripture: "Rejoice in the Lord always. I will say it again: Rejoice!" - Philippians 4:4 (NIV)

Devotional: Today, let us explore the theme of embracing God's purpose in times of rejoicing. Rejoicing is a way to express our gratitude and praise to God for His goodness. Reflect on the significance of finding joy in Him and celebrating His faithfulness. Take a moment to pray and ask God to help you cultivate a joyful heart, regardless of the circumstances. Let gratitude for His love and the joy that comes from delighting in Him fill your heart.

Reflection: In your journal, write about the impact of embracing God's purpose in times of rejoicing. How can you intentionally cultivate a joyful heart and celebrate God's goodness in every situation? How does the act of embracing God's purpose in times of rejoicing contribute to your overall sense of gratitude, worship, and spiritual joy? How can you use your rejoicing to reflect God's love and bring joy to others through your humble and joyful attitude?

Prayer: Gracious God, I thank You for Your goodness and the joy that comes from delighting in You. Help me to rejoice in You always, regardless of the circumstances. Show me how to reflect Your love and bring joy through my humble and joyful heart. Fill my heart with gratitude for Your faithfulness and the joy that comes from embracing Your purpose in times of rejoicing. In Jesus' name, I pray. Amen.

DAY 83

EMBRACING GOD'S PURPOSE IN TIMES OF HEALING

Scripture: "Heal me, Lord, and I will be healed; save me and I will be saved, for you are the one I praise." - Jeremiah 17:14 (NIV)

Devotional: Today, let us focus on embracing God's purpose in times of healing. Whether physical, emotional, or spiritual, healing is a testament to God's restorative power. Reflect on the significance of praising Him for His healing touch. Take a moment to pray and ask God for His healing in every aspect of your life. Let gratitude for His restoration and the joy that comes from experiencing His healing power fill your heart.

Reflection: In your journal, write about the impact of embracing God's purpose in times of healing. How can you intentionally praise Him for His healing touch in your life? How does the act of embracing God's purpose in times of healing contribute to your overall sense of gratitude, hope, and spiritual renewal? How can you use your experience of His healing to reflect God's love and bring joy to others through your humble and grateful attitude?

Prayer: Heavenly Father, I thank You for Your healing touch and the joy that comes from experiencing Your restoration. Help me to praise You for Your healing in every aspect of my life. Show me how to reflect Your love and bring joy through my humble and grateful response to Your healing. Fill my heart with gratitude for Your presence and the joy that comes from embracing Your purpose in times of healing. In Jesus' name, I pray. Amen.

DAY 84

EMBRACING GOD'S PURPOSE IN TIMES OF DOUBT

Scripture: "Immediately the boy's father exclaimed, 'I do believe; help me overcome my unbelief!'" - Mark 9:24 (NIV)

Devotional: Today, let us explore the theme of embracing God's purpose in times of doubt. Doubts are a natural part of faith, and God invites us to bring them to Him. Reflect on the significance of seeking His help to overcome unbelief. Take a moment to pray and ask God to strengthen your faith and help you find assurance in His promises. Let gratitude for His patience and the joy that comes from growing in faith fill your heart.

Reflection: In your journal, write about the impact of embracing God's purpose in times of doubt. How can you intentionally seek His help to overcome unbelief and find assurance in His promises? How does the act of embracing God's purpose in times of doubt contribute to your overall sense of growth, trust, and spiritual maturity? How can you use your experience of overcoming doubts to reflect God's love and bring joy to others through your humble and persevering attitude?

Prayer: Gracious God, I thank You for Your patience and the joy that comes from finding assurance in Your promises. Help me to seek Your help to overcome doubts and grow in faith. Show me how to reflect Your love and bring joy through my humble and persevering response to uncertainty. Fill my heart with gratitude for Your presence and the joy that comes from embracing Your purpose in times of doubt. In Jesus' name, I pray. Amen.

DAY 85

EMBRACING GOD'S PURPOSE IN RETIREMENT

Scripture: "Even to your old age and gray hairs, I am he, I am he who will sustain you. I have made you and I will carry you; I will sustain you and I will rescue you." - Isaiah 46:4 (NIV)

Devotional: Today, let us focus on embracing God's purpose in retirement. As you enter this new season of life, know that God's plan for you is still unfolding. Reflect on the significance of embracing this phase with trust and a willingness to continue serving Him. Take a moment to pray and ask God to help you discover His purpose in retirement, knowing that He will sustain and guide you. Let gratitude for His faithfulness throughout your life and the joy that comes from embracing His plan for this new chapter fill your heart.

Reflection: In your journal, write about the impact of embracing God's purpose in retirement. How can you intentionally seek His guidance and discover new ways to serve Him in this season of life? How does the act of embracing God's purpose in retirement contribute to your overall sense of fulfillment, purpose, and spiritual growth? How can you use your retirement years to reflect God's love and bring joy to others through your humble and available attitude?

Prayer: Heavenly Father, I thank You for Your faithfulness throughout my life and the joy that comes from embracing Your purpose in retirement. Help me to seek Your guidance and discover new ways to serve You in this season. Show me how to reflect Your love and bring joy through my humble and available heart. Fill my heart with gratitude for Your sustaining grace and the joy that comes from embracing Your purpose in retirement. In Jesus' name, I pray. Amen.

DAY 86

EMBRACING GOD'S PURPOSE IN CAREER AND WORK

Scripture: "Whatever you do, work at it with all your heart, as working for the Lord, not for human masters." - Colossians 3:23 (NIV)

Devotional: Today, let us explore the theme of embracing God's purpose in career and work. Our professional pursuits can become a platform to honor and glorify God. Reflect on the significance of working with excellence and integrity as an offering to the Lord. Take a moment to pray and ask God to help you find purpose and fulfillment in your career, knowing that your work is ultimately for Him. Let gratitude for the opportunities and the joy that comes from aligning your work with His will fill your heart.

Reflection: In your journal, write about the impact of embracing God's purpose in career and work. How can you intentionally approach your work with excellence and integrity, seeing it as an offering to the Lord? How does the act of embracing God's purpose in your career contribute to your overall sense of purpose, impact, and spiritual influence? How can you use your professional endeavors to reflect God's love and bring joy to others through your humble and diligent attitude?

Prayer: Gracious God, I thank You for the opportunities and the joy that comes from aligning my career with Your purpose. Help me to work with excellence and integrity, seeing my vocation as an offering to You. Show me how to reflect Your love and bring joy through my humble and diligent work. Fill my heart with gratitude for the chance to serve You through my career and the joy that comes from embracing Your purpose in my work. In Jesus' name, I pray. Amen.

DAY 87

EMBRACING GOD'S PURPOSE IN MARRIAGE

Scripture: "Therefore what God has joined together, let no one separate." - Mark 10:9 (NIV)

Devotional: Today, let us explore the theme of embracing God's purpose in marriage. For those who are married, this sacred union is an opportunity to love, honor, and serve one another according to God's plan. Reflect on the significance of embracing His purpose in your marriage, seeking unity and mutual growth. Take a moment to pray and ask God to help you strengthen your marriage with love, grace, and selflessness. Let gratitude for the gift of marriage and the joy that comes from aligning with His design fill your heart.

Reflection: In your journal, write about the impact of embracing God's purpose in marriage. How can you intentionally love, honor, and serve your spouse according to His plan? How does the act of embracing God's purpose in your marriage contribute to your overall sense of commitment, intimacy, and spiritual partnership? How can you use your marriage to reflect God's love and bring joy to others through your humble and sacrificial attitude?

Prayer: Gracious God, I thank You for the gift of marriage and the joy that comes from aligning with Your purpose. Help me to love, honor, and serve my spouse according to Your plan. Show me how to reflect Your love and bring joy through my humble and sacrificial love in marriage. Fill my heart with gratitude for the gift of my spouse and the joy that comes from embracing Your purpose in marriage. In Jesus' name, I pray. Amen.

DAY 88

EMBRACING GOD'S PURPOSE THROUGH VOLUNTEERING

Scripture: "Each of you should use whatever gift you have received to serve others, as faithful stewards of God's grace in its various forms." - 1 Peter 4:10 (NIV)

Devotional: Today, let us explore the theme of embracing God's purpose through volunteering. Volunteering is a meaningful way to use our gifts to serve others and make a difference. Reflect on the significance of using your time and talents to bless those in need. Take a moment to pray and ask God to help you find opportunities to volunteer and serve with a humble and compassionate heart. Let gratitude for the chance to be His instrument of grace and the joy that comes from selfless service fill your heart.

Reflection: In your journal, write about the impact of embracing God's purpose through volunteering. How can you intentionally seek opportunities to use your gifts to serve others and make a difference in their lives? How does the act of embracing God's purpose through volunteering contribute to your overall sense of fulfillment, compassion, and impact in your community? How can you use your selfless service to reflect God's love and bring joy to others through your humble and devoted attitude?

Prayer: Gracious God, I thank You for the opportunity to serve others through volunteering and the joy that comes from being Your instrument of grace. Help me to seek opportunities to use my gifts to bless those in need. Show me how to reflect Your love and bring joy through my humble and devoted service. Fill my heart with gratitude for the chance to make a difference and the joy that comes from embracing Your purpose through volunteering. In Jesus' name, I pray. Amen.

DAY 89

EMBRACING GOD'S PURPOSE IN SINGLENESS

Scripture: "Delight yourself in the Lord, and he will give you the desires of your heart." - Psalm 37:4 (NIV)

Devotional: Today, let us focus on embracing God's purpose in singleness. For those who are single, this season can be an opportunity to find contentment and fulfillment in the Lord. Reflect on the significance of delighting in God and seeking His will above all else. Take a moment to pray and ask God to help you find joy and purpose in your singleness, trusting that He knows the desires of your heart. Let gratitude for His provision and the joy that comes from embracing His timing fill your heart.

Reflection: In your journal, write about the impact of embracing God's purpose in singleness. How can you intentionally find contentment and fulfillment in the Lord during this season of your life? How does the act of embracing God's purpose in singleness contribute to your overall sense of joy, purpose, and trust in His plan? How can you use your singleness to reflect God's love and bring joy to others through your humble and wholehearted attitude?

Prayer: Heavenly Father, I thank You for the gift of singleness and the joy that comes from finding contentment in You. Help me to delight in You and seek Your will above all else. Show me how to reflect Your love and bring joy through my humble and wholehearted embrace of Your purpose in singleness. Fill my heart with gratitude for Your provision and the joy that comes from embracing Your timing. In Jesus' name, I pray. Amen.

DAY 90

EMBRACING GOD'S PURPOSE IN RESTORING BROKEN RELATIONSHIPS

Scripture: "Bear with each other and forgive one another if any of you has a grievance against someone. Forgive as the Lord forgave you." - Colossians 3:13 (NIV)

Devotional: Today, let us focus on embracing God's purpose in restoring broken relationships. As human beings, we may encounter conflicts and strained connections, but God calls us to pursue reconciliation and forgiveness. Reflect on the significance of embracing forgiveness as a way to fulfill His purpose for your life. Take a moment to pray and ask God to help you extend grace and seek restoration in fractured relationships. Let gratitude for His forgiveness and the joy that comes from reconciled connections fill your heart.

Reflection: In your journal, write about the impact of embracing God's purpose in restoring broken relationships. How can you intentionally extend grace and seek reconciliation in fractured connections? How does the act of embracing God's purpose in restoring broken relationships contribute to your overall sense of healing, empathy, and unity within your relationships? How can you use your commitment to forgiveness to reflect God's love and bring joy to others through your humble and empathetic attitude?

Prayer: Heavenly Father, I thank You for the gift of forgiveness and the joy that comes from reconciled relationships. Help me to extend grace and seek restoration in fractured connections. Show me how to reflect Your love and bring joy through my commitment to forgiveness. Fill my heart with gratitude for Your forgiveness and the joy that comes from embracing Your purpose in restoring broken relationships. In Jesus' name, I pray. Amen.

DAY 91

SEEKING GOD'S GUIDANCE FOR PURPOSE

Scripture: "Trust in the LORD with all your heart and lean not on your own understanding; in all your ways submit to him, and he will make your paths straight." - Proverbs 3:5-6 (NIV)

Devotional: Today, let us explore the theme of finding purpose in life by seeking God's guidance. Embrace the idea that true purpose is discovered when we trust in the Lord and align our lives with His will. Reflect on the times when God has directed your path and brought clarity to your purpose. Take a moment to pray and surrender your desires and plans to God, asking Him to reveal His purpose for your life. Let gratitude for the opportunity to seek and find purpose in Him fill your heart.

Reflection: In your journal, write about your journey of seeking purpose in life. How has God guided you? What steps can you take to align your life with His purpose? How can you trust in Him more fully in your quest for purpose?

Prayer: Heavenly Father, I desire to find true purpose in my life. I submit myself to Your guidance and trust in Your wisdom. Show me Your purpose for me and empower me to live it out faithfully. In Jesus' name, I pray. Amen.

DAY 92

EMBRACING YOUR UNIQUE GIFTS AND TALENTS

Scripture: "Each of you should use whatever gift you have received to serve others, as faithful stewards of God's grace in its various forms." - 1 Peter 4:10 (NIV)

Devotional: Today, let us explore the theme of finding purpose in life by embracing your unique gifts and talents. Embrace gratitude for the specific abilities and strengths that God has bestowed upon you. Reflect on the ways in which you can use these gifts to serve others and bring glory to God. Take a moment to pray and ask God to reveal how you can best utilize your gifts to fulfill your purpose. Let gratitude for the gift of your unique abilities fill your heart.

Reflection: In your journal, make a list of your gifts and talents. How can you use them to make a positive impact on others? How can you align your passions with your purpose? How can you continuously develop and refine your skills to better serve God and others?

Prayer: Gracious God, I am grateful for the unique gifts and talents You have given me. Help me to use them wisely and for the benefit of others. Guide me in aligning my passions with Your purpose for my life. In Jesus' name, I pray. Amen.

DAY 93

DISCOVERING MEANING IN SERVING OTHERS

Scripture: "For even the Son of Man did not come to be served, but to serve, and to give his life as a ransom for many." - Mark 10:45 (NIV)

Devotional: Today, let us explore the theme of finding purpose in life through serving others. Embrace gratitude for the opportunity to make a difference in the lives of those around you. Reflect on the times when serving others has brought fulfillment and a sense of purpose. Take a moment to pray and ask God to open your eyes to the needs of others and to guide you in serving with a genuine heart. Let gratitude for the privilege of serving others fill your heart.

Reflection: In your journal, write about a specific experience where serving others brought you a sense of purpose. How did it impact your perspective on life? How can you make intentional choices to serve others in your daily life?

Prayer: Loving God, I thank You for the opportunity to serve others. Open my eyes to the needs around me and help me to serve with a joyful heart. Guide me in making a meaningful impact in the lives of those I encounter. In Jesus' name, I pray. Amen.

DAY 94

SEEKING GOD'S WILL FOR YOUR CAREER

Scripture: "Commit to the LORD whatever you do, and he will establish your plans." - Proverbs 16:3 (NIV)

Devotional: Today, let us explore the theme of finding purpose in life through seeking God's will for your career. Embrace the idea that your work can be a meaningful expression of your purpose. Reflect on the times when God has provided guidance and opened doors in your professional journey. Take a moment to pray and surrender your career aspirations to God, asking Him to align your path with His will. Let gratitude for the opportunity to seek and find purpose in your career fill your heart.

Reflection: In your journal, write about your career aspirations and how they align with your sense of purpose. How can you seek God's guidance in making career decisions? How can you use your work to make a positive impact in the world?

Prayer: Heavenly Father, I commit my career to You. Guide me in making decisions that align with Your will and purpose for my life. Open doors of opportunity that will enable me to use my talents for Your glory. In Jesus' name, I pray. Amen.

DAY 95

FINDING PURPOSE IN RELATIONSHIPS

Scripture: "Dear children, let us not love with words or speech but with actions and in truth." - 1 John 3:18 (NIV)

Devotional: Today, let us explore the theme of finding purpose in life through meaningful relationships. Embrace gratitude for the people God has placed in your life and the opportunity to love and serve them. Reflect on the ways in which your relationships bring purpose and fulfillment. Take a moment to pray and ask God to deepen your connections with others and to guide you in being a source of love and support. Let gratitude for the gift of relationships and their purpose in your life fill your heart.

Reflection: In your journal, write about the meaningful relationships in your life. How do they contribute to your sense of purpose? How can you invest in and nurture these relationships more intentionally? How can you be a source of love and support to others?

Prayer: Loving God, thank You for the gift of relationships. Help me to value and invest in the people You have placed in my life. Guide me in being a source of love, encouragement, and support to others. In Jesus' name, I pray. Amen.

DAY 96

SEEKING GOD'S PURPOSE IN SEASONS OF WAITING

Scripture: "Wait for the LORD; be strong and take heart and wait for the LORD." - Psalm 27:14 (NIV)

Devotional: Today, let us explore the theme of finding purpose in life during seasons of waiting. Embrace gratitude for the opportunity to trust God's timing and learn valuable lessons in the process. Reflect on the times when waiting has brought growth and deeper dependence on God. Take a moment to pray and ask God to reveal His purpose in the waiting and to strengthen you in the midst of uncertainty. Let gratitude for the lessons and growth in seasons of waiting fill your heart.

Reflection: In your journal, write about a specific season of waiting in your life. How did it shape your character and perspective? What lessons did you learn during that time? How can you trust God's purpose and timing in your current season of waiting?

Prayer: Patient God, teach me to wait with a hopeful heart. Help me to trust Your purpose in seasons of waiting and to grow in faith and patience. Strengthen me as I lean on You in uncertainty. In Jesus' name, I pray. Amen.

DAY 97

EMBRACING CHANGE AS A CATALYST FOR PURPOSE

Scripture: "See, I am doing a new thing! Now it springs up; do you not perceive it? I am making a way in the wilderness and streams in the wasteland." - Isaiah 43:19 (NIV)

Devotional: Today, let us explore the theme of finding purpose in life by embracing change. Embrace gratitude for the opportunities that change brings to discover new paths and purposes. Reflect on the times when unexpected changes have led you to new and fulfilling experiences. Take a moment to pray and ask God to help you embrace change with a spirit of openness and trust in His guiding hand. Let gratitude for the transformative power of change and its role in finding purpose fill your heart.

Reflection: In your journal, write about a significant change or transition in your life. How did it shape your journey and reveal new purposes? How can you embrace change with faith and resilience? How can you actively seek God's guidance in times of change?

Prayer: God of new beginnings, help me to embrace change with faith and openness. Guide me in discerning Your purpose in seasons of transition. Give me the courage and resilience to step into new paths and experiences that align with Your will. In Jesus' name, I pray. Amen.

DAY 98

FINDING PURPOSE IN OVERCOMING CHALLENGES

Scripture: "I can do all this through him who gives me strength." - Philippians 4:13 (NIV)

Devotional: Today, let us explore the theme of finding purpose in life through overcoming challenges. Embrace gratitude for the opportunities to grow and develop resilience in the face of difficulties. Reflect on the times when you have overcome obstacles and experienced personal growth as a result. Take a moment to pray and ask God to give you strength and perseverance to face challenges with a purpose-driven mindset. Let gratitude for the lessons learned and the strength gained through overcoming challenges fill your heart.

Reflection: In your journal, write about a specific challenge or setback that you have overcome. How did it shape your character and purpose? What lessons did you learn during that time? How can you use your experiences to encourage and inspire others facing similar challenges?

Prayer: Mighty God, thank You for the strength You provide to overcome challenges. Help me to face difficulties with resilience and a purpose-driven mindset. Guide me in using my experiences to encourage and support others. In Jesus' name, I pray. Amen.

DAY 99

SEEKING ETERNAL PURPOSE IN THE MIDST OF EARTHLY PURSUITS

Scripture: "Set your minds on things above, not on earthly things." - Colossians 3:2 (NIV)

Devotional: Today, let us explore the theme of finding eternal purpose in the midst of earthly pursuits. Embrace gratitude for the opportunities to invest in things that have lasting significance. Reflect on the times when you have pursued earthly goals and experienced the need for a deeper, eternal purpose. Take a moment to pray and ask God to align your heart and mind with His eternal perspective. Let gratitude for the opportunity to seek and find purpose that transcends earthly pursuits fill your heart.

Reflection: In your journal, write about the tension between earthly pursuits and eternal purpose in your life. How can you seek God's guidance in aligning your priorities? How can you invest in things that have lasting significance? How can you live with an eternal perspective in your daily pursuits?

Prayer: Heavenly Father, guide me in setting my mind on things above. Help me to pursue earthly goals with an eternal purpose in mind. Show me how to invest in things that have lasting significance. In Jesus' name, I pray. Amen.

DAY 100

REFLECTING ON YOUR PURPOSE JOURNEY

Scripture: "I have fought the good fight, I have finished the race, I have kept the faith." - 2 Timothy 4:7 (NIV)

Devotional: Today, let us reflect on your purpose journey. Embrace gratitude for the growth, insights, and experiences you have gained along the way. Reflect on the progress you have made in discovering and living out your purpose. Take a moment to pray and ask God to continue guiding you as you journey towards a fulfilling and purposeful life. Let gratitude for the transformative journey of purpose fill your heart.

Reflection: In your journal, write about your purpose journey so far. How have you grown and evolved? What lessons have you learned along the way? How can you continue seeking God's guidance in fulfilling your purpose?

Prayer: Gracious God, thank You for the transformative journey of purpose. Guide me as I continue to seek and live out Your purpose for my life. Open my eyes to new possibilities and empower me to make a positive impact in the world. In Jesus' name, I pray. Amen.

DAY 101

CULTIVATING A GRATEFUL HEART FOR HAPPINESS

Scripture: "Give thanks in all circumstances; for this is God's will for you in Christ Jesus." - 1 Thessalonians 5:18 (NIV)

Devotional: Today, let us explore the theme of finding happiness through cultivating a grateful heart. Embrace gratitude as a key to experiencing joy and contentment in every circumstance. Reflect on the blessings in your life, both big and small. Take a moment to pray and thank God for His abundant goodness. Let gratitude fill your heart and set the foundation for a happy and fulfilling life.

Reflection: In your journal, write down five things you are grateful for today. How does gratitude affect your perspective and overall happiness? How can you cultivate a grateful heart in your daily life?

Prayer: Gracious God, I thank You for the many blessings in my life. Help me to cultivate a grateful heart and find happiness in the midst of every circumstance. Open my eyes to the goodness around me and enable me to live with gratitude. In Jesus' name, I pray. Amen.

DAY 102

FINDING JOY IN SIMPLE PLEASURES

Scripture: "The joy of the LORD is your strength." - Nehemiah 8:10 (NIV)

Devotional: Today, let us focus on finding happiness through embracing the simple pleasures of life. Joy can be found in the beauty of nature, a warm conversation with a friend, or a moment of stillness. Reflect on the simple pleasures that bring you joy and contentment. Take a moment to appreciate these moments of happiness and offer a prayer of gratitude for the joy they bring to your life.

Reflection: In your journal, make a list of simple pleasures that bring you joy. How can you intentionally incorporate these moments into your daily life? How can you share these simple pleasures with others?

Prayer: God of joy, thank You for the simple pleasures that bring happiness to my life. Help me to appreciate these moments and find joy in the ordinary. Teach me to share these moments with others and spread happiness wherever I go. In Jesus' name, I pray. Amen.

DAY 103

CHOOSING A POSITIVE ATTITUDE FOR LASTING HAPPINESS

Scripture: "Finally, brothers and sisters, whatever is true, whatever is noble, whatever is right, whatever is pure, whatever is lovely, whatever is admirable—if anything is excellent or praiseworthy—think about such things." - Philippians 4:8 (NIV)

Devotional: Today, let us explore the theme of choosing a positive attitude as a pathway to lasting happiness. Our thoughts and attitudes have a significant impact on our overall well-being. Reflect on the power of positive thinking and how it can shape your perspective. Take a moment to pray and ask God to help you focus on the positive aspects of life and cultivate a joyful attitude.

Reflection: In your journal, write about a time when choosing a positive attitude made a difference in your happiness. How can you intentionally shift your mindset to focus on positive and uplifting thoughts? How can you encourage and support others in adopting a positive attitude?

Prayer: God of positivity, I thank You for the power of a positive attitude. Help me to focus on what is true, noble, right, pure, lovely, admirable, excellent, and praiseworthy. Fill my heart with joy and guide me in spreading positivity to those around me. In Jesus' name, I pray. Amen.

DAY 104

FINDING HAPPINESS THROUGH ACTS OF KINDNESS

Scripture: "A generous person will prosper; whoever refreshes others will be refreshed." - Proverbs 11:25 (NIV)

Devotional: Today, let us focus on finding happiness through acts of kindness. When we extend love and kindness to others, we not only bring joy to their lives but also experience a sense of fulfillment ourselves. Reflect on the impact of small acts of kindness and how they can brighten someone's day. Take a moment to pray and ask God to guide you in acts of kindness, spreading happiness to those around you.

Reflection: In your journal, write about a time when an act of kindness brought happiness to someone's life. How can you incorporate intentional acts of kindness into your daily routine? How can you make a positive difference in the lives of others through simple gestures?

Prayer: Loving God, help me to be an instrument of kindness and love in this world. Guide me in finding opportunities to bring happiness to others through acts of kindness. Fill my heart with compassion and generosity. In Jesus' name, I pray. Amen.

DAY 105

CONTENTMENT AS THE KEY TO HAPPINESS

Scripture: "I have learned to be content whatever the circumstances." - Philippians 4:11 (NIV)

Devotional: Today, let us explore the theme of contentment as the key to happiness. True happiness does not come from external circumstances but from an inner state of contentment. Reflect on the areas of your life where contentment can bring lasting joy. Take a moment to pray and ask God to help you cultivate contentment and find happiness in all circumstances.

Reflection: In your journal, write about a time when practicing contentment brought happiness into your life. How can you cultivate contentment in areas where you struggle? How can you encourage others to embrace a mindset of contentment?

Prayer: God of contentment, teach me to find joy in all circumstances. Help me to cultivate a heart of gratitude and contentment, knowing that true happiness is found in You. Grant me the strength to resist comparison and embrace the blessings You have given me. In Jesus' name, I pray. Amen.

DAY 106

LETTING GO OF COMPARISONS FOR AUTHENTIC HAPPINESS

Scripture: "Do not conform to the pattern of this world but be transformed by the renewing of your mind." - Romans 12:2 (NIV)

Devotional: Today, let us focus on letting go of comparisons as a pathway to authentic happiness. In a world that often encourages comparison and the pursuit of perfection, finding true happiness lies in embracing our uniqueness. Reflect on the dangers of comparison and how it can rob us of joy. Take a moment to pray and ask God to help you celebrate your own journey and find contentment in who you are.

Reflection: In your journal, write about a time when letting go of comparisons brought authentic happiness into your life. How can you cultivate a mindset of self-acceptance and appreciation for your unique qualities? How can you support and encourage others in embracing their own journey?

Prayer: Heavenly Father, free me from the trap of comparison. Help me to embrace my own journey and find happiness in who I am. Renew my mind and enable me to appreciate the beauty of others without feeling diminished. In Jesus' name, I pray. Amen.

DAY 107

NURTURING MEANINGFUL RELATIONSHIPS FOR LASTING HAPPINESS

Scripture: "Two are better than one, because they have a good return for their labor." - Ecclesiastes 4:9 (NIV)

Devotional: Today, let us explore the theme of nurturing meaningful relationships as a source of lasting happiness. Our connections with loved ones bring joy, support, and fulfillment to our lives. Reflect on the importance of cultivating healthy and loving relationships. Take a moment to pray and ask God to help you invest in and prioritize your relationships, finding happiness in the bonds you share.

Reflection: In your journal, write about the meaningful relationships in your life and how they contribute to your happiness. How can you nurture and strengthen these connections? How can you show love and appreciation to the people who bring happiness into your life?

Prayer: Loving God, I thank You for the gift of meaningful relationships. Help me to invest in and nurture the bonds I share with others. Guide me in showing love and appreciation to those who bring happiness into my life. In Jesus' name, I pray. Amen.

DAY 108

UNCOVERING JOY IN FORGIVENESS

Scripture: "Bear with each other and forgive one another if any of you has a grievance against someone. Forgive as the Lord forgave you." - Colossians 3:13 (NIV)

Devotional: Today, let us focus on uncovering joy through forgiveness. Holding onto grudges and bitterness only weighs us down and robs us of happiness. Reflect on the power of forgiveness and its ability to bring freedom and healing. Take a moment to pray and ask God to help you forgive those who have hurt you, releasing any resentment and finding joy in the process.

Reflection: In your journal, write about a time when forgiveness brought joy and healing into your life. How can you practice forgiveness more readily in your relationships? How can you extend forgiveness to yourself and embrace the freedom it brings?

Prayer: Gracious God, teach me the power of forgiveness. Help me to release resentment and find joy in the act of forgiving. Enable me to extend forgiveness to others and experience the healing it brings. In Jesus' name, I pray. Amen.

DAY 109

EMBRACING SOLITUDE FOR INNER HAPPINESS

Scripture: "But Jesus often withdrew to lonely places and prayed." - Luke 5:16 (NIV)

Devotional: Today, let us explore the theme of embracing solitude as a means to inner happiness. In the busyness of life, finding moments of stillness and solitude can rejuvenate our spirits and bring clarity. Reflect on the importance of creating space for quiet reflection and connection with God. Take a moment to pray and ask God to help you carve out moments of solitude, finding happiness in the stillness.

Reflection: In your journal, write about a time when solitude brought you inner happiness and spiritual renewal. How can you create intentional moments of solitude in your daily life? How can you deepen your connection with God through quiet reflection?

Prayer: God of solitude, help me to find happiness in moments of stillness. Guide me in creating space for quiet reflection and connection with You. Fill my heart with Your peace and joy as I embrace solitude. In Jesus' name, I pray. Amen.

DAY 110

LIVING WITH PURPOSE FOR TRUE HAPPINESS

Scripture: "Commit to the LORD whatever you do, and he will establish your plans." - Proverbs 16:3 (NIV)

Devotional: Today, let us focus on living with purpose as the pathway to true happiness. When we align our lives with God's will and commit our actions to Him, we find fulfillment and deep joy. Reflect on the importance of living intentionally and seeking God's guidance in all that you do. Take a moment to pray and surrender your plans to God, asking Him to establish your steps and fill your life with purpose and happiness.

Reflection: In your journal, write about the relationship between purpose and happiness in your life. How can you live more intentionally and align your actions with God's will? How can you find happiness in the pursuit of your true purpose?

Prayer: Heavenly Father, guide me in living a purposeful life. Help me to seek Your will in all that I do and to find happiness in the pursuit of my true purpose. Establish my plans and fill my heart with joy as I live for You. In Jesus' name, I pray. Amen.

DAY 111

EMBRACING YOUR PASSIONS AND TALENTS FOR PURPOSE

Scripture: "Each of you should use whatever gift you have received to serve others, as faithful stewards of God's grace in its various forms." - 1 Peter 4:10 (NIV)

Devotional: Today, let us explore the theme of finding purpose in life through embracing your passions and talents. God has uniquely gifted you with abilities and interests that can be used to make a positive impact. Reflect on the passions and talents that ignite your soul. Take a moment to pray and ask God to reveal how you can use these gifts to fulfill your purpose and serve others. Let gratitude for your passions and talents fill your heart as you seek to live a purpose-driven life.

Reflection: In your journal, write about your passions and talents. How can you use them to make a difference in the world? How can you align your interests with your purpose? How can you actively develop and utilize your gifts for the glory of God and the benefit of others?

Prayer: Gracious God, thank You for the unique passions and talents You have given me. Help me to use them faithfully and for the good of others. Guide me in aligning my interests with Your purpose and using my gifts to make a positive impact. In Jesus' name, I pray. Amen.

DAY 112

FINDING PURPOSE IN EVERYDAY WORK

Scripture: "So whether you eat or drink or whatever you do, do it all for the glory of God." - 1 Corinthians 10:31 (NIV)

Devotional: Today, let us focus on finding purpose in our everyday work. Whether it's in a career, as a student, or in caring for a family, our daily tasks and responsibilities can contribute to a greater purpose. Reflect on the impact of your work and how it aligns with God's plan. Take a moment to pray and ask God to show you how your work can be a meaningful expression of your purpose. Let gratitude for the opportunity to find purpose in your everyday tasks fill your heart.

Reflection: In your journal, write about your current work or daily responsibilities. How can you infuse purpose into these tasks? How can you glorify God through your work? How can you make a positive impact on those around you in your everyday life?

Prayer: Heavenly Father, thank You for the opportunity to find purpose in my everyday work. Help me to see the value and meaning in my tasks and responsibilities. Guide me in using my work as a platform to glorify You and make a positive impact on those around me. In Jesus' name, I pray. Amen.

DAY 113

SEEKING GOD'S GUIDANCE FOR LIFE DECISIONS

Scripture: "Trust in the LORD with all your heart and lean not on your own understanding; in all your ways submit to him, and he will make your paths straight." - Proverbs 3:5-6 (NIV)

Devotional: Today, let us explore the theme of seeking God's guidance for life decisions. When we surrender our plans to God and trust in His leading, we can walk confidently in our purpose. Reflect on the decisions you are facing and the importance of seeking God's wisdom. Take a moment to pray and ask God to guide your steps and reveal His purpose for your life. Let gratitude for His guidance and the assurance of His presence fill your heart.

Reflection: In your journal, write about a specific decision you are currently facing. How can you seek God's guidance in this situation? What steps can you take to align your plans with His will? How can you trust Him more fully in your journey of discovering and living out your purpose?

Prayer: Loving God, I surrender my decisions to You. Guide me in seeking Your wisdom and following Your leading. Help me to trust in Your guidance and align my plans with Your will. Thank You for Your presence and faithfulness in my purpose journey. In Jesus' name, I pray. Amen.

DAY 114

EMBRACING CHALLENGES AS OPPORTUNITIES FOR GROWTH

Scripture: "Consider it pure joy, my brothers and sisters, whenever you face trials of many kinds, because you know that the testing of your faith produces perseverance." - James 1:2-3 (NIV)

Devotional: Today, let us focus on embracing challenges as opportunities for growth in our purpose journey. While challenges may be difficult, they can shape us into the person God intends us to be. Reflect on the trials you have faced and the growth that has resulted. Take a moment to pray and ask God to help you view challenges through the lens of purpose and embrace them as catalysts for personal development. Let gratitude for the lessons learned and the strength gained through challenges fill your heart.

Reflection: In your journal, write about a specific challenge or setback you have encountered. How did it shape your character and purpose? How can you embrace challenges with faith and resilience? How can you allow God to work through difficulties to refine and mold you for His purpose?

Prayer: Heavenly Father, I thank You for the growth that comes through challenges. Help me to view difficulties through the lens of purpose and embrace them as opportunities for personal development. Grant me the faith and resilience to face challenges with courage and trust in Your plans. In Jesus' name, I pray. Amen.

DAY 115

FINDING PURPOSE IN SEASONS OF WAITING

Scripture: "Wait for the LORD; be strong and take heart and wait for the LORD." - Psalm 27:14 (NIV)

Devotional: Today, let us explore the theme of finding purpose in life during seasons of waiting. Waiting can be challenging, but it is in these times that God often shapes and prepares us for what is to come. Reflect on the importance of patience and trust in the waiting seasons of life. Take a moment to pray and ask God to reveal His purpose in the waiting and to strengthen you in the midst of uncertainty. Let gratitude for the lessons and growth in seasons of waiting fill your heart.

Reflection: In your journal, write about a specific season of waiting in your life. How did it shape your journey and reveal new purposes? How can you trust God's purpose and timing in your current season of waiting? How can you actively seek His guidance and continue to grow while you wait?

Prayer: Patient God, teach me to wait with a hopeful heart. Help me to trust Your purpose in seasons of waiting and to grow in faith and patience. Strengthen me as I lean on You in uncertainty and guide me as I seek Your guidance in this waiting season. In Jesus' name, I pray. Amen.

DAY 116

ALIGNING YOUR PRIORITIES WITH GOD'S PURPOSE

Scripture: "But seek first his kingdom and his righteousness, and all these things will be given to you as well." - Matthew 6:33 (NIV)

Devotional: Today, let us focus on aligning our priorities with God's purpose for our lives. When we seek God's kingdom first, our lives take on a greater sense of meaning and fulfillment. Reflect on the areas where your priorities may need realignment. Take a moment to pray and ask God to help you prioritize His will above all else and find joy in living out His purpose. Let gratitude for His guidance and the clarity He brings to your priorities fill your heart.

Reflection: In your journal, write about your current priorities and how they align with God's purpose. Are there areas that need adjustment? How can you actively seek God's kingdom and righteousness in your daily life? How can you make intentional choices to live in alignment with His purpose?

Prayer: Gracious God, I surrender my priorities to You. Guide me in aligning my life with Your purpose. Help me to seek Your kingdom and righteousness above all else. Grant me the wisdom to make choices that honor You and bring true fulfillment. In Jesus' name, I pray. Amen.

DAY 117

DISCOVERING PURPOSE THROUGH REFLECTION AND SELF-DISCOVERY

Scripture: "Search me, God, and know my heart; test me and know my anxious thoughts. See if there is any offensive way in me, and lead me in the way everlasting." - Psalm 139:23-24 (NIV)

Devotional: Today, let us explore the theme of discovering purpose through reflection and self-discovery. By understanding ourselves better, we can uncover our unique calling and contribution to the world. Reflect on the importance of self-reflection and inviting God into the process of self-discovery. Take a moment to pray and ask God to reveal insights about your strengths, passions, and purpose. Let gratitude for the opportunity to embark on a journey of self-discovery and purpose fill your heart.

Reflection: In your journal, write about the ways you can engage in self-reflection and self-discovery. How can you uncover your strengths, passions, and purpose? How can you invite God into this process? How can you actively pursue personal growth and self-awareness?

Prayer: Loving God, search me and know my heart. Guide me in self-reflection and self-discovery. Show me my strengths, passions, and purpose. Lead me in the way everlasting as I seek to align my life with Your will. Thank You for the gift of self-awareness and the journey of discovering my purpose. In Jesus' name, I pray. Amen.

DAY 118

FINDING PURPOSE IN YOUR UNIQUE STORY

Scripture: "I praise you because I am fearfully and wonderfully made; your works are wonderful, I know that full well." - Psalm 139:14 (NIV)

Devotional: Today, let us focus on finding purpose in your unique story. God has intricately woven together the experiences, talents, and challenges of your life to shape your purpose. Reflect on your journey and the ways in which your story can inspire and impact others. Take a moment to pray and ask God to reveal His purpose in the chapters of your life. Let gratitude for the beauty and significance of your unique story fill your heart.

Reflection: In your journal, write about the significant moments and experiences that have shaped your life. How can you use your story to make a positive impact on others? How can you embrace your uniqueness and find purpose in the chapters of your life? How can you encourage others to embrace their own stories and seek God's purpose within them?

Prayer: Heavenly Father, I thank You for the unique story of my life. Help me to embrace my experiences, talents, and challenges as part of Your purpose for me. Guide me in using my story to inspire and impact others for Your glory. Fill my heart with gratitude for the chapters of my life and the purpose they hold. In Jesus' name, I pray. Amen.

DAY 119

SERVING OTHERS AS A PATHWAY TO PURPOSE

Scripture: "For even the Son of Man did not come to be served, but to serve, and to give his life as a ransom for many." - Mark 10:45 (NIV)

Devotional: Today, let us explore the theme of finding purpose in life through serving others. When we extend love and compassion to those in need, we reflect the heart of Christ and discover our own purpose. Reflect on the opportunities you have to serve and make a difference in the lives of others. Take a moment to pray and ask God to show you how you can use your gifts and resources to serve others and fulfill your purpose. Let gratitude for the privilege of serving others fill your heart.

Reflection: In your journal, write about a time when serving others brought a sense of purpose and fulfillment. How can you actively seek out opportunities to serve in your daily life? How can you use your unique gifts and resources to make a positive impact in the world? How can you live with a servant's heart and emulate Christ's example?

Prayer: Loving God, thank You for the opportunity to serve others. Open my eyes to the needs around me and empower me to serve with a joyful heart. Guide me in making a meaningful impact in the lives of those I encounter. Fill my heart with gratitude for the privilege of serving and the purpose it brings. In Jesus' name, I pray. Amen.

DAY 120

SEEKING GOD'S PURPOSE ABOVE YOUR OWN DESIRES

Scripture: "For I know the plans I have for you," declares the LORD, "plans to prosper you and not to harm you, plans to give you hope and a future." - Jeremiah 29:11 (NIV)

Devotional: Today, let us focus on seeking God's purpose above our own desires. True fulfillment comes when we align our desires with His plans for our lives. Reflect on the importance of surrendering your dreams and aspirations to God and trusting in His perfect plan. Take a moment to pray and ask God to help you release your own agenda and embrace His purpose for you. Let gratitude for His loving guidance and the hope of a future filled with purpose fill your heart.

Reflection: In your journal, write about your desires and dreams. How can you surrender them to God's will? How can you seek His guidance in aligning your desires with His purpose? How can you trust in His plans even when they differ from your own? How can you live with a surrendered heart and open hands, ready to embrace His purpose for your life?

Prayer: Heavenly Father, I surrender my desires and dreams to You. Help me to seek Your purpose above my own. Guide me in aligning my heart with Your will and trusting in Your perfect plan. Fill me with gratitude for Your loving guidance and the hope of a future filled with purpose. In Jesus' name, I pray. Amen.

DAY 121

EMBRACING YOUR UNIQUE CALLING

Scripture: "For we are God's handiwork, created in Christ Jesus to do good works, which God prepared in advance for us to do." - Ephesians 2:10 (NIV)

Devotional: Today, let us explore the theme of embracing your unique calling. God has created you with specific gifts, passions, and a purpose. Reflect on the ways in which your calling aligns with God's plan for your life. Take a moment to pray and ask God to reveal His calling and empower you to walk in it. Let gratitude for the privilege of being a vessel for God's good works fill your heart.

Reflection: In your journal, write about the aspects of your life that you feel drawn to and passionate about. How do these align with God's purpose for you? How can you actively embrace and pursue your unique calling? How can you use your gifts and talents to make a positive impact on others?

Prayer: Loving Father, I thank You for creating me with a unique calling and purpose. Open my eyes to the ways in which my gifts and passions align with Your plan for my life. Empower me to walk confidently in my calling, bringing glory to Your name through my actions. In Jesus' name, I pray. Amen.

DAY 122

TRUSTING GOD'S TIMING FOR YOUR PURPOSE

Scripture: "He has made everything beautiful in its time." - Ecclesiastes 3:11 (NIV)

Devotional: Today, let us focus on trusting God's timing for your purpose. It can be challenging when we desire to fulfill our purpose but must wait for the right season. Reflect on the importance of patience and trust in God's perfect timing. Take a moment to pray and ask God to help you surrender your timeline to Him and trust that He will bring your purpose to fruition in His perfect time. Let gratitude for His sovereignty and faithfulness fill your heart as you wait with hope.

Reflection: In your journal, write about an area of your life where you are waiting for God's timing in fulfilling your purpose. How can you actively cultivate patience and trust during this season? How can you use this waiting period as an opportunity for personal growth and preparation? How can you seek God's guidance and embrace His plan while you wait?

Prayer: Heavenly Father, I surrender my timeline to You. Help me to trust Your perfect timing for my purpose. Grant me patience and peace as I wait for Your plan to unfold. Teach me valuable lessons and prepare me for the fulfillment of my purpose. In Jesus' name, I pray. Amen.

DAY 123

FINDING PURPOSE IN YOUR RELATIONSHIPS

Scripture: "Love one another deeply, from the heart." - 1 Peter 1:22 (NIV)

Devotional: Today, let us explore the theme of finding purpose in your relationships. Our connections with others offer opportunities for growth, support, and love. Reflect on the importance of nurturing healthy and meaningful relationships. Take a moment to pray and ask God to help you cultivate purposeful connections with those around you. Let gratitude for the people in your life and the purpose they bring fill your heart.

Reflection: In your journal, write about the significant relationships in your life and the ways in which they contribute to your purpose. How can you invest in and strengthen these connections? How can you show love and support to those who bring purpose into your life? How can you be intentional in making a positive impact on others through your relationships?

Prayer: Loving God, thank You for the relationships in my life. Help me to nurture and strengthen the connections that contribute to my purpose. Guide me in showing love and support to those who bring purpose into my life. Teach me how to make a positive impact on others through my relationships. In Jesus' name, I pray. Amen.

DAY 124

SEEKING GOD'S WILL IN YOUR DECISIONS

Scripture: "Your word is a lamp for my feet, a light on my path." - Psalm 119:105 (NIV)

Devotional: Today, let us focus on seeking God's will in your decisions. When we align our choices with His plan, we walk confidently in our purpose. Reflect on the importance of seeking His guidance and wisdom in every decision you make. Take a moment to pray and ask God to lead you and reveal His will for your life. Let gratitude for His guidance and the assurance of walking in His purpose fill your heart.

Reflection: In your journal, write about a decision you are currently facing. How can you seek God's will and guidance in this situation? What steps can you take to align your choices with His purpose? How can you trust in His leading and make decisions that honor Him?

Prayer: Heavenly Father, I seek Your will in all that I do. Guide me and reveal Your purpose for my life. Grant me the wisdom and discernment to make choices that align with Your plan. Fill me with gratitude for Your guidance and the assurance of walking in Your purpose. In Jesus' name, I pray. Amen.

DAY 125

FINDING PURPOSE IN YOUR UNIQUE PERSONALITY

Scripture: "I praise you because I am fearfully and wonderfully made; your works are wonderful, I know that full well." - Psalm 139:14 (NIV)

Devotional: Today, let us explore the theme of finding purpose in your unique personality. God has created you with distinct traits and characteristics that contribute to His plan for your life. Reflect on the ways in which your personality can be used to bring glory to God and fulfill your purpose. Take a moment to pray and ask God to help you embrace and utilize your unique qualities for His purposes. Let gratitude for the gift of your personality and the purpose it holds fill your heart.

Reflection: In your journal, write about the unique traits and characteristics of your personality. How can you use these qualities to make a positive impact on others? How can you embrace and develop your personality for God's purposes? How can you allow Him to shape and refine your character as you walk in your purpose?

Prayer: Gracious God, I thank You for fearfully and wonderfully creating me. Help me to embrace and utilize the unique traits and characteristics of my personality for Your glory. Guide me in developing and refining my character as I walk in Your purpose. Fill my heart with gratitude for the gift of my personality and the purpose it holds. In Jesus' name, I pray. Amen.

DAY 126

MAKING A DIFFERENCE IN YOUR COMMUNITY

Scripture: "Let us not become weary in doing good, for at the proper time we will reap a harvest if we do not give up." - Galatians 6:9 (NIV)

Devotional: Today, let us focus on making a difference in your community. God has placed you in your specific community for a purpose. Reflect on the needs around you and the ways in which you can contribute to the well-being of others. Take a moment to pray and ask God to show you how you can actively engage in acts of kindness, service, and love within your community. Let gratitude for the opportunity to bring positive change and make a difference fill your heart.

Reflection: In your journal, write about the specific needs and challenges in your community. How can you contribute to the well-being of others? How can you actively engage in acts of kindness, service, and love within your community? How can you inspire others to join you in making a positive impact?

Prayer: Loving God, guide me in making a difference in my community. Show me the needs around me and how I can contribute to the well-being of others. Empower me to engage in acts of kindness, service, and love. Fill my heart with gratitude for the opportunity to bring positive change and make a difference. In Jesus' name, I pray. Amen.

DAY 127

EMBRACING YOUR ROLE AS A LIGHT IN THE WORLD

Scripture: "You are the light of the world. A town built on a hill cannot be hidden." - Matthew 5:14 (NIV)

Devotional: Today, let us explore the theme of embracing your role as a light in the world. As a follower of Christ, you have the opportunity to shine His light and make a positive impact on those around you. Reflect on the significance of your influence and the ways in which you can bring hope, love, and encouragement to others. Take a moment to pray and ask God to help you be a source of light and inspiration in the world. Let gratitude for the privilege of being a vessel for His light fill your heart.

Reflection: In your journal, write about the ways in which you can be a light in the world. How can you bring hope, love, and encouragement to those around you? How can you use your words and actions to reflect Christ's light? How can you be intentional in making a positive impact on others?

Prayer: Heavenly Father, I thank You for calling me to be a light in the world. Help me to shine Your light in all that I do. Guide me in bringing hope, love, and encouragement to those around me. Empower me to make a positive impact and reflect Your character. In Jesus' name, I pray. Amen.

DAY 128

FINDING PURPOSE IN YOUR JOURNEY OF FAITH

Scripture: "And without faith it is impossible to please God, because anyone who comes to him must believe that he exists and that he rewards those who earnestly seek him." - Hebrews 11:6 (NIV)

Devotional: Today, let us focus on finding purpose in your journey of faith. Your relationship with God is a vital part of your purpose and identity. Reflect on the significance of your faith and the ways in which it shapes your purpose. Take a moment to pray and ask God to deepen your faith and reveal His plan for your life. Let gratitude for the journey of faith and the rewards of seeking Him earnestly fill your heart.

Reflection: In your journal, write about the role of faith in your purpose journey. How does your faith shape your perspective and choices? How can you deepen your relationship with God and trust Him more fully in your journey? How can you encourage others in their own faith and purpose journeys?

Prayer: Loving God, I thank You for the journey of faith and the purpose it brings to my life. Deepen my relationship with You and strengthen my faith. Guide me in trusting You more fully in my purpose journey. Fill my heart with gratitude for the rewards of seeking You earnestly. In Jesus' name, I pray. Amen.

DAY 129

OVERCOMING OBSTACLES ON THE PATH TO PURPOSE

Scripture: "I can do all this through him who gives me strength." - Philippians 4:13 (NIV)

Devotional: Today, let us explore the theme of overcoming obstacles on the path to purpose. Challenges and setbacks are a natural part of life, but they do not define our purpose. Reflect on the ways in which you can navigate through obstacles with faith and perseverance. Take a moment to pray and ask God to strengthen you, grant you wisdom, and help you overcome any hindrances on your purpose journey. Let gratitude for His faithfulness and the assurance of His strength fill your heart.

Reflection: In your journal, write about a specific obstacle or challenge you are facing on your purpose journey. How can you navigate through it with faith and perseverance? How can you lean on God's strength and wisdom? How can you grow and learn from obstacles, allowing them to refine and shape you for your purpose?

Prayer: Heavenly Father, I thank You for Your strength that enables me to overcome obstacles. Grant me wisdom, perseverance, and faith as I navigate challenges on my purpose journey. Help me to rely on Your strength and learn from each obstacle I face. Fill my heart with gratitude for Your faithfulness and the assurance that You are with me every step of the way. In Jesus' name, I pray. Amen.

DAY 130

FINDING PURPOSE IN YOUR TALENTS AND ABILITIES

Scripture: "Each of you should use whatever gift you have received to serve others, as faithful stewards of God's grace in its various forms." - 1 Peter 4:10 (NIV)

Devotional: Today, let us focus on finding purpose in your talents and abilities. God has uniquely gifted you with specific skills and strengths that can be used to impact others. Reflect on the ways in which your talents can be aligned with His purpose. Take a moment to pray and ask God to reveal how you can use your abilities to serve others and fulfill your purpose. Let gratitude for the gifts you have been entrusted with and the privilege of being a faithful steward fill your heart.

Reflection: In your journal, write about your talents and abilities. How can you use them to serve others and make a positive impact? How can you develop and maximize your skills for God's purposes? How can you be a faithful steward of the gifts entrusted to you?

Prayer: Gracious God, I thank You for the talents and abilities You have given me. Help me to use them faithfully and for the benefit of others. Guide me in developing and maximizing my skills for Your purposes. Fill my heart with gratitude for the privilege of being a faithful steward. In Jesus' name, I pray. Amen.

DAY 131

IMPACTING FUTURE GENERATIONS FOR GOD'S KINGDOM

Scripture: "One generation commends your works to another; they tell of your mighty acts." - Psalm 145:4 (NIV)

Devotional: Today, let us explore the theme of impacting future generations for God's kingdom. Your life and purpose have the potential to leave a lasting legacy. Reflect on the significance of your influence on those who come after you. Take a moment to pray and ask God to help you be intentional in passing on your faith, values, and purpose to the next generation. Let gratitude for the opportunity to impact future generations and leave a lasting legacy fill your heart.

Reflection: In your journal, write about the ways in which you can impact future generations for God's kingdom. How can you pass on your faith, values, and purpose to the next generation? How can you invest in the lives of children, youth, or young adults? How can you leave a lasting legacy of love, faith, and purpose?

Prayer: Heavenly Father, I desire to impact future generations for Your kingdom. Guide me in passing on my faith, values, and purpose to the next generation. Show me how to invest in the lives of children, youth, or young adults. Fill my heart with gratitude for the opportunity to leave a lasting legacy. In Jesus' name, I pray. Amen.

DAY 132

CONTENTMENT IN YOUR PURPOSE JOURNEY

Scripture: "I have learned to be content whatever the circumstances." - Philippians 4:11 (NIV)

Devotional: Today, let us focus on finding contentment in your purpose journey. Contentment does not mean complacency, but rather a deep sense of satisfaction and peace in the midst of your pursuit of purpose. Reflect on the importance of finding joy and fulfillment in each step of the journey, even when it doesn't unfold as expected. Take a moment to pray and ask God to help you cultivate contentment and gratitude in your purpose journey. Let gratitude for His provision and guidance fill your heart.

Reflection: In your journal, write about the areas in your purpose journey where you struggle to find contentment. How can you cultivate gratitude and satisfaction in each step? How can you trust God's timing and plan even when things don't go as expected? How can you find joy and fulfillment in the present moment?

Prayer: Loving Father, help me to find contentment in my purpose journey. Teach me to trust Your timing and plan. Cultivate gratitude and joy in each step, even when it doesn't unfold as expected. Fill my heart with gratitude for Your provision and guidance. In Jesus' name, I pray. Amen.

DAY 133

MAKING SACRIFICES FOR YOUR PURPOSE

Scripture: "Then he said to them all: 'Whoever wants to be my disciple must deny themselves and take up their cross daily and follow me.'" - Luke 9:23 (NIV)

Devotional: Today, let us explore the theme of making sacrifices for your purpose. Following God's plan often requires us to let go of our own desires and comfort. Reflect on the sacrifices you may need to make in order to fully embrace your purpose. Take a moment to pray and ask God to give you the strength and willingness to make sacrifices for His sake. Let gratitude for the opportunity to lay down your own desires and follow Him fill your heart.

Reflection: In your journal, write about the sacrifices you may need to make in order to fulfill your purpose. How can you let go of your own desires and comfort? How can you align your life with God's plan, even when it requires sacrifice? How can you find peace and fulfillment in surrendering to His purpose?

Prayer: Gracious God, I surrender my desires and comfort to You. Give me the strength and willingness to make sacrifices for Your sake. Help me to align my life with Your plan, even when it requires sacrifice. Fill my heart with gratitude for the privilege of following You. In Jesus' name, I pray. Amen.

DAY 134

OVERCOMING SELF-DOUBT IN PURSUIT OF PURPOSE

Scripture: "I can do all this through him who gives me strength." - Philippians 4:13 (NIV)

Devotional: Today, let us focus on overcoming self-doubt in pursuit of purpose. Doubts and insecurities can hinder us from fully embracing our purpose. Reflect on the truth that you are capable and equipped through Christ's strength. Take a moment to pray and ask God to help you overcome self-doubt and step confidently into your purpose. Let gratitude for His empowering presence and the assurance of His strength fill your heart.

Reflection: In your journal, write about the areas where you struggle with self-doubt in your purpose journey. How can you renew your mind with God's truth and trust in His strength? How can you silence the voice of self-doubt and step boldly into your purpose? How can you encourage others who may be facing similar doubts?

Prayer: Heavenly Father, I confess my self-doubts to You. Renew my mind with Your truth and help me to trust in Your strength. Empower me to silence the voice of doubt and step boldly into my purpose. Fill my heart with gratitude for Your empowering presence. In Jesus' name, I pray. Amen.

DAY 135

RECEIVING AND EXTENDING GRACE ON YOUR PURPOSE JOURNEY

Scripture: "Let us then approach God's throne of grace with confidence, so that we may receive mercy and find grace to help us in our time of need." - Hebrews 4:16 (NIV)

Devotional: Today, let us explore the theme of receiving and extending grace on your purpose journey. God's grace sustains and empowers us as we seek to fulfill our purpose. Reflect on the significance of receiving His mercy and grace in your life. Take a moment to pray and ask God to help you extend grace to yourself and others on the journey. Let gratitude for His unending grace and the privilege of extending it to others fill your heart.

Reflection: In your journal, write about the areas where you need to receive and extend grace on your purpose journey. How can you embrace God's mercy and grace in your life? How can you show grace to yourself when facing setbacks or challenges? How can you extend grace and forgiveness to others who may have hurt or disappointed you?

Prayer: Loving God, I thank You for Your abundant grace and mercy. Help me to receive Your grace and extend it to myself and others on my purpose journey. Teach me how to show grace when facing setbacks or challenges. Empower me to extend grace and forgiveness to those who have hurt or disappointed me. In Jesus' name, I pray. Amen.

DAY 136

THE JOY OF NOURISHING FOOD

Scripture: "So whether you eat or drink or whatever you do, do it all for the glory of God." - 1 Corinthians 10:31 (NIV)

Devotional: Today, let's find joy in the nourishment of food. Take time to savor a delicious meal, appreciating the flavors and the nourishment it provides for your body. Embrace the joy of sharing a meal with loved ones and giving thanks to God for the abundance of His provision.

Reflection: In your journal, write about the joy you find in nourishing food. How can you approach meals with gratitude and mindfulness, recognizing the goodness of God's creation in the variety of flavors and ingredients? How can you make mealtimes a time of joy, connection, and reflection on God's provision in your life?

Prayer: Gracious God, I thank You for the joy of nourishing food. As I partake in delicious meals, help me to savor the flavors and embrace the nourishment they provide. May mealtimes be an opportunity to give thanks to You for Your abundant provision and to share joyful moments with loved ones. In Jesus' name, I pray. Amen.

DAY 137

SURRENDERING YOUR PLANS TO GOD'S PURPOSE

Scripture: "In their hearts humans plan their course, but the LORD establishes their steps." - Proverbs 16:9 (NIV)

Devotional: Today, let us explore the theme of surrendering your plans to God's purpose. Our plans may be well-intentioned, but ultimately, God's purpose and timing prevail. Reflect on the importance of surrendering your plans and trusting in His divine guidance. Take a moment to pray and ask God to align your desires with His purpose and grant you the wisdom to surrender to His leading. Let gratitude for His sovereignty and the assurance of His perfect plan fill your heart.

Reflection: In your journal, write about the areas where you struggle to surrender your plans to God's purpose. How can you align your desires with His plan? How can you actively surrender your plans and trust in His leading? How can you find peace and fulfillment in His perfect plan?

Prayer: Gracious God, I surrender my plans to Your purpose. Align my desires with Your plan and grant me the wisdom to surrender to Your leading. Help me to trust in Your divine guidance and find peace in Your perfect plan. Fill my heart with gratitude for Your sovereignty. In Jesus' name, I pray. Amen.

DAY 138

FINDING PURPOSE IN YOUR EVERYDAY RESPONSIBILITIES

Scripture: "And whatever you do, whether in word or deed, do it all in the name of the Lord Jesus, giving thanks to God the Father through him." - Colossians 3:17 (NIV)

Devotional: Today, let us focus on finding purpose in your everyday responsibilities. Your actions and attitudes in the small things of life can have a significant impact. Reflect on the importance of living each moment for the glory of God. Take a moment to pray and ask God to help you find purpose in your daily tasks and responsibilities. Let gratitude for the privilege of serving Him in the ordinary moments of life fill your heart.

Reflection: In your journal, write about the everyday responsibilities and tasks that may sometimes feel mundane. How can you approach them with purpose and a desire to honor God? How can you serve Him faithfully in the small things? How can you find joy and fulfillment in the ordinary moments of life?

Prayer: Heavenly Father, I thank You for the everyday responsibilities and tasks that fill my life. Help me to approach them with purpose and a desire to honor You. Teach me how to serve You faithfully in the small things. Fill my heart with gratitude for the privilege of serving You in the ordinary moments of life. In Jesus' name, I pray. Amen.

DAY 139

EMBRACING GROWTH AND CHANGE ON YOUR PURPOSE JOURNEY

Scripture: "See, I am doing a new thing! Now it springs up; do you not perceive it? I am making a way in the wilderness and streams in the wasteland." - Isaiah 43:19 (NIV)

Devotional: Today, let us explore the theme of embracing growth and change on your purpose journey. God often leads us through seasons of change and growth to shape us for His purposes. Reflect on the opportunities for growth and transformation that arise on your journey. Take a moment to pray and ask God to help you embrace change and be open to His leading. Let gratitude for the new things He is doing and the ways He is shaping you fill your heart.

Reflection: In your journal, write about a specific area of growth or change you are currently experiencing on your purpose journey. How can you embrace the process and be open to God's leading? What lessons and opportunities for transformation do you perceive in this season? How can you actively seek His guidance and purpose amidst the changes?

Prayer: Loving Father, I thank You for the opportunities for growth and change on my purpose journey. Help me to embrace the process and be open to Your leading. Guide me in perceiving the lessons and transformation that You have for me in this season. Fill my heart with gratitude for the new things You are doing and the ways You are shaping me. In Jesus' name, I pray. Amen.

DAY 140

REST AND RENEWAL FOR A PURPOSEFUL LIFE

Scripture: "Come to me, all you who are weary and burdened, and I will give you rest." - Matthew 11:28 (NIV)

Devotional: Today, let us focus on the theme of rest and renewal for a purposeful life. In the busyness of pursuing our purpose, it is important to find rest and allow ourselves to be renewed. Reflect on the significance of rest in your life and the ways in which it enables you to live purposefully. Take a moment to pray and ask God to help you prioritize rest and find balance in your pursuit of purpose. Let gratitude for the rest and renewal that He provides fill your heart.

Reflection: In your journal, write about the importance of rest in your purpose journey. How can you prioritize rest and self-care in your daily life? How can you create space for renewal and rejuvenation? How can you find a healthy balance between productivity and rest?

Prayer: Heavenly Father, I thank You for the gift of rest and renewal. Help me to prioritize rest and self-care in my purpose journey. Guide me in finding a healthy balance between productivity and rest. Fill my heart with gratitude for the rest and renewal that You provide. In Jesus' name, I pray. Amen.

DAY 141

EMBRACING YOUR UNIQUENESS

Scripture: "I praise you because I am fearfully and wonderfully made; your works are wonderful, I know that full well." - Psalm 139:14 (NIV)

Devotional: Today, let us explore the theme of embracing your uniqueness. God has created you with a set of gifts, talents, and experiences that make you unique. Reflect on the beauty of your individuality and the ways in which your uniqueness contributes to your purpose. Take a moment to pray and thank God for the specific qualities that make you who you are. Let gratitude for the privilege of being fearfully and wonderfully made fill your heart.

Reflection: In your journal, write about the unique qualities, talents, and experiences that make you who you are. How can you embrace and celebrate your individuality? How can you use your unique attributes to fulfill your purpose and make a difference in the world? How can you appreciate the uniqueness of others and support them in their own purpose journeys?

Prayer: Heavenly Father, I thank You for fearfully and wonderfully creating me. Help me to embrace and celebrate my uniqueness. Guide me in using my unique qualities, talents, and experiences to fulfill my purpose. Teach me how to appreciate the uniqueness of others and support them in their purpose journeys. In Jesus' name, I pray. Amen.

DAY 142

FINDING PURPOSE IN SEASONS OF REST

Scripture: "He makes me lie down in green pastures, he leads me beside quiet waters, he refreshes my soul." - Psalm 23:2-3 (NIV)

Devotional: Today, let us focus on finding purpose in seasons of rest. Rest is an essential part of a balanced and purposeful life. Reflect on the importance of taking time to rest, recharge, and connect with God. Take a moment to pray and ask God to help you prioritize rest and find moments of rejuvenation in your daily life. Let gratitude for the gift of rest and the opportunity to be refreshed in His presence fill your heart.

Reflection: In your journal, write about the value of rest in your purpose journey. How can you create intentional moments of rest in your daily routine? How can you connect with God and allow Him to refresh your soul? How can you find joy and fulfillment in the seasons of rest, knowing that they contribute to your overall well-being and purpose?

Prayer: Loving God, I thank You for the gift of rest. Help me to prioritize moments of rest and rejuvenation in my purpose journey. Guide me in connecting with You and finding refreshment for my soul. Fill my heart with gratitude for the seasons of rest and the opportunity to be renewed in Your presence. In Jesus' name, I pray. Amen.

DAY 143

FINDING INSPIRATION IN BOOKS AND ART

Scripture: "All Scripture is God-breathed and is useful for teaching, rebuking, correcting, and training in righteousness." - 2 Timothy 3:16 (NIV)

Devotional: Today, let's find joy in the inspiration of books and art. Whether it's reading a good book, visiting an art gallery, or creating something with your own hands, books and art have the power to uplift and ignite our creativity. Take time to immerse yourself in literature and art that brings joy and speaks to your soul.

Reflection: In your journal, write about the books and artworks that have inspired you recently. How do these creative expressions enrich your understanding of life and God's creation? How can you make time for reading and appreciating art as a source of joy and growth in your life? How can you use your own creativity to inspire others?

Prayer: Creative God, I thank You for the inspiration found in books and art. As I engage with literature and creative expressions, help me to find joy and meaning in these forms of inspiration. May they deepen my understanding of Your creation and stir my own creativity to glorify You. In Jesus' name, I pray. Amen.

DAY 144

DISCOVERING PURPOSE IN EVERYDAY MOMENTS

Scripture: "And whatever you do, whether in word or deed, do it all in the name of the Lord Jesus, giving thanks to God the Father through him." - Colossians 3:17 (NIV)

Devotional: Today, let us focus on discovering purpose in everyday moments. Our purpose is not limited to grand achievements but can be found in the small, ordinary actions of our daily lives. Reflect on the significance of living each moment with intention and for the glory of God. Take a moment to pray and ask God to help you find purpose and meaning in the everyday moments. Let gratitude for the opportunity to serve and honor God in the ordinary fill your heart.

Reflection: In your journal, write about the everyday moments in which you can discover purpose. How can you bring intention and meaning to your daily actions? How can you serve and honor God in the small tasks and interactions of life? How can you find joy and fulfillment in the present moment, knowing that each moment contributes to your overall purpose?

Prayer: Heavenly Father, I desire to find purpose in the everyday moments of my life. Help me to bring intention and meaning to my daily actions. Guide me in serving and honoring You in the small tasks and interactions. Fill my heart with gratitude for the opportunity to glorify You in the ordinary. In Jesus' name, I pray. Amen.

DAY 145

CULTIVATING A HEART OF GRATITUDE

Scripture: "Give thanks to the LORD, for he is good; his love endures forever." - 1 Chronicles 16:34 (NIV)

Devotional: Today, let us explore the theme of cultivating a heart of gratitude. Gratitude opens our eyes to the blessings and purposeful moments in our lives. Reflect on the importance of cultivating a grateful heart and the ways in which gratitude can transform your perspective. Take a moment to pray and thank God for His goodness and the abundant blessings in your life. Let gratitude for His faithfulness and provision fill your heart.

Reflection: In your journal, write about the blessings and purposeful moments in your life that you are grateful for. How can you cultivate a heart of gratitude and express thanks to God each day? How does gratitude impact your perspective and overall sense of purpose? How can you share your gratitude with others and inspire them to embrace gratitude in their own lives?

Prayer: Gracious God, I thank You for Your goodness and the abundant blessings in my life. Teach me to cultivate a heart of gratitude and to express thanks to You daily. Help me to see the purposeful moments in my life and the ways You are working. Fill my heart with gratitude for Your faithfulness and provision. In Jesus' name, I pray. Amen.

DAY 146

USING YOUR PAST FOR A PURPOSEFUL FUTURE

Scripture: "And we know that in all things God works for the good of those who love him, who have been called according to his purpose." - Romans 8:28 (NIV)

Devotional: Today, let us focus on using your past for a purposeful future. God can redeem and use our past experiences, both positive and challenging, to shape us for His purposes. Reflect on the ways in which your past has shaped your present and how it can contribute to your purposeful future. Take a moment to pray and ask God to help you see the lessons and opportunities for growth in your past. Let gratitude for His redemptive work and the hope of a purposeful future fill your heart.

Reflection: In your journal, write about the significant experiences or lessons from your past that have shaped your present journey. How can you use these experiences for a purposeful future? How can you find healing and redemption in areas of your past that may still hold pain or regret? How can you share your story with others to encourage and inspire them in their own purpose journeys?

Prayer: Heavenly Father, I thank You for Your redemptive work in my past. Help me to see the lessons and opportunities for growth that my past holds. Guide me in using my experiences for a purposeful future. Bring healing and redemption to areas of my past that may still hold pain or regret. Fill my heart with gratitude for the hope of a purposeful future. In Jesus' name, I pray. Amen.

DAY 147

SEEKING GOD'S GUIDANCE IN DECISION-MAKING

Scripture: "Trust in the LORD with all your heart and lean not on your own understanding; in all your ways submit to him, and he will make your paths straight." - Proverbs 3:5-6 (NIV)

Devotional: Today, let us explore the theme of seeking God's guidance in decision-making. Your purpose journey involves making choices and decisions along the way. Reflect on the importance of seeking God's wisdom and guidance in every decision you face. Take a moment to pray and ask God to give you clarity, discernment, and peace as you make decisions aligned with His purpose for your life. Let gratitude for His guidance and the assurance of His faithfulness fill your heart.

Reflection: In your journal, write about a decision you are currently facing on your purpose journey. How can you seek God's guidance and wisdom in this decision? How can you align your choices with His purpose for your life? How can you cultivate a heart of surrender and trust as you make decisions? How can you find peace in knowing that He will make your paths straight?

Prayer: Loving God, I seek Your guidance in every decision I face. Grant me clarity, discernment, and peace as I make choices aligned with Your purpose. Help me to submit all my ways to You and trust in Your leading. Fill my heart with gratitude for Your guidance and the assurance of Your faithfulness. In Jesus' name, I pray. Amen.

DAY 148

SERVING OTHERS WITH COMPASSION

Scripture: "Each of you should use whatever gift you have received to serve others, as faithful stewards of God's grace in its various forms." - 1 Peter 4:10 (NIV)

Devotional: Today, let us focus on serving others with compassion. Your purpose is intimately connected to serving and making a difference in the lives of others. Reflect on the importance of using your gifts and resources to bless and uplift those around you. Take a moment to pray and ask God to help you cultivate a heart of compassion and to show you practical ways to serve others with love. Let gratitude for the privilege of being a vessel of God's grace and compassion fill your heart.

Reflection: In your journal, write about the ways in which you can serve others with compassion. How can you use your gifts, resources, and time to bless and uplift those around you? How can you show love and kindness in practical ways? How can you make a positive impact on the lives of others through your acts of service?

Prayer: Heavenly Father, I thank You for the privilege of serving others. Help me to cultivate a heart of compassion and to use my gifts, resources, and time to bless and uplift those around me. Show me practical ways to demonstrate love and kindness. Fill my heart with gratitude for the privilege of being a vessel of Your grace and compassion. In Jesus' name, I pray. Amen.

DAY 149

ENJOYING THE COMPANY OF LOVED ONES

Scripture: "Two are better than one, because they have a good return for their labor." - Ecclesiastes 4:9 (NIV)

Devotional: Today, let's focus on the joy of spending time with loved ones. Whether it's family, friends, or colleagues, the presence of those we cherish enriches our lives. Take time to connect with your loved ones, whether in person or through a phone call or video chat. Embrace the joy and support that comes from meaningful relationships.

Reflection: In your journal, write about the joy you find in the company of loved ones. How do these relationships add depth and meaning to your life? How can you prioritize quality time with those you care about, even in the midst of a busy schedule? How can you be a source of joy and encouragement to your loved ones?

Prayer: Heavenly Father, I thank You for the joy of meaningful relationships with my loved ones. As I spend time with them, help me to cherish and nurture these connections. May our interactions bring joy and support to each other's lives, reflecting Your love and care for us all. In Jesus' name, I pray. Amen.

Day 150

Finding Purpose in Times of Waiting

Scripture: "Wait for the LORD; be strong and take heart and wait for the LORD." - Psalm 27:14 (NIV)

Devotional: Today, let us focus on finding purpose in times of waiting. Waiting can often be a challenging and uncertain season, but it is not without purpose. Reflect on the ways in which waiting can refine your character, deepen your trust in God, and prepare you for the fulfillment of His plans. Take a moment to pray and ask God to help you embrace patience and find purpose in the waiting seasons of your life. Let gratitude for His faithfulness and the lessons learned in times of waiting fill your heart.

Reflection: In your journal, write about a specific season of waiting you are currently experiencing. How can you embrace patience and find purpose in this season? What lessons and character qualities do you perceive are being refined in your waiting? How can you actively seek God's guidance and purpose in the waiting seasons of your life?

Prayer: Heavenly Father, I thank You for Your faithfulness in times of waiting. Help me to embrace patience and find purpose in the seasons of waiting. Guide me in perceiving the lessons and character refinement that You have for me. Teach me how to actively seek Your guidance and purpose in these waiting seasons. Fill my heart with gratitude for Your faithfulness and the assurance that You are working even in times of waiting. In Jesus' name, I pray. Amen.

DAY 151

CULTIVATING A HEART OF GENEROSITY

Scripture: "Each of you should give what you have decided in your heart to give, not reluctantly or under compulsion, for God loves a cheerful giver." - 2 Corinthians 9:7 (NIV)

Devotional: Today, let us explore the theme of cultivating a heart of generosity. Generosity is an essential aspect of a purposeful life, as it allows us to share God's blessings with others. Reflect on the significance of giving, not only in terms of material possessions but also in offering love, kindness, and encouragement to those around you. Take a moment to pray and ask God to help you cultivate a generous heart and to show you practical ways to give to others. Let gratitude for His abundant blessings and the joy of giving fill your heart.

Reflection: In your journal, write about the ways in which you can cultivate a heart of generosity. How can you give of your time, resources, and talents to bless others? How can you offer love, kindness, and encouragement to those in need? How can you make a positive impact on the lives of others through your generosity?

Prayer: Gracious God, I thank You for Your abundant blessings in my life. Help me to cultivate a generous heart and to give to others with joy and love. Show me practical ways to use my time, resources, and talents to bless those around me. Teach me how to offer love, kindness, and encouragement to those in need. Fill my heart with gratitude for the privilege of making a positive impact through my generosity. In Jesus' name, I pray. Amen.

Day 152

Nurturing Relationships on Your Purpose Journey

Scripture: "Two are better than one, because they have a good return for their labor: If either of them falls down, one can help the other up." - Ecclesiastes 4:9-10 (NIV)

Devotional: Today, let us focus on nurturing relationships on your purpose journey. We are not meant to walk this journey alone but in community with others. Reflect on the importance of cultivating healthy and supportive relationships that can encourage, challenge, and uplift you on your purpose journey. Take a moment to pray and ask God to guide you in nurturing meaningful connections and to show you how you can be a blessing to others in their own purpose journeys. Let gratitude for the gift of relationships and the power of community fill your heart.

Reflection: In your journal, write about the relationships in your life that support and encourage you in your purpose journey. How can you nurture and strengthen these relationships? How can you be intentional in seeking out community and connecting with like-minded individuals? How can you be a source of encouragement and support to others on their purpose journeys?

Prayer: Heavenly Father, I thank You for the relationships in my life that support and encourage me. Guide me in nurturing and strengthening these connections. Show me how to seek out community and connect with like-minded individuals who can uplift me on my purpose journey. Teach me how to be a source of encouragement and support to others in their own purpose journeys. Fill my heart with gratitude for the gift of relationships and the power of community. In Jesus' name, I pray. Amen.

DAY 153

DISCOVERING PURPOSE IN SEASONS OF SUFFERING

Scripture: "Not only so, but we also glory in our sufferings, because we know that suffering produces perseverance; perseverance, character; and character, hope." - Romans 5:3-4 (NIV)

Devotional: Today, let us explore the theme of discovering purpose in seasons of suffering. Suffering is a reality of life, but even in the midst of pain and hardship, God can bring purpose and transformation. Reflect on the ways in which suffering can produce perseverance, character, and hope in your life. Take a moment to pray and ask God to help you find meaning and purpose in the midst of your suffering. Let gratitude for His presence and the growth that comes through difficult seasons fill your heart.

Reflection: In your journal, write about a specific season of suffering or hardship you have experienced. How can you find purpose and meaning in the midst of your pain? How has suffering shaped your character and brought forth perseverance? How can you find hope and trust God's faithfulness even in the most challenging circumstances?

Prayer: Gracious God, I thank You for Your presence and strength in times of suffering. Help me to find purpose and meaning in the midst of my pain. Teach me how to trust Your faithfulness and find hope in difficult circumstances. Fill my heart with gratitude for the growth and transformation that can come through seasons of suffering. In Jesus' name, I pray. Amen.

DAY 154

HONORING GOD IN YOUR WORK

Scripture: "Whatever you do, work at it with all your heart, as working for the Lord, not for human masters." - Colossians 3:23 (NIV)

Devotional: Today, let us focus on honoring God in your work. Your occupation, whether paid or unpaid, provides opportunities to glorify God and serve others. Reflect on the significance of approaching your work with excellence, integrity, and a heart that seeks to honor God. Take a moment to pray and ask God to help you view your work as a means of worship and service to Him. Let gratitude for the privilege of using your skills and talents to make a difference fill your heart.

Reflection: In your journal, write about the ways in which you can honor God in your work. How can you approach your tasks with excellence, integrity, and a heart that seeks to glorify Him? How can you be a positive influence and serve others through your work? How can you find joy and fulfillment in using your skills and talents for His purposes?

Prayer: Heavenly Father, I desire to honor You in my work. Help me to approach my tasks with excellence, integrity, and a heart that seeks to glorify You. Guide me in being a positive influence and serving others through my work. Fill my heart with gratitude for the privilege of using my skills and talents to make a difference. In Jesus' name, I pray. Amen.

DAY 155

THE JOY OF GIVING AND SERVING OTHERS

Scripture: "Each of you should give what you have decided in your heart to give, not reluctantly or under compulsion, for God loves a cheerful giver." - 2 Corinthians 9:7 (NIV)

Devotional: Today, let's find joy in giving and serving others. Whether it's a small act of kindness or a larger gesture, giving with a cheerful heart not only blesses others but also brings joy to our own lives. Take time to serve someone in need, lend a helping hand, or simply share a kind word. Embrace the joy that comes from being a blessing to others.

Reflection: In your journal, write about the joy you experience when giving and serving others. How does serving with a cheerful heart impact your perspective on life's simplicity and purpose? How can you actively seek opportunities to give and serve in your community and beyond? How can you inspire others to find joy in acts of kindness?

Prayer: Gracious God, I thank You for the joy that comes from giving and serving others. Help me to embrace opportunities to be a blessing to those in need, serving with a cheerful heart. May my acts of kindness reflect Your love and bring joy to others, revealing the simplicity of Your message of love. In Jesus' name, I pray. Amen.

Day 156

Embracing Music's Soothing Melody

Scripture: "He put a new song in my mouth, a hymn of praise to our God. Many will see and fear the Lord and put their trust in him." - Psalm 40:3 (NIV)

Devotional: Today, let's focus on the uplifting power of music. Whether you play an instrument, sing, or simply listen to melodies, music has the ability to soothe and uplift our souls. Take time to engage with your favorite tunes or explore new songs that bring joy to your heart. Allow the harmonies and lyrics to draw you closer to God and bring peace to your spirit.

Reflection: In your journal, write about the impact of music on your emotions and mindset. How does music help you find joy and comfort in life's simplicity? How can you incorporate more music into your daily routine to uplift your spirit and find solace in God's presence? How can you use music to encourage and inspire others?

Prayer: Dear Lord, I thank You for the gift of music and its ability to uplift my soul. As I listen to melodies and sing songs of praise, draw me closer to You and fill me with joy and peace. May the music I embrace be a reflection of Your love and bring comfort to others. In Jesus' name, I pray. Amen.

DAY 157

SEEKING CONFIRMATION IN GOD'S WORD

Scripture: "Your word is a lamp for my feet, a light on my path." - Psalm 119:105 (NIV)

Devotional: Today, let us explore the theme of seeking confirmation in God's Word. The Bible is a source of guidance and wisdom as you seek to follow God's purpose for your life. Reflect on the importance of immersing yourself in Scripture and allowing it to illuminate your path. Take a moment to pray and ask God to speak to you through His Word, confirming His purpose and direction in your life. Let gratitude for the truth and guidance found in the Scriptures fill your heart.

Reflection: In your journal, write about a specific area of your life where you desire confirmation from God's Word. How can you immerse yourself in Scripture and seek His guidance? What passages or promises can you cling to as you navigate your purpose journey? How can you apply the principles and teachings of the Bible to your daily life?

Prayer: Loving God, I thank You for Your Word and the guidance it provides. Speak to me through the Scriptures and confirm Your purpose and direction in my life. Help me to immerse myself in Your Word and apply its principles to my daily life. Fill my heart with gratitude for the truth and guidance found in Your Word. In Jesus' name, I pray. Amen.

DAY 158

FINDING BEAUTY IN NATURE

Scripture: "The heavens declare the glory of God; the skies proclaim the work of his hands." - Psalm 19:1 (NIV)

Devotional: Today, let's focus on finding beauty in nature. Take a moment to step outside and observe the world around you. Look at the intricate details of a flower, the majesty of the mountains, or the vastness of the ocean. Reflect on how God's creation reveals His glory and creativity. Let the simplicity and wonder of nature uplift your spirit and fill your heart with gratitude.

Reflection: In your journal, write about the beauty of nature you encountered today. How did it uplift your spirit and remind you of God's greatness? How can you intentionally incorporate time in nature into your daily life to find joy and peace? How can you use your appreciation for nature's beauty to bring joy and encouragement to others?

Prayer: Creator God, I thank You for the beauty of nature that surrounds me. As I marvel at Your creation, help me to recognize Your handiwork and find joy in the simplicity of nature. Guide me to cherish and protect the environment, reflecting Your love and care for the world. In Jesus' name, I pray. Amen.

DAY 159

FINDING PURPOSE IN TRIALS

Scripture: "Consider it pure joy, my brothers and sisters, whenever you face trials of many kinds, because you know that the testing of your faith produces perseverance." - James 1:2-3 (NIV)

Devotional: Today, let us explore the theme of finding purpose in trials. Trials and challenges can shape and refine us, strengthening our faith and character. Reflect on the ways in which God can use difficult seasons to develop perseverance and deepen your trust in Him. Take a moment to pray and ask God to help you find purpose and growth in the midst of trials. Let gratitude for His faithfulness and the transformative power of trials fill your heart.

Reflection: In your journal, write about a specific trial or challenge you are currently facing. How can you find purpose and growth in the midst of this trial? How can you trust God's faithfulness and rely on His strength? How can you encourage and support others who may be going through similar trials?

Prayer: Loving God, I thank You for Your presence and strength in times of trials. Help me to find purpose and growth in the midst of my challenges. Teach me to trust Your faithfulness and rely on Your strength. Guide me in encouraging and supporting others who may be going through similar trials. Fill my heart with gratitude for the transformative power of trials. In Jesus' name, I pray. Amen.

Day 160

Recognizing God's Guidance Through Prayer

Scripture: "This is the confidence we have in approaching God: that if we ask anything according to his will, he hears us." - 1 John 5:14 (NIV)

Devotional: Today, let us focus on recognizing God's guidance through prayer. Prayer is a powerful means of communication with God, allowing you to seek His guidance and align your desires with His will. Reflect on the significance of cultivating a consistent and fervent prayer life as you navigate your purpose journey. Take a moment to pray and ask God to help you recognize His voice and leading through prayer. Let gratitude for the privilege of prayer and the assurance of His listening ear fill your heart.

Reflection: In your journal, write about the role of prayer in seeking and recognizing God's guidance. How can you cultivate a consistent and fervent prayer life? How can you align your desires with His will through prayer? How can you actively listen for His voice and discern His leading? How can you find peace and assurance in knowing that He hears and answers your prayers?

Prayer: Heavenly Father, I thank You for the privilege of prayer and the opportunity to seek Your guidance. Help me to cultivate a consistent and fervent prayer life. Teach me how to align my desires with Your will through prayer. Guide me in actively listening for Your voice and discerning Your leading. Fill my heart with gratitude for the assurance that You hear and answer my prayers. In Jesus' name, I pray. Amen.

DAY 161

TRUSTING GOD'S TIMING

Scripture: "But those who hope in the LORD will renew their strength. They will soar on wings like eagles; they will run and not grow weary, they will walk and not be faint." - Isaiah 40:31 (NIV)

Devotional: Today, let us explore the theme of trusting God's timing. It can be challenging to wait for the fulfillment of His promises and the unfolding of His purpose. Reflect on the importance of placing your hope in the Lord and finding strength in His perfect timing. Take a moment to pray and ask God to help you trust His timing and find contentment in the present moment. Let gratitude for His faithfulness and the assurance of His plans fill your heart.

Reflection: In your journal, write about an area of your life where you struggle to trust God's timing. How can you place your hope in the Lord and find strength in His perfect timing? What lessons or growth might He be cultivating in you during this season of waiting? How can you cultivate contentment and joy in the present moment, knowing that He is in control?

Prayer: Gracious Father, I struggle to trust Your timing in certain areas of my life. Help me to place my hope in You and find strength in Your perfect timing. Teach me the lessons and growth You desire to cultivate in me during seasons of waiting. Guide me in finding contentment and joy in the present moment, knowing that You are in control. Fill my heart with gratitude for Your faithfulness and the assurance of Your plans. In Jesus' name, I pray. Amen.

DAY 162

STEPPING OUT IN FAITH

Scripture: "Trust in the LORD with all your heart and lean not on your own understanding; in all your ways submit to him, and he will make your paths straight." - Proverbs 3:5-6 (NIV)

Devotional: Today, let us focus on stepping out in faith. Following God's purpose often requires taking bold steps and trusting Him beyond our understanding. Reflect on the importance of trusting in the Lord with all your heart and surrendering your plans to His guidance. Take a moment to pray and ask God to help you step out in faith, even when it feels uncomfortable or uncertain. Let gratitude for His faithfulness and the assurance of His guidance fill your heart.

Reflection: In your journal, write about a specific area of your life where you need to step out in faith. How can you trust in the Lord with all your heart and lean not on your own understanding? What steps can you take to submit your plans and desires to Him? How can you find peace and confidence in knowing that He will make your paths straight?

Prayer: Heavenly Father, I desire to step out in faith and follow Your purpose for my life. Help me to trust in You with all my heart and surrender my plans to Your guidance. Guide me in taking bold steps even when it feels uncomfortable or uncertain. Fill my heart with gratitude for Your faithfulness and the assurance of Your guidance. In Jesus' name, I pray. Amen.

DAY 163

WALKING IN OBEDIENCE

Scripture: "For we are God's handiwork, created in Christ Jesus to do good works, which God prepared in advance for us to do." - Ephesians 2:10 (NIV)

Devotional: Today, let us explore the theme of walking in obedience. God has prepared good works for you to do as part of His purpose for your life. Reflect on the importance of aligning your actions and decisions with His will. Take a moment to pray and ask God to reveal His specific plans and assignments for you. Let gratitude for the privilege of being His handiwork and the joy of serving Him through obedience fill your heart.

Reflection: In your journal, write about the areas of your life where you need to walk in obedience to God's will. How can you align your actions and decisions with His purpose? What steps can you take to follow His leading and fulfill the good works He has prepared for you? How can you find joy and fulfillment in serving Him through obedience?

Prayer: Loving Father, I desire to walk in obedience to Your will. Show me the areas of my life where I need to align my actions and decisions with Your purpose. Reveal Your specific plans and assignments for me. Guide me in following Your leading and fulfilling the good works You have prepared for me. Fill my heart with gratitude for the privilege of being Your handiwork and the joy of serving You through obedience. In Jesus' name, I pray. Amen.

DAY 164

OVERCOMING OBSTACLES WITH FAITH

Scripture: "Jesus looked at them and said, 'With man this is impossible, but with God all things are possible.'" - Matthew 19:26 (NIV)

Devotional: Today, let us focus on overcoming obstacles with faith. Along your purpose journey, you may encounter challenges and barriers that seem insurmountable. Reflect on the power of faith in the face of impossibilities and the assurance that nothing is too difficult for God. Take a moment to pray and ask God to increase your faith and help you overcome obstacles with His strength. Let gratitude for His limitless power and the hope of His intervention fill your heart.

Reflection: In your journal, write about the obstacles or challenges you are currently facing on your purpose journey. How can you approach these difficulties with faith and trust in God's power? What steps can you take to overcome obstacles, knowing that nothing is impossible with Him? How can you encourage and inspire others to face their own obstacles with faith?

Prayer: Heavenly Father, I face obstacles and challenges on my purpose journey. Increase my faith and help me to trust in Your limitless power. Guide me in taking steps to overcome these obstacles, knowing that nothing is impossible with You. Teach me how to encourage and inspire others to face their own obstacles with faith. Fill my heart with gratitude for Your intervention and the hope that comes from trusting in You. In Jesus' name, I pray. Amen.

DAY 165

EMBRACING A SPIRIT OF PERSEVERANCE

Scripture: "And let us run with perseverance the race marked out for us." - Hebrews 12:1 (NIV)

Devotional: Today, let us explore the theme of embracing a spirit of perseverance. Following God's purpose requires endurance and steadfastness. Reflect on the importance of pressing on, even in the face of challenges and setbacks. Take a moment to pray and ask God to fill you with perseverance and strengthen your resolve to continue running the race marked out for you. Let gratitude for His sustaining power and the rewards of perseverance fill your heart.

Reflection: In your journal, write about the areas of your purpose journey where you need to embrace a spirit of perseverance. How can you cultivate endurance and steadfastness in the midst of challenges? What strategies can you employ to stay focused on God's purpose and keep moving forward? How can you find encouragement and support from fellow believers as you persevere?

Prayer: Gracious Father, I face challenges and setbacks on my purpose journey. Fill me with perseverance and strengthen my resolve to continue running the race marked out for me. Help me to cultivate endurance and steadfastness in the face of difficulties. Guide me in staying focused on Your purpose and finding encouragement from fellow believers. Fill my heart with gratitude for Your sustaining power and the rewards that come from perseverance. In Jesus' name, I pray. Amen.

DAY 166

WALKING HUMBLY BEFORE GOD

Scripture: "He has shown you, O mortal, what is good. And what does the LORD require of you? To act justly and to love mercy and to walk humbly with your God." - Micah 6:8 (NIV)

Devotional: Today, let us focus on walking humbly before God. Humility is essential in following His purpose for our lives. Reflect on the importance of recognizing your dependence on God and acknowledging His sovereignty. Take a moment to pray and ask God to help you cultivate a humble heart that is receptive to His guidance. Let gratitude for His grace and the privilege of walking with Him fill your heart.

Reflection: In your journal, write about the areas of your life where you need to cultivate humility before God. How can you act justly, love mercy, and walk humbly with Him? What steps can you take to embrace a posture of humility and surrender? How can you grow in your dependence on Him and acknowledge His sovereignty in all aspects of your life?

Prayer: Loving Father, I desire to walk humbly before You. Help me to recognize my dependence on You and acknowledge Your sovereignty. Teach me how to act justly, love mercy, and cultivate a humble heart that is receptive to Your guidance. Fill my heart with gratitude for Your grace and the privilege of walking with You. In Jesus' name, I pray. Amen.

DAY 167

DISCERNING GOD'S VOICE

Scripture: "My sheep listen to my voice; I know them, and they follow me." - John 10:27 (NIV)

Devotional: Today, let us explore the theme of discerning God's voice. As you follow His purpose for your life, it is crucial to discern His leading and distinguish His voice amidst the noise of the world. Reflect on the importance of cultivating a listening ear and a sensitive heart to His promptings. Take a moment to pray and ask God to help you discern His voice and follow Him faithfully. Let gratitude for the intimacy of His relationship and the guidance of His voice fill your heart.

Reflection: In your journal, write about the ways in which you can cultivate a listening ear to discern God's voice. How can you create space for silence and solitude to hear Him clearly? What practices can you adopt to grow in sensitivity to His promptings? How can you align your thoughts and desires with His Word to ensure you are following His voice?

Prayer: Heavenly Father, I desire to discern Your voice amidst the noise of the world. Help me to cultivate a listening ear and a sensitive heart to Your promptings. Guide me in creating space for silence and solitude to hear You clearly. Teach me how to align my thoughts and desires with Your Word. Fill my heart with gratitude for the intimacy of our relationship and the guidance of Your voice. In Jesus' name, I pray. Amen.

DAY 168

EMBRACING A SPIRIT OF CONTENTMENT

Scripture: "I have learned to be content whatever the circumstances." - Philippians 4:11 (NIV)

Devotional: Today, let us focus on embracing a spirit of contentment. Contentment is vital in following God's purpose, as it frees us from the constant pursuit of worldly desires. Reflect on the importance of finding satisfaction in God alone, regardless of your circumstances. Take a moment to pray and ask God to help you cultivate a contented heart that rests in His provision and sufficiency. Let gratitude for His faithfulness and the peace that comes from contentment fill your heart.

Reflection: In your journal, write about the areas of your life where you struggle with contentment. How can you find satisfaction in God alone and release the pursuit of worldly desires? What steps can you take to cultivate a contented heart that rests in His provision and sufficiency? How can you encourage and inspire others to embrace a spirit of contentment?

Prayer: Gracious God, I struggle with contentment in certain areas of my life. Help me to find satisfaction in You alone and release the pursuit of worldly desires. Teach me how to cultivate a contented heart that rests in Your provision and sufficiency. Guide me in encouraging and inspiring others to embrace a spirit of contentment. Fill my heart with gratitude for Your faithfulness and the peace that comes from contentment. In Jesus' name, I pray. Amen.

DAY 169

SEEKING GOD'S KINGDOM FIRST

Scripture: "But seek first his kingdom and his righteousness, and all these things will be given to you as well." - Matthew 6:33 (NIV)

Devotional: Today, let us explore the theme of seeking God's kingdom first. Aligning your life with His purpose requires prioritizing His kingdom and righteousness above all else. Reflect on the significance of placing Him at the center of your life and allowing His will to guide your choices and actions. Take a moment to pray and ask God to help you seek His kingdom first in all that you do. Let gratitude for His provision and the fulfillment that comes from seeking His kingdom fill your heart.

Reflection: In your journal, write about the ways in which you can seek God's kingdom first in your daily life. How can you prioritize His will and righteousness above all else? What adjustments or sacrifices might be necessary to align your choices and actions with His purpose? How can you find peace and assurance in knowing that He will provide for all your needs?

Prayer: Heavenly Father, I desire to seek Your kingdom first in all that I do. Help me to prioritize Your will and righteousness above all else. Guide me in making the necessary adjustments and sacrifices to align my choices and actions with Your purpose. Fill my heart with gratitude for Your provision and the fulfillment that comes from seeking Your kingdom. In Jesus' name, I pray. Amen.

DAY 170

EMBRACING GOD'S UNFOLDING PLAN

Scripture: "For I know the plans I have for you," declares the LORD, "plans to prosper you and not to harm you, plans to give you hope and a future." - Jeremiah 29:11 (NIV)

Devotional: Today, let us focus on embracing God's unfolding plan. His plans for your life are far greater and more intricate than you can imagine. Reflect on the importance of trusting His sovereignty and surrendering to His timing. Take a moment to pray and ask God to help you embrace His plan, even when it may seem uncertain or different from your own expectations. Let gratitude for His goodness, hope, and the assurance of a future in His hands fill your heart.

Reflection: In your journal, write about the areas of your life where you struggle to embrace God's unfolding plan. How can you trust His sovereignty and surrender to His timing? What steps can you take to align your desires with His greater purpose? How can you find peace and hope in knowing that His plans are always for your good?

Prayer: Gracious Father, I struggle to embrace Your unfolding plan in certain areas of my life. Help me to trust Your sovereignty and surrender to Your timing. Guide me in aligning my desires with Your greater purpose. Fill my heart with gratitude for Your goodness, hope, and the assurance of a future in Your hands. In Jesus' name, I pray. Amen.

DAY 171

REFLECTING GOD'S LOVE TO OTHERS

Scripture: "Dear friends, let us love one another, for love comes from God." - 1 John 4:7 (NIV)

Devotional: Today, let us explore the theme of reflecting God's love to others. Following His purpose involves showing love and kindness to those around us. Reflect on the significance of being a vessel of His love and extending grace to others. Take a moment to pray and ask God to help you love others as He loves you. Let gratitude for His unconditional love and the privilege of being an instrument of His love fill your heart.

Reflection: In your journal, write about the ways in which you can reflect God's love to others in your daily life. How can you extend kindness, compassion, and grace to those around you? How can you be intentional in showing His love through your words and actions? How can you make a positive impact on the lives of others by reflecting His love?

Prayer: Heavenly Father, I thank You for Your unconditional love for me. Help me to reflect Your love to others in my daily life. Teach me how to extend kindness, compassion, and grace to those around me. Guide me in being intentional in showing Your love through my words and actions. Fill my heart with gratitude for the privilege of being an instrument of Your love. In Jesus' name, I pray. Amen.

Day 172

Finding Joy in God's Presence

Scripture: "You make known to me the path of life; you will fill me with joy in your presence, with eternal pleasures at your right hand." - Psalm 16:11 (NIV)

Devotional: Today, let us focus on finding joy in God's presence. The pursuit of His purpose is not meant to be joyless but filled with His presence and delight. Reflect on the importance of seeking His face and finding joy in the intimacy of His presence. Take a moment to pray and ask God to fill you with His joy as you walk in His purpose. Let gratitude for the joy and eternal pleasures found in His presence fill your heart.

Reflection: In your journal, write about the ways in which you can find joy in God's presence. How can you cultivate a deeper relationship with Him? How can you make space for quiet moments of worship and communion with Him? How can you let His joy overflow into every aspect of your life, reflecting His presence to others?

Prayer: Loving Father, I desire to find joy in Your presence as I walk in Your purpose. Fill me with Your joy and help me to seek Your face. Teach me how to cultivate a deeper relationship with You. Guide me in making space for quiet moments of worship and communion with You. Fill my heart with gratitude for the joy and eternal pleasures found in Your presence. In Jesus' name, I pray. Amen.

DAY 173

EMBRACING THE JOURNEY, TRUSTING THE DESTINATION

Scripture: "Trust in the LORD with all your heart and lean not on your own understanding; in all your ways submit to him, and he will make your paths straight." - Proverbs 3:5-6 (NIV)

Devotional: Today, let us explore the theme of embracing the journey and trusting the destination. Following God's purpose is a lifelong journey filled with twists, turns, and unexpected detours. Reflect on the importance of trusting in the Lord with all your heart, even when the path seems unclear or different from your expectations. Take a moment to pray and ask God to help you embrace the journey, knowing that He is faithful to guide you to the destination. Let gratitude for His faithfulness and the assurance of His straight paths fill your heart.

Reflection: In your journal, write about the areas of your purpose journey where you struggle to embrace the journey and trust the destination. How can you lean not on your own understanding but instead trust in the Lord with all your heart? How can you submit all your ways to Him and seek His guidance along the way? How can you find peace and confidence in knowing that He will make your paths straight?

Prayer: Heavenly Father, I struggle to embrace the journey and trust the destination in certain areas of my purpose journey. Help me to lean not on my own understanding but trust in You with all my heart. Guide me in submitting all my ways to You and seeking Your guidance along the way. Fill my heart with gratitude for Your faithfulness and the assurance that You will make my paths straight. In Jesus' name, I pray. Amen.

DAY 174

GRATITUDE FOR EVERYDAY BLESSINGS

Scripture: "Give thanks to the LORD, for he is good; his love endures forever." - 1 Chronicles 16:34 (NIV)

Devotional: Today, let us focus on gratitude for everyday blessings. Joy can be found in recognizing and appreciating the small blessings that fill our lives each day. Reflect on the importance of cultivating a heart of gratitude and acknowledging God's goodness in the seemingly ordinary moments. Take a moment to pray and thank God for the everyday blessings He provides. Let gratitude for His love and faithfulness fill your heart and bring forth joy.

Reflection: In your journal, write about the everyday blessings you often overlook. How can you cultivate a heart of gratitude and increase your awareness of these blessings? How can you express your thanks to God and share His goodness with others? How does recognizing everyday blessings contribute to your overall sense of joy?

Prayer: Heavenly Father, I thank You for the everyday blessings that fill my life. Help me to cultivate a heart of gratitude and increase my awareness of Your goodness in the seemingly ordinary moments. Teach me to express my thanks to You and share Your goodness with others. Fill my heart with gratitude for Your love and faithfulness, and let that gratitude overflow into joy. In Jesus' name, I pray. Amen.

DAY 175

FINDING JOY IN CREATION

Scripture: "The heavens declare the glory of God; the skies proclaim the work of his hands." - Psalm 19:1 (NIV)

Devotional: Today, let us explore the theme of finding joy in creation. God's handiwork is evident all around us, and it can bring us great joy and wonder. Reflect on the beauty and intricacy of the natural world and the opportunity to connect with God through His creation. Take a moment to pray and thank God for the wonders of His creation. Let gratitude for His creativity and the joy that comes from experiencing His handiwork fill your heart.

Reflection: In your journal, write about the aspects of nature that bring you joy and awe. How can you intentionally connect with God through His creation? How does immersing yourself in nature and appreciating its beauty contribute to your sense of joy? How can you be a good steward of the earth and care for the environment as an expression of gratitude to God?

Prayer: Loving Creator, I thank You for the wonders of Your creation. Help me to connect with You through the beauty and intricacy of the natural world. Teach me to appreciate and care for the earth as an expression of gratitude to You. Fill my heart with gratitude for Your creativity and the joy that comes from experiencing Your handiwork. In Jesus' name, I pray. Amen.

DAY 176

CULTIVATING JOYFUL RELATIONSHIPS

Scripture: "A friend loves at all times, and a brother is born for a time of adversity." - Proverbs 17:17 (NIV)

Devotional: Today, let us focus on cultivating joyful relationships. Meaningful connections with others can bring immense joy and fulfillment to our lives. Reflect on the importance of nurturing relationships, showing love, and building supportive communities. Take a moment to pray and thank God for the gift of relationships and the joy they bring. Let gratitude for the people in your life and the joy that comes from deep connections fill your heart.

Reflection: In your journal, write about the relationships that bring you joy and support. How can you nurture and invest in these relationships? How can you show love and kindness to those around you? How can you foster a sense of community and build meaningful connections? How does having joyful relationships contribute to your overall sense of joy?

Prayer: Gracious God, I thank You for the gift of relationships and the joy they bring to my life. Help me to nurture and invest in the relationships that matter. Teach me to show love and kindness to those around me. Guide me in fostering a sense of community and building meaningful connections. Fill my heart with gratitude for the people in my life and the joy that comes from deep connections. In Jesus' name, I pray. Amen.

DAY 177

JOY IN SERVING OTHERS

Scripture: "Each of you should use whatever gift you have received to serve others, as faithful stewards of God's grace in its various forms." - 1 Peter 4:10 (NIV)

Devotional: Today, let us explore the theme of joy in serving others. Using our gifts and talents to bless others brings not only joy to them but also joy to our own hearts. Reflect on the opportunities you have to serve and make a positive impact on the lives of others. Take a moment to pray and ask God to show you how you can serve others with joy and gratitude. Let the joy of selfless service and the gratitude for being a steward of His grace fill your heart.

Reflection: In your journal, write about the ways in which you can serve others with joy. How can you use your gifts and talents to make a positive impact? How can you cultivate a heart of gratitude as you serve? How does serving others contribute to your overall sense of joy?

Prayer: Heavenly Father, I thank You for the opportunities to serve others and make a positive impact. Show me how I can use my gifts and talents to bless those around me. Help me to cultivate a heart of gratitude as I serve. Fill my heart with the joy of selfless service and the gratitude for being a steward of Your grace. In Jesus' name, I pray. Amen.

DAY 178

FINDING BEAUTY IN NATURE

Scripture: "The heavens declare the glory of God; the skies proclaim the work of his hands." - Psalm 19:1 (NIV)

Devotional: Today, let's focus on finding beauty in nature. Take a moment to step outside and observe the world around you. Look at the intricate details of a flower, the majesty of the mountains, or the vastness of the ocean. Reflect on how God's creation reveals His glory and creativity. Let the simplicity and wonder of nature uplift your spirit and fill your heart with gratitude.

Reflection: In your journal, write about the beauty of nature you encountered today. How did it uplift your spirit and remind you of God's greatness? How can you intentionally incorporate time in nature into your daily life to find joy and peace? How can you use your appreciation for nature's beauty to bring joy and encouragement to others?

Prayer: Creator God, I thank You for the beauty of nature that surrounds me. As I marvel at Your creation, help me to recognize Your handiwork and find joy in the simplicity of nature. Guide me to cherish and protect the environment, reflecting Your love and care for the world. In Jesus' name, I pray. Amen.

DAY 179

JOY IN THE MIDST OF CHALLENGES

Scripture: "Consider it pure joy, my brothers and sisters, whenever you face trials of many kinds because you know that the testing of your faith produces perseverance." - James 1:2-3 (NIV)

Devotional: Today, let us explore the theme of finding joy in the midst of challenges. Joy is not dependent on our circumstances but can be experienced even in the midst of trials. Reflect on the opportunity for growth, resilience, and deeper faith that challenges can bring. Take a moment to pray and ask God to help you find joy in the face of difficulties. Let gratitude for His presence, the lessons learned, and the strength gained through challenges fill your heart.

Reflection: In your journal, write about the challenges you are currently facing and how you can find joy in the midst of them. How can you lean on God's strength and grace during difficult times? How can you maintain a hopeful and joyful perspective, trusting that God is working all things together for your good? How can you inspire and encourage others to find joy in the face of challenges?

Prayer: Gracious Father, I thank You for the opportunity to find joy in the midst of challenges. Help me to lean on Your strength and grace during difficult times. Teach me to maintain a hopeful and joyful perspective, trusting in Your faithfulness. Fill my heart with gratitude for Your presence, the lessons learned, and the strength gained through challenges. In Jesus' name, I pray. Amen.

DAY 180

JOY IN SURRENDERING TO GOD'S WILL

Scripture: "Then Jesus said to his disciples, 'Whoever wants to be my disciple must deny themselves and take up their cross and follow me.'" - Matthew 16:24 (NIV)

Devotional: Today, let us focus on finding joy in surrendering to God's will. Surrendering our own plans and desires to align with His purpose can bring a deep sense of joy and fulfillment. Reflect on the importance of denying ourselves, taking up our cross, and following Jesus wholeheartedly. Take a moment to pray and ask God to help you surrender to His will with joy and obedience. Let gratitude for His guidance, provision, and the joy of walking in His purpose fill your heart.

Reflection: In your journal, write about areas of your life where you struggle to surrender to God's will. How can you deny yourself, take up your cross, and follow Him more faithfully? What steps can you take to align your desires with His purpose? How does surrendering to God's will contribute to your overall sense of joy?

Prayer: Heavenly Father, I desire to find joy in surrendering to Your will. Help me to deny myself, take up my cross, and follow You wholeheartedly. Guide me in aligning my desires with Your purpose. Fill my heart with gratitude for Your guidance, provision, and the joy of walking in Your purpose. In Jesus' name, I pray. Amen.

DAY 181

JOY IN FORGIVENESS

Scripture: "Bear with each other and forgive one another if any of you has a grievance against someone. Forgive as the Lord forgave you." - Colossians 3:13 (NIV)

Devotional: Today, let us explore the theme of finding joy in forgiveness. Holding onto grudges and harboring unforgiveness only weighs us down, but forgiving others brings freedom and joy. Reflect on the power of forgiveness, both in receiving God's forgiveness and extending it to others. Take a moment to pray and ask God to help you cultivate a forgiving heart. Let gratitude for His forgiveness and the joy that comes from releasing others from the burden of unforgiveness fill your heart.

Reflection: In your journal, write about any areas where you are holding onto unforgiveness. How can you surrender those grievances to God and choose forgiveness? How does extending forgiveness contribute to your own sense of joy and freedom? How can you encourage others to embrace the joy of forgiveness?

Prayer: Loving Father, I thank You for Your forgiveness and grace in my life. Help me to cultivate a forgiving heart towards others. Show me any areas where I am holding onto unforgiveness, and teach me to surrender those grievances to You. Fill my heart with gratitude for Your forgiveness and the joy that comes from releasing others from the burden of unforgiveness. In Jesus' name, I pray. Amen.

DAY 182

JOY IN WORSHIP

Scripture: "Worship the LORD with gladness; come before him with joyful songs." - Psalm 100:2 (NIV)

Devotional: Today, let us focus on finding joy in worship. Worshiping God is an opportunity to express our love and adoration for Him and experience His presence. Reflect on the importance of worship as a source of joy and connection with God. Take a moment to pray and thank God for the gift of worship. Let gratitude for His goodness and the joy that comes from praising Him with a glad heart fill your heart.

Reflection: In your journal, write about the ways in which you can cultivate a deeper sense of joy in worship. How can you approach worship with a glad heart and a spirit of gratitude? How can you make worship a daily practice, even beyond attending church services? How does worship contribute to your overall sense of joy and fulfillment?

Prayer: Heavenly Father, I thank You for the gift of worship. Help me to cultivate a deeper sense of joy as I come before You with a glad heart. Teach me to approach worship with gratitude and sincerity. Guide me in making worship a daily practice, allowing it to bring me closer to You. Fill my heart with gratitude for Your goodness and the joy that comes from praising You. In Jesus' name, I pray. Amen.

DAY 183

JOY IN GENEROSITY

Scripture: "Each of you should give what you have decided in your heart to give, not reluctantly or under compulsion, for God loves a cheerful giver." - 2 Corinthians 9:7 (NIV)

Devotional: Today, let us explore the theme of finding joy in generosity. Giving selflessly and sacrificially not only blesses others but also brings joy to our own hearts. Reflect on the joy that comes from being generous with your time, resources, and love. Take a moment to pray and ask God to help you cultivate a generous and cheerful spirit. Let gratitude for His abundant provision and the joy that comes from giving fill your heart.

Reflection: In your journal, write about the areas in which you can practice generosity. How can you give of your time, talents, and resources to bless others? How can you cultivate a cheerful and willing heart in your acts of generosity? How does being generous contribute to your overall sense of joy and fulfillment?

Prayer: Gracious God, I thank You for Your abundant provision in my life. Help me to cultivate a generous and cheerful spirit. Show me how I can give of my time, talents, and resources to bless others. Teach me to give without reluctance or compulsion but with a joyful heart. Fill my heart with gratitude for Your provision and the joy that comes from giving. In Jesus' name, I pray. Amen.

DAY 184

JOY IN CELEBRATION

Scripture: "This is the day the LORD has made; let us rejoice and be glad in it." - Psalm 118:24 (NIV)

Devotional: Today, let us focus on finding joy in celebration. Life is filled with moments worth celebrating, both big and small. Reflect on the importance of rejoicing in the blessings, victories, and milestones of life. Take a moment to pray and thank God for the gift of celebration. Let gratitude for His faithfulness and the joy that comes from celebrating His goodness fill your heart.

Reflection: In your journal, write about the ways in which you can cultivate a spirit of celebration in your life. How can you rejoice in the blessings, victories, and milestones, both for yourself and for others? How can you create a culture of celebration in your relationships and community? How does celebrating contribute to your overall sense of joy and gratitude?

Prayer: Loving Father, I thank You for the gift of celebration. Help me to cultivate a spirit of joy and gratitude as I rejoice in Your blessings, victories, and milestones. Show me how to create a culture of celebration in my relationships and community. Fill my heart with gratitude for Your faithfulness and the joy that comes from celebrating Your goodness. In Jesus' name, I pray. Amen.

DAY 185

JOY IN GOD'S WORD

Scripture: "The precepts of the LORD are right, giving joy to the heart. The commands of the LORD are radiant, giving light to the eyes." - Psalm 19:8 (NIV)

Devotional: Today, let us explore the theme of finding joy in God's Word. The Bible is a source of wisdom, guidance, and joy. Reflect on the importance of spending time in Scripture and allowing it to illuminate your path and bring joy to your heart. Take a moment to pray and thank God for the gift of His Word. Let gratitude for His truth and the joy that comes from meditating on His Word fill your heart.

Reflection: In your journal, write about the ways in which you can cultivate a deeper sense of joy in reading and studying God's Word. How can you approach Scripture with reverence and openness to His teachings? How can you make regular time for reflection and meditation on His Word? How does immersing yourself in God's Word contribute to your overall sense of joy and spiritual growth?

Prayer: Heavenly Father, I thank You for the gift of Your Word. Help me to cultivate a deeper sense of joy as I read and study Scripture. Show me how to approach Your Word with reverence and openness to Your teachings. Guide me in making regular time for reflection and meditation on Your Word. Fill my heart with gratitude for Your truth and the joy that comes from immersing myself in Your Word. In Jesus' name, I pray. Amen.

DAY 186

JOY IN HOPE

Scripture: "May the God of hope fill you with all joy and peace as you trust in him, so that you may overflow with hope by the power of the Holy Spirit." - Romans 15:13 (NIV)

Devotional: Today, let us focus on finding joy in hope. Our hope in God brings us joy and peace, even in the midst of challenges. Reflect on the assurance and confidence that come from trusting in God's promises. Take a moment to pray and thank God for the hope He provides. Let gratitude for His faithfulness and the joy that comes from trusting in His hope fill your heart.

Reflection: In your journal, write about the ways in which you can cultivate a deeper sense of joy in hope. How can you anchor your hope in God's promises and rely on His faithfulness? How can you encourage and uplift others with the hope that you have in Christ? How does having hope contribute to your overall sense of joy and perseverance?

Prayer: Gracious God, I thank You for the hope You provide. Help me to cultivate a deeper sense of joy as I anchor my hope in Your promises. Show me how to rely on Your faithfulness and trust in Your plan. Teach me to encourage and uplift others with the hope that I have in Christ. Fill my heart with gratitude for Your faithfulness and the joy that comes from trusting in Your hope. In Jesus' name, I pray. Amen.

DAY 187

JOY IN SURRENDERING CONTROL

Scripture: "Commit your way to the LORD; trust in him and he will do this." - Psalm 37:5 (NIV)

Devotional: Today, let us explore the theme of finding joy in surrendering control. Surrendering our plans and desires to God can bring peace and joy, knowing that He is in control. Reflect on the freedom and trust that come from releasing control and submitting to His will. Take a moment to pray and ask God to help you surrender control with joy and confidence. Let gratitude for His guidance and the joy that comes from trusting in His sovereignty fill your heart.

Reflection: In your journal, write about areas of your life where you struggle to surrender control to God. How can you commit your way to the Lord and trust in Him more fully? What steps can you take to release control and embrace His plan for your life? How does surrendering control contribute to your overall sense of joy and peace?

Prayer: Loving Father, I struggle to surrender control in certain areas of my life. Help me to commit my way to You and trust in Your guidance. Show me how to release control and embrace Your plan for me with joy and confidence. Fill my heart with gratitude for Your sovereignty and the joy that comes from trusting in You. In Jesus' name, I pray. Amen.

Day 188

Joy in Stillness and Rest

Scripture: "He says, 'Be still, and know that I am God; I will be exalted among the nations, I will be exalted in the earth.'" - Psalm 46:10 (NIV)

Devotional: Today, let us focus on finding joy in stillness and rest. In the busyness of life, it is essential to find moments of quiet and rest in God's presence. Reflect on the peace and joy that come from being still and knowing that He is God. Take a moment to pray and thank God for the gift of stillness and rest. Let gratitude for His presence and the joy that comes from resting in Him fill your heart.

Reflection: In your journal, write about the ways in which you can cultivate stillness and rest in your life. How can you create space for quiet moments of reflection and rejuvenation? How can you prioritize rest and self-care as a means to experience joy? How does finding stillness and rest contribute to your overall sense of joy and well-being?

Prayer: Heavenly Father, I thank You for the gift of stillness and rest. Help me to cultivate moments of quiet and reflection in my life. Show me how to prioritize rest and self-care as a means to experience joy and rejuvenation. Fill my heart with gratitude for Your presence and the joy that comes from resting in You. In Jesus' name, I pray. Amen.

DAY 189

JOY IN TRUSTING GOD'S TIMING

Scripture: "But do not forget this one thing, dear friends: With the Lord a day is like a thousand years, and a thousand years are like a day." - 2 Peter 3:8 (NIV)

Devotional: Today, let us explore the theme of finding joy in trusting God's timing. His timing is perfect, even when it may seem slow or different from our own expectations. Reflect on the importance of patience and trust in His sovereign plan. Take a moment to pray and ask God to help you trust His timing with joy and confidence. Let gratitude for His faithfulness and the joy that comes from surrendering to His timing fill your heart.

Reflection: In your journal, write about areas of your life where you struggle to trust God's timing. How can you cultivate patience and surrender to His sovereign plan? What steps can you take to align your desires with His timing? How does trusting God's timing contribute to your overall sense of joy and peace?

Prayer: Gracious God, I struggle to trust Your timing in certain areas of my life. Help me to cultivate patience and surrender to Your sovereign plan. Show me how to align my desires with Your timing. Fill my heart with gratitude for Your faithfulness and the joy that comes from trusting in You. In Jesus' name, I pray. Amen.

Day 190

Joy in Encouragement and Affirmation

Scripture: "Therefore encourage one another and build each other up, just as in fact you are doing." - 1 Thessalonians 5:11 (NIV)

Devotional: Today, let us focus on finding joy in encouragement and affirmation. The power of uplifting words and support can bring great joy to both the giver and the receiver. Reflect on the importance of building others up and expressing love and affirmation. Take a moment to pray and thank God for the gift of encouragement. Let gratitude for His love and the joy that comes from uplifting others fill your heart.

Reflection: In your journal, write about the ways in which you can cultivate a spirit of encouragement and affirmation. How can you use your words to build others up and express love? How can you create a culture of support and positivity in your relationships and community? How does offering encouragement and affirmation contribute to your overall sense of joy and fulfillment?

Prayer: Loving Father, I thank You for the gift of encouragement and affirmation. Help me to cultivate a spirit of uplifting others with my words and actions. Show me how to express love and build others up. Guide me in creating a culture of support and positivity in my relationships and community. Fill my heart with gratitude for Your love and the joy that comes from uplifting others. In Jesus' name, I pray. Amen.

DAY 191

JOY IN COMPASSIONATE SERVICE

Scripture: "If anyone has material possessions and sees a brother or sister in need but has no pity on them, how can the love of God be in that person? Dear children, let us not love with words or speech but with actions and in truth." - 1 John 3:17-18 (NIV)

Devotional: Today, let us explore the theme of finding joy in compassionate service. Serving others with love and compassion not only blesses them but also brings joy and fulfillment to our own hearts. Reflect on the importance of showing Christ's love through acts of service and meeting the needs of others. Take a moment to pray and ask God to help you serve with a compassionate heart. Let gratitude for His love and the joy that comes from selfless service fill your heart.

Reflection: In your journal, write about the ways in which you can cultivate a heart of compassionate service. How can you extend a helping hand to those in need? How can you show Christ's love through your actions and in truth? How does serving others with compassion contribute to your overall sense of joy and purpose?

Prayer: Gracious God, I thank You for the opportunity to serve others with compassion. Help me to cultivate a heart of selfless service. Show me how to extend a helping hand to those in need and demonstrate Your love through my actions. Fill my heart with gratitude for Your love and the joy that comes from serving others. In Jesus' name, I pray. Amen.

DAY 192

JOY IN CREATION

Scripture: "The heavens declare the glory of God; the skies proclaim the work of his hands." - Psalm 19:1 (NIV)

Devotional: Today, let us focus on finding joy in creation. God's handiwork is evident all around us, and it can bring us great joy and wonder. Reflect on the beauty and intricacy of the natural world and the opportunity to connect with God through His creation. Take a moment to pray and thank God for the wonders of His creation. Let gratitude for His creativity and the joy that comes from experiencing His handiwork fill your heart.

Reflection: In your journal, write about the aspects of nature that bring you joy and awe. How can you intentionally connect with God through His creation? How does immersing yourself in nature and appreciating its beauty contribute to your sense of joy? How can you be a good steward of the earth and care for the environment as an expression of gratitude to God?

Prayer: Loving Creator, I thank You for the wonders of Your creation. Help me to connect with You through the beauty and intricacy of the natural world. Teach me to appreciate and care for the earth as an expression of gratitude to You. Fill my heart with gratitude for Your creativity and the joy that comes from experiencing Your handiwork. In Jesus' name, I pray. Amen.

DAY 193

JOY IN AUTHENTIC RELATIONSHIPS

Scripture: "Therefore encourage one another and build each other up, just as in fact you are doing." - 1 Thessalonians 5:11 (NIV)

Devotional: Today, let us explore the theme of finding joy in authentic relationships. Genuine connections with others bring deep joy and fulfillment to our lives. Reflect on the importance of building authentic relationships based on trust, love, and support. Take a moment to pray and thank God for the gift of meaningful relationships. Let gratitude for the people in your life and the joy that comes from authentic connections fill your heart.

Reflection: In your journal, write about the relationships that bring you joy and support. How can you nurture and invest in these relationships? How can you show love and kindness to those around you? How can you foster a sense of authenticity and vulnerability in your connections? How do authentic relationships contribute to your overall sense of joy and well-being?

Prayer: Heavenly Father, I thank You for the gift of authentic relationships. Help me to nurture and invest in the relationships that matter. Teach me to show love and kindness to those around me. Guide me in fostering a sense of authenticity and vulnerability in my connections. Fill my heart with gratitude for the people in my life and the joy that comes from authentic relationships. In Jesus' name, I pray. Amen.

DAY 194

JOY IN CONTENTMENT

Scripture: "I am not saying this because I am in need, for I have learned to be content whatever the circumstances." - Philippians 4:11 (NIV)

Devotional: Today, let us focus on finding joy in contentment. True joy is not dependent on external circumstances but comes from a heart of contentment and gratitude. Reflect on the importance of cultivating a spirit of contentment and finding satisfaction in God's provision. Take a moment to pray and thank God for His faithfulness and the blessings in your life. Let gratitude for His provision and the joy that comes from contentment fill your heart.

Reflection: In your journal, write about the areas in which you struggle to find contentment. How can you shift your focus from what you lack to what you have? How can you cultivate gratitude and embrace a spirit of contentment? How does finding contentment contribute to your overall sense of joy and peace?

Prayer: Gracious God, I thank You for Your provision in my life. Help me to cultivate a spirit of contentment and gratitude. Show me how to shift my focus from what I lack to what I have. Teach me to find joy in Your faithfulness and the blessings You have bestowed upon me. Fill my heart with gratitude for Your provision and the joy that comes from contentment. In Jesus' name, I pray. Amen.

DAY 195

JOY IN FELLOWSHIP

Scripture: "Let us hold unswervingly to the hope we profess, for he who promised is faithful. And let us consider how we may spur one another on toward love and good deeds, not giving up meeting together, as some are in the habit of doing, but encouraging one another—and all the more as you see the Day approaching." - Hebrews 10:23-25 (NIV)

Devotional: Today, let us explore the theme of finding joy in fellowship. Gathering with fellow believers and sharing in community brings great joy and encouragement. Reflect on the importance of engaging in fellowship, spurring one another on toward love and good deeds. Take a moment to pray and thank God for the gift of Christian community. Let gratitude for the people in your life and the joy that comes from fellowship fill your heart.

Reflection: In your journal, write about the ways in which you can cultivate a deeper sense of joy in fellowship. How can you engage more fully in Christian community? How can you encourage and support others in their faith journeys? How does participating in fellowship contribute to your overall sense of joy and spiritual growth?

Prayer: Loving Father, I thank You for the gift of Christian community and the joy that comes from fellowship. Help me to engage more fully in the community of believers. Show me how to encourage and support others in their faith journeys. Fill my heart with gratitude for the people in my life and the joy that comes from sharing in fellowship. In Jesus' name, I pray. Amen.

DAY 196

JOY IN GOD'S FAITHFULNESS

Scripture: "The LORD is my strength and my shield; my heart trusts in him, and he helps me. My heart leaps for joy, and with my song I praise him." - Psalm 28:7 (NIV)

Devotional: Today, let us focus on finding joy in God's faithfulness. He is our strength, our shield, and our helper. Reflect on the ways in which God has been faithful in your life, providing strength and support. Take a moment to pray and thank God for His unwavering faithfulness. Let gratitude for His presence and the joy that comes from trusting in His faithfulness fill your heart.

Reflection: In your journal, write about the ways in which you have experienced God's faithfulness. How can you cultivate a deeper sense of trust in Him? How can you rely on His strength and provision in every area of your life? How does knowing and experiencing God's faithfulness contribute to your overall sense of joy and confidence?

Prayer: Gracious God, I thank You for Your unwavering faithfulness in my life. Help me to cultivate a deeper sense of trust in You. Show me how to rely on Your strength and provision in every area of my life. Fill my heart with gratitude for Your presence and the joy that comes from trusting in Your faithfulness. In Jesus' name, I pray. Amen.

DAY 197

JOY IN GIVING THANKS

Scripture: "Give thanks to the LORD, for he is good; his love endures forever." - Psalm 107:1 (NIV)

Devotional: Today, let us explore the theme of finding joy in giving thanks. Gratitude is a powerful attitude that brings joy and shifts our perspective. Reflect on the goodness of God and the countless blessings in your life. Take a moment to pray and thank God for His love and faithfulness. Let gratitude for His goodness and the joy that comes from giving thanks fill your heart.

Reflection: In your journal, write about the ways in which you can cultivate a heart of gratitude. How can you develop a daily practice of giving thanks to God? How can you express gratitude to others and appreciate the small blessings in life? How does a spirit of thankfulness contribute to your overall sense of joy and contentment?

Prayer: Loving Father, I thank You for Your goodness and faithfulness in my life. Help me to cultivate a heart of gratitude. Show me how to develop a daily practice of giving thanks to You. Teach me to appreciate the small blessings and express gratitude to others. Fill my heart with gratitude for Your love and the joy that comes from giving thanks. In Jesus' name, I pray. Amen.

DAY 198

JOY IN GOD'S PRESENCE

Scripture: "You make known to me the path of life; you will fill me with joy in your presence, with eternal pleasures at your right hand." - Psalm 16:11 (NIV)

Devotional: Today, let us focus on finding joy in God's presence. In His presence, there is fullness of joy and eternal pleasures. Reflect on the privilege and delight of being in communion with God. Take a moment to pray and thank God for His constant presence in your life. Let gratitude for His love and the joy that comes from experiencing His presence fill your heart.

Reflection: In your journal, write about the ways in which you can cultivate a deeper sense of joy in God's presence. How can you make space for quiet moments of prayer and reflection? How can you seek His presence in your daily life and activities? How does experiencing God's presence contribute to your overall sense of joy and peace?

Prayer: Heavenly Father, I thank You for the privilege and delight of experiencing Your presence. Help me to cultivate a deeper sense of joy in Your presence. Show me how to make space for quiet moments of prayer and reflection. Guide me in seeking Your presence in my daily life and activities. Fill my heart with gratitude for Your love and the joy that comes from experiencing Your presence. In Jesus' name, I pray. Amen.

DAY 199

JOY IN PERSEVERANCE

Scripture: "Consider it pure joy, my brothers and sisters, whenever you face trials of many kinds because you know that the testing of your faith produces perseverance." - James 1:2-3 (NIV)

Devotional: Today, let us explore the theme of finding joy in perseverance. Trials and challenges are opportunities for growth and character development. Reflect on the joy that comes from enduring and persevering through difficulties. Take a moment to pray and ask God to give you the strength and perseverance to overcome obstacles. Let gratitude for His faithfulness and the joy that comes from persevering fill your heart.

Reflection: In your journal, write about the areas in your life where you need to persevere. How can you develop a mindset of joy and resilience in the face of trials? How can you rely on God's strength and grace to overcome challenges? How does perseverance contribute to your overall sense of joy and spiritual maturity?

Prayer: Gracious God, I thank You for the opportunity to grow and develop character through perseverance. Help me to develop a mindset of joy and resilience in the face of trials. Give me the strength and perseverance to overcome obstacles. Fill my heart with gratitude for Your faithfulness and the joy that comes from enduring. In Jesus' name, I pray. Amen.

DAY 200

JOY IN ETERNAL PERSPECTIVE

Scripture: "For our light and momentary troubles are achieving for us an eternal glory that far outweighs them all. So we fix our eyes not on what is seen, but on what is unseen, since what is seen is temporary, but what is unseen is eternal." - 2 Corinthians 4:17-18 (NIV)

Devotional: Today, let us focus on finding joy in an eternal perspective. Our present troubles and challenges are temporary compared to the eternal glory that awaits us. Reflect on the hope and joy that come from fixing your eyes on what is unseen. Take a moment to pray and thank God for the assurance of His eternal promises. Let gratitude for His faithfulness and the joy that comes from an eternal perspective fill your heart.

Reflection: In your journal, write about the ways in which you can cultivate an eternal perspective in your daily life. How can you shift your focus from temporary circumstances to the eternal truths of God's promises? How can you live with hope and joy, knowing that your present trials are achieving eternal glory? How does an eternal perspective contribute to your overall sense of joy and purpose?

Prayer: Heavenly Father, I thank You for the assurance of Your eternal promises. Help me to cultivate an eternal perspective in my daily life. Show me how to shift my focus from temporary circumstances to the eternal truths of Your Word. Teach me to live with hope and joy, knowing that my present trials are achieving eternal glory. Fill my heart with gratitude for Your faithfulness and the joy that comes from an eternal perspective. In Jesus' name, I pray. Amen.

DAY 201

JOY IN COOKING AND SHARING MEALS

Scripture: "And day by day, attending the temple together and breaking bread in their homes, they received their food with glad and generous hearts." - Acts 2:46 (NIV)

Devotional: Today, let us explore the theme of finding joy in cooking and sharing meals. Food has a way of bringing people together, fostering connection, and creating joyful memories. Reflect on the joy and satisfaction you experience when you prepare a delicious meal and share it with loved ones. Take a moment to pray and thank God for the gift of nourishment and the joy it brings. Let gratitude for His provision and the joy that comes from cooking and sharing meals fill your heart.

Reflection: In your journal, write about the joy and love you experience when you cook and share meals with others. How can you intentionally make time to create delicious dishes and gather around the table with loved ones? How does the act of cooking and sharing meals contribute to your overall sense of connection and gratitude for God's provision? How can you use these moments to reflect God's love and bring joy to others through the gift of hospitality?

Prayer: Loving Father, I thank You for the gift of nourishment and the joy it brings to my life. Help me to intentionally create delicious meals and share them with loved ones. Show me how to use the gift of hospitality to reflect Your love. Fill my heart with gratitude for Your provision and the joy that comes from cooking and sharing meals. In Jesus' name, I pray. Amen.

DAY 202

JOY IN GRATITUDE

Scripture: "Give thanks in all circumstances; for this is God's will for you in Christ Jesus." - 1 Thessalonians 5:18 (NIV)

Devotional: Today, let us explore the theme of finding joy in gratitude. Gratitude is a powerful attitude that shifts our focus from what we lack to the blessings we have. Reflect on the importance of cultivating a heart of gratitude and expressing thanks to God and others. Take a moment to pray and thank God for His goodness and provision. Let gratitude for His faithfulness and the joy that comes from a grateful heart fill your heart.

Reflection: In your journal, write about the ways in which you can cultivate a spirit of gratitude. How can you develop a daily practice of giving thanks to God? How can you express gratitude to others and appreciate the small blessings in life? How does a grateful heart contribute to your overall sense of joy and contentment?

Prayer: Gracious God, I thank You for Your goodness and provision in my life. Help me to cultivate a spirit of gratitude. Show me how to develop a daily practice of giving thanks to You. Teach me to appreciate the small blessings and express gratitude to others. Fill my heart with gratitude for Your faithfulness and the joy that comes from a grateful heart. In Jesus' name, I pray. Amen.

DAY 203

JOY IN CREATIVITY

Scripture: "So God created mankind in his own image, in the image of God he created them; male and female he created them." - Genesis 1:27 (NIV)

Devotional: Today, let us explore the theme of finding joy in creativity. As beings made in the image of a creative God, we are endowed with the ability to express ourselves and bring beauty into the world. Reflect on the joy and fulfillment you experience when you engage in creative pursuits, whether it be painting, writing, crafting, or any other form of artistic expression. Take a moment to pray and thank God for the gift of creativity and the joy it brings. Let gratitude for His inspiration and the joy that comes from engaging in creative endeavors fill your heart.

Reflection: In your journal, write about the joy and satisfaction you experience when you engage in creative activities. How can you intentionally make time to nurture your creative side and explore different forms of expression? How does the act of creating contribute to your overall sense of purpose and self-discovery? How can you use your creativity to reflect God's beauty and bring joy to others through sharing your artistic gifts?

Prayer: Heavenly Father, I thank You for the gift of creativity and the joy it brings to my life. Help me to make time to engage in creative pursuits and express myself through different forms of artistry. Show me how to nurture my creative side and explore new avenues of expression. Fill my heart with gratitude for Your inspiration and the joy that comes from embracing creativity. In Jesus' name, I pray. Amen.

DAY 204

JOY IN LAUGHTER

Scripture: "A cheerful heart is good medicine, but a crushed spirit dries up the bones." - Proverbs 17:22 (NIV)

Devotional: Today, let us explore the theme of finding joy in laughter. Laughter is a gift from God that brings lightness and joy to our hearts. Reflect on the importance of embracing humor and finding moments of laughter in your life. Take a moment to pray and thank God for the joy and healing power of laughter. Let gratitude for His sense of humor and the joy that comes from laughter fill your heart.

Reflection: In your journal, write about the ways in which you can cultivate a spirit of laughter and joy. How can you find moments of humor and lightness in your daily life? How can you share laughter with others and create a joyful atmosphere? How does embracing laughter contribute to your overall sense of joy and well-being?

Prayer: Loving Father, I thank You for the gift of laughter. Help me to cultivate a spirit of joy and humor in my life. Show me how to find moments of laughter and lightness in my daily experiences. Teach me to share laughter with others and create a joyful atmosphere. Fill my heart with gratitude for Your sense of humor and the joy that comes from laughter. In Jesus' name, I pray. Amen.

DAY 205

JOY IN FRIENDSHIP

Scripture: "A friend loves at all times, and a brother is born for a time of adversity." - Proverbs 17:17 (NIV)

Devotional: Today, let us focus on finding joy in friendship. True friendships bring support, encouragement, and joy to our lives. Reflect on the gift of friendship and the impact of meaningful connections. Take a moment to pray and thank God for the friends He has placed in your life. Let gratitude for their presence and the joy that comes from deep friendships fill your heart.

Reflection: In your journal, write about the friendships that bring you joy and support. How can you nurture and invest in these friendships? How can you be a friend who loves at all times and offers support during challenging seasons? How do meaningful friendships contribute to your overall sense of joy and well-being?

Prayer: Gracious God, I thank You for the gift of friendship and the joy it brings to my life. Help me to nurture and invest in the friendships that matter. Show me how to be a friend who loves at all times and offers support during challenging seasons. Fill my heart with gratitude for the friends You have placed in my life and the joy that comes from deep connections. In Jesus' name, I pray. Amen.

DAY 206

JOY IN VOLUNTEERING

Scripture: "Each of you should use whatever gift you have received to serve others, as faithful stewards of God's grace in its various forms." - 1 Peter 4:10 (NIV)

Devotional: Today, let us focus on finding joy in volunteering. The act of selflessly serving others and making a positive impact in their lives can bring a deep sense of fulfillment and joy. Reflect on the joy and satisfaction you experience when you extend a helping hand to those in need. Take a moment to pray and thank God for the opportunities to serve and the joy it brings. Let gratitude for His grace and the joy that comes from volunteering fill your heart.

Reflection: In your journal, write about the joy and purpose you experience when you volunteer. How can you intentionally seek opportunities to serve and make a positive impact in your community? How does the act of volunteering contribute to your overall sense of fulfillment and compassion for others? How can you use your gifts and talents to reflect God's love and bring joy to those you serve?

Prayer: Heavenly Father, I thank You for the opportunities to serve and the joy it brings to my life. Help me to intentionally seek ways to make a positive impact in the lives of others. Show me how to use my gifts and talents to serve with compassion. Fill my heart with gratitude for Your grace and the joy that comes from volunteering. In Jesus' name, I pray. Amen.

DAY 207

JOY IN MUSIC AND WORSHIP

Scripture: "Sing to him, sing praise to him; tell of all his wonderful acts." - Psalm 105:2 (NIV)

Devotional: Today, let us focus on finding joy in music and worship. Music has the power to uplift our spirits and draw us closer to God. Reflect on the joy that comes from engaging in worship through singing, playing instruments, or listening to worship songs. Take a moment to pray and thank God for the gift of music and the ability to worship Him. Let gratitude for His presence and the joy that comes from music and worship fill your heart.

Reflection: In your journal, write about the ways in which you can incorporate music and worship into your daily life. How can you create moments of musical worship that bring joy and draw you closer to God? How does engaging in music and worship contribute to your overall sense of joy and spiritual connection?

Prayer: Loving Father, I thank You for the gift of music and the joy it brings to my heart. Help me to incorporate music and worship into my daily life. Show me how to create moments of musical worship that draw me closer to You. Fill my heart with gratitude for Your presence and the joy that comes from engaging in music and worship. In Jesus' name, I pray. Amen.

DAY 208

JOY IN SIMPLICITY

Scripture: "But seek first his kingdom and his righteousness, and all these things will be given to you as well." - Matthew 6:33 (NIV)

Devotional: Today, let us explore the theme of finding joy in simplicity. In a world filled with busyness and distractions, simplicity brings clarity and contentment. Reflect on the importance of prioritizing God's kingdom and seeking His righteousness above all else. Take a moment to pray and ask God to help you embrace a simpler lifestyle that brings joy and peace. Let gratitude for His provision and the joy that comes from simplicity fill your heart.

Reflection: In your journal, write about the areas of your life where you can simplify and focus on what truly matters. How can you prioritize your relationship with God and align your priorities with His kingdom? How can you create space for rest, reflection, and meaningful connections? How does embracing simplicity contribute to your overall sense of joy and fulfillment?

Prayer: Gracious God, I thank You for Your provision and the joy that comes from simplicity. Help me to simplify my life and focus on what truly matters. Show me how to prioritize Your kingdom and seek Your righteousness above all else. Teach me to create space for rest, reflection, and meaningful connections. Fill my heart with gratitude for Your provision and the joy that comes from embracing simplicity. In Jesus' name, I pray. Amen.

DAY 209

JOY IN PRACTICING GRATITUDE

Scripture: "Give thanks in all circumstances; for this is God's will for you in Christ Jesus." - 1 Thessalonians 5:18 (NIV)

Devotional: Today, let us explore the theme of finding joy in practicing gratitude. Gratitude is a powerful practice that shifts our focus to the blessings and goodness in our lives. Reflect on the joy and contentment you experience when you intentionally cultivate a heart of gratitude. Take a moment to pray and thank God for His abundant blessings and the joy they bring. Let gratitude for His faithfulness and the joy that comes from practicing gratitude fill your heart.

Reflection: In your journal, write about the joy and peace you experience when you practice gratitude. How can you intentionally cultivate a grateful heart and recognize the blessings in your life, both big and small? How does the act of practicing gratitude contribute to your overall sense of contentment and trust in God's provision? How can you use this practice to bring joy to others and inspire them to cultivate gratitude in their own lives?

Prayer: Gracious God, I thank You for Your abundant blessings and the joy they bring to my life. Help me to cultivate a grateful heart and recognize Your goodness in all circumstances. Show me how to practice gratitude in my daily life. Fill my heart with gratitude for Your faithfulness and the joy that comes from practicing gratitude. In Jesus' name, I pray. Amen.

Day 210

Joy in Exploring Nature

Scripture: "The heavens declare the glory of God; the skies proclaim the work of his hands." - Psalm 19:1 (NIV)

Devotional: Today, let us focus on finding joy in exploring nature. The beauty and wonders of the natural world can bring a sense of awe, peace, and gratitude for God's creation. Reflect on the joy and wonder you experience when you immerse yourself in nature and appreciate its intricate details. Take a moment to pray and thank God for the gift of the outdoors and the joy it brings. Let gratitude for His creativity and the joy that comes from exploring nature fill your heart.

Reflection: In your journal, write about the joy and serenity you experience when you immerse yourself in nature. How can you intentionally make time to connect with the natural world and explore its beauty? How does the act of being in nature contribute to your overall sense of awe and reverence for God's creation? How can you use these moments to reflect on His glory and find joy in the simplicity of His natural wonders?

Prayer: Loving Father, I thank You for the gift of nature and the joy it brings to my life. Help me to intentionally make time to explore and connect with the outdoors. Show me how to find awe and gratitude in the beauty of Your creation. Fill my heart with gratitude for Your creativity and the joy that comes from immersing myself in nature. In Jesus' name, I pray. Amen.

DAY 211

JOY IN SUNSETS

Scripture: "From the rising of the sun to the place where it sets, the name of the Lord is to be praised." - Psalm 113:3 (NIV)

Devotional: Today, let us focus on finding joy in sunsets. There is something truly awe-inspiring about the beauty of a setting sun. Reflect on the colors, the stillness, and the sense of wonder that accompanies a sunset. Take a moment to pray and thank God for the gift of sunsets and the joy they bring to your heart. Let gratitude for His creation and the joy that comes from experiencing sunsets fill your heart.

Reflection: In your journal, write about the joy and peace you experience when you witness a beautiful sunset. How can you make time in your daily routine to intentionally appreciate and savor the beauty of sunsets? How does connecting with nature and its simple wonders contribute to your overall sense of joy and gratitude?

Prayer: Loving Creator, I thank You for the gift of sunsets and the joy they bring. Help me to make time to witness and appreciate the beauty of sunsets. Show me how to connect with nature and its simple wonders. Fill my heart with gratitude for Your creation and the joy that comes from experiencing sunsets. In Jesus' name, I pray. Amen.

DAY 212

JOY IN RAIN

Scripture: "Answer me when I call to you, my righteous God. Give me relief from my distress; have mercy on me and hear my prayer." - Psalm 4:1 (NIV)

Devotional: Today, let us explore the theme of finding joy in rain. Rain showers have the power to bring refreshment and renewal to the earth. Reflect on the sound of raindrops, the smell of petrichor, and the feeling of gentle precipitation. Take a moment to pray and thank God for the gift of rain and the joy it brings. Let gratitude for His provision and the joy that comes from rain fill your heart.

Reflection: In your journal, write about the joy and peace you experience when it rains. How can you intentionally embrace and appreciate the rain in your life? How does the symbolism of rain as a source of cleansing and growth resonate with your spiritual journey? How does finding joy in simple natural phenomena contribute to your overall sense of gratitude and contentment?

Prayer: Gracious God, I thank You for the gift of rain and the joy it brings. Help me to embrace and appreciate the rain in my life. Show me how to find beauty and symbolism in the gentle precipitation. Fill my heart with gratitude for Your provision and the joy that comes from rain. In Jesus' name, I pray. Amen.

DAY 213

JOY IN FRESHLY BREWED COFFEE OR TEA

Scripture: "Taste and see that the Lord is good; blessed is the one who takes refuge in him." - Psalm 34:8 (NIV)

Devotional: Today, let us focus on finding joy in a freshly brewed cup of coffee or tea. There is something comforting and invigorating about the aroma and taste of a well-prepared hot beverage. Reflect on the simple pleasure of savoring a warm cup in your hands. Take a moment to pray and thank God for the gift of coffee or tea and the joy it brings to your day. Let gratitude for His provision and the joy that comes from this simple pleasure fill your heart.

Reflection: In your journal, write about the joy and tranquility you experience when you enjoy a freshly brewed cup of coffee or tea. How can you intentionally create space in your routine to savor and appreciate this simple pleasure? How can you use this time to pause, reflect, and connect with God? How does finding joy in the simple act of drinking coffee or tea contribute to your overall sense of gratitude and mindfulness?

Prayer: Loving Father, I thank You for the gift of coffee or tea and the joy it brings to my day. Help me to create space in my routine to savor and appreciate this simple pleasure. Show me how to use this time to pause, reflect, and connect with You. Fill my heart with gratitude for Your provision and the joy that comes from this simple act. In Jesus' name, I pray. Amen.

DAY 214

JOY IN A GOOD BOOK

Scripture: "Your word is a lamp for my feet, a light on my path." - Psalm 119:105 (NIV)

Devotional: Today, let us explore the theme of finding joy in a good book. Reading is a beautiful way to learn, escape, and engage the imagination. Reflect on the joy and inspiration you find when engrossed in a captivating story or thought-provoking literature. Take a moment to pray and thank God for the gift of books and the joy they bring to your life. Let gratitude for knowledge, storytelling, and the joy that comes from reading fill your heart.

Reflection: In your journal, write about the joy and enrichment you experience when reading a good book. How can you prioritize reading as a source of growth and relaxation in your life? How can you explore different genres and authors to expand your perspectives? How does finding joy in the simple act of reading contribute to your overall sense of fulfillment and intellectual nourishment?

Prayer: Heavenly Father, I thank You for the gift of books and the joy they bring to my life. Help me to prioritize reading as a source of growth and relaxation. Show me how to explore different genres and authors to expand my perspectives. Fill my heart with gratitude for knowledge, storytelling, and the joy that comes from reading. In Jesus' name, I pray. Amen.

DAY 215

JOY IN COOKING OR BAKING

Scripture: "So whether you eat or drink or whatever you do, do it all for the glory of God." - 1 Corinthians 10:31 (NIV)

Devotional: Today, let us focus on finding joy in cooking or baking. The act of preparing food can be a creative and nourishing experience. Reflect on the joy and satisfaction that come from experimenting with ingredients and sharing a delicious meal with loved ones. Take a moment to pray and thank God for the gift of food, the ability to cook or bake, and the joy it brings to your life. Let gratitude for His provision and the joy that comes from this simple act fill your heart.

Reflection: In your journal, write about the joy and fulfillment you experience when you cook or bake. How can you intentionally embrace the process and find joy in creating meals for yourself and others? How can you use this time to connect with God's provision and appreciate the flavors and textures of different ingredients? How does finding joy in the simple act of cooking or baking contribute to your overall sense of gratitude and hospitality?

Prayer: Gracious God, I thank You for the gift of food and the joy it brings to my life. Help me to embrace the process of cooking or baking and find joy in creating meals. Show me how to connect with Your provision and appreciate the flavors and textures of different ingredients. Fill my heart with gratitude for Your provision and the joy that comes from this simple act. In Jesus' name, I pray. Amen.

DAY 216

JOY IN NATURE WALKS

Scripture: "The earth is the LORD's, and everything in it, the world, and all who live in it." - Psalm 24:1 (NIV)

Devotional: Today, let us explore the theme of finding joy in nature walks. Nature has a way of rejuvenating our souls and reminding us of God's incredible creation. Reflect on the peace and awe you experience when surrounded by the beauty of the natural world. Take a moment to pray and thank God for the gift of nature and the joy it brings to your life. Let gratitude for His creation and the joy that comes from connecting with nature fill your heart.

Reflection: In your journal, write about the joy and serenity you experience when taking a walk in nature. How can you intentionally carve out time to immerse yourself in the beauty of the outdoors? How can you engage your senses and appreciate the intricate details of God's creation? How does finding joy in the simple act of nature walks contribute to your overall sense of wonder and spiritual connection?

Prayer: Heavenly Father, I thank You for the gift of nature and the joy it brings to my life. Help me to carve out time to immerse myself in the beauty of the outdoors. Show me how to engage my senses and appreciate the intricate details of Your creation. Fill my heart with gratitude for Your creation and the joy that comes from connecting with nature. In Jesus' name, I pray. Amen.

DAY 217

JOY IN ART AND CREATIVITY

Scripture: "In the beginning, God created the heavens and the earth." - Genesis 1:1 (NIV)

Devotional: Today, let us focus on finding joy in art and creativity. God is the ultimate Creator, and He has blessed us with the ability to express ourselves artistically. Reflect on the joy and fulfillment you find when engaged in creative pursuits. Take a moment to pray and thank God for the gift of art and the joy it brings to your life. Let gratitude for His creativity and the joy that comes from embracing your artistic side fill your heart.

Reflection: In your journal, write about the joy and inspiration you experience when engaging in art or creative activities. How can you make time to explore your creativity and embrace different art forms? How can you use your artistic abilities to glorify God and bless others? How does finding joy in the simple act of art and creativity contribute to your overall sense of fulfillment and self-expression?

Prayer: Loving Creator, I thank You for the gift of art and the joy it brings to my life. Help me to make time to explore my creativity and embrace different art forms. Show me how to use my artistic abilities to glorify You and bless others. Fill my heart with gratitude for Your creativity and the joy that comes from embracing my artistic side. In Jesus' name, I pray. Amen.

DAY 218

JOY IN ENGAGING IN PHYSICAL ACTIVITY

Scripture: "Do you not know that your bodies are temples of the Holy Spirit, who is in you, whom you have received from God? You are not your own." - 1 Corinthians 6:19 (NIV)

Devotional: Today, let us explore the theme of finding joy in engaging in physical activity. Taking care of our bodies and staying active contributes to our overall well-being and brings joy through movement. Reflect on the joy and vitality you experience when you engage in physical exercise. Take a moment to pray and thank God for the gift of a healthy body and the joy it brings. Let gratitude for His provision and the joy that comes from physical activity fill your heart.

Reflection: In your journal, write about the joy and energy you experience when you engage in physical activity. How can you intentionally make time for exercise and prioritize your health and well-being? How does the act of being physically active contribute to your overall sense of vitality and gratitude for the gift of a healthy body? How can you use your physical strength and well-being to honor God and bring joy to others through acts of service and care?

Prayer: Heavenly Father, I thank You for the gift of a healthy body and the joy it brings to my life. Help me to make time for physical activity and prioritize my well-being. Show me how to honor You through taking care of my body. Fill my heart with gratitude for Your provision and the joy that comes from engaging in physical activity. In Jesus' name, I pray. Amen.

DAY 219

JOY IN A WARM HUG

Scripture: "Greet one another with a holy kiss." - Romans 16:16 (NIV)

Devotional: Today, let us focus on finding joy in a warm hug. Hugs are a powerful way to express love, comfort, and connection. Reflect on the joy and warmth you experience when embracing someone in a heartfelt hug. Take a moment to pray and thank God for the gift of physical touch and the joy it brings to your life. Let gratitude for relationships and the joy that comes from a warm hug fill your heart.

Reflection: In your journal, write about the joy and comfort you experience when giving or receiving a warm hug. How can you intentionally offer hugs as a gesture of love and support to those around you? How does physical touch contribute to your sense of connection and well-being? How does finding joy in the simple act of a warm hug contribute to your overall sense of love and compassion?

Prayer: Heavenly Father, I thank You for the gift of physical touch and the joy it brings to my life. Help me to offer hugs as a gesture of love and support to those around me. Show me how to connect with others through the power of a warm embrace. Fill my heart with gratitude for relationships and the joy that comes from a warm hug. In Jesus' name, I pray. Amen.

DAY 220

JOY IN KIND WORDS

Scripture: "**Gracious words are a honeycomb, sweet to the** soul and healing to the bones." - Proverbs 16:24 (NIV)

Devotional: Today, let us explore the theme of finding joy in kind words. Our words have the power to uplift, encourage, and bring joy to others. Reflect on the joy and impact you experience when speaking or receiving kind and affirming words. Take a moment to pray and thank God for the gift of language and the joy it brings to your life. Let gratitude for the ability to express kindness and the joy that comes from uplifting others fill your heart.

Reflection: In your journal, write about the joy and fulfillment you experience when speaking kind words or receiving them from others. How can you intentionally use your words to encourage, uplift, and bring joy to those around you? How does the act of speaking kind words contribute to your overall sense of love and compassion? How can you cultivate a habit of speaking life-giving words in your daily interactions?

Prayer: Loving God, I thank You for the gift of language and the joy it brings to my life. Help me to use my words to uplift, encourage, and bring joy to others. Show me how to cultivate a habit of speaking kind and life-giving words. Fill my heart with gratitude for the ability to express kindness and the joy that comes from uplifting others. In Jesus' name, I pray. Amen.

DAY 221

JOY IN SMILING

Scripture: "A happy heart makes the face cheerful, but heartache crushes the spirit." - Proverbs 15:13 (NIV)

Devotional: Today, let us focus on finding joy in smiling. Smiling is a simple yet powerful act that has the ability to brighten someone's day and uplift our own spirits. Reflect on the joy and warmth you experience when smiling or witnessing a genuine smile from others. Take a moment to pray and thank God for the gift of smiles and the joy they bring to your life. Let gratitude for relationships and the joy that comes from a simple smile fill your heart.

Reflection: In your journal, write about the joy and positivity you experience when smiling or making others smile. How can you intentionally wear a smile and spread joy to those around you? How does the act of smiling contribute to your overall sense of happiness and well-being? How can you cultivate a habit of smiling more frequently and embracing the joy it brings?

Prayer: Gracious God, I thank You for the gift of smiles and the joy they bring to my life. Help me to wear a smile and spread joy to those around me. Show me how to cultivate a habit of smiling and embracing the joy it brings. Fill my heart with gratitude for relationships and the joy that comes from a simple smile. In Jesus' name, I pray. Amen.

DAY 222

JOY IN PETTING ANIMALS

Scripture: "The righteous care for the needs of their animals, but the kindest acts of the wicked are cruel." - Proverbs 12:10 (NIV)

Devotional: Today, let us explore the theme of finding joy in petting animals. The companionship and unconditional love of pets can bring immense joy to our lives. Reflect on the joy and comfort you experience when spending time with animals and showing them affection. Take a moment to pray and thank God for the gift of animals and the joy they bring to your life. Let gratitude for the bond between humans and animals and the joy that comes from their presence fill your heart.

Reflection: In your journal, write about the joy and connection you experience when petting animals. How can you intentionally spend time with animals and show them love and care? How does the presence of animals contribute to your overall sense of joy and well-being? How can you cultivate a heart that regards the lives of animals and appreciates the beauty of God's creation?

Prayer: Heavenly Father, I thank You for the gift of animals and the joy they bring to my life. Help me to spend time with animals and show them love and care. Show me how to appreciate the bond between humans and animals. Fill my heart with gratitude for the presence of animals and the joy that comes from their companionship. In Jesus' name, I pray. Amen.

DAY 223

JOY IN JOURNALING

Scripture: "Your word is a lamp for my feet, a light on my path." - Psalm 119:105 (NIV)

Devotional: Today, let us focus on finding joy in journaling. Writing down our thoughts, prayers, and reflections can bring clarity and joy to our lives. Reflect on the joy and therapeutic effects of pouring your heart onto paper. Take a moment to pray and thank God for the gift of words and the joy they bring to your life. Let gratitude for the act of journaling and the joy that comes from self-expression fill your heart.

Reflection: In your journal, write about the joy and fulfillment you experience when journaling. How can you make time in your day to reflect, write, and connect with your inner thoughts and emotions? How does the act of journaling contribute to your overall sense of self-discovery and spiritual growth? How can you use journaling as a tool to deepen your relationship with God?

Prayer: Loving Father, I thank You for the gift of words and the joy they bring to my life. Help me to make time for journaling and self-reflection. Show me how to use this practice to connect with my inner thoughts and emotions. Fill my heart with gratitude for the act of journaling and the joy that comes from self-expression. In Jesus' name, I pray. Amen.

Day 224

Joy in Gazing at the Stars

Scripture: "When I consider your heavens, the work of your fingers, the moon and the stars, which you have set in place. 4 what is mankind that you are mindful of them,human beings that you care for them?" - Psalm 8:3-4 (NIV)

Devotional: Today, let us explore the theme of finding joy in gazing at the stars. The vastness and beauty of the night sky can evoke a sense of wonder and humility in us. Reflect on the joy and awe you experience when gazing at the stars and contemplating God's creation. Take a moment to pray and thank God for the gift of the night sky and the joy it brings to your life. Let gratitude for His majesty and the joy that comes from stargazing fill your heart.

Reflection: In your journal, write about the joy and wonder you experience when gazing at the stars. How can you create moments to observe the night sky and marvel at its beauty? How does contemplating the vastness of the universe and God's creation deepen your faith and sense of purpose? How does finding joy in the simple act of stargazing contribute to your overall sense of awe and reverence?

Prayer: Gracious God, I thank You for the gift of the night sky and the joy it brings to my life. Help me to create moments to observe and marvel at the stars. Show me how to contemplate Your creation and find wonder in its vastness. Fill my heart with gratitude for Your majesty and the joy that comes from stargazing. In Jesus' name, I pray. Amen.

DAY 225

JOY IN LEARNING SOMETHING NEW

Scripture: "Give instruction to the wise, and they will be still wiser; teach the righteous and they will increase in learning." - Proverbs 9:9 (NIV)

Devotional: Today, let us focus on finding joy in learning something new. Lifelong learning opens doors to new opportunities, expands our knowledge, and brings a sense of accomplishment. Reflect on the joy and curiosity you experience when you engage in learning and acquiring new skills. Take a moment to pray and thank God for the gift of wisdom and the joy it brings. Let gratitude for His guidance and the joy that comes from learning something new fill your heart.

Reflection: In your journal, write about the joy and fulfillment you experience when you learn something new. How can you intentionally make time for personal growth and explore areas of interest that inspire you? How does the act of learning contribute to your overall sense of empowerment and intellectual stimulation? How can you use your newfound knowledge and skills to bring joy to others and make a positive impact in the world?

Prayer: Gracious God, I thank You for the gift of wisdom and the joy it brings to my life. Help me to intentionally make time for personal growth and learning. Show me how to explore new areas of interest and expand my knowledge. Fill my heart with gratitude for Your guidance and the joy that comes from learning something new. In Jesus' name, I pray. Amen.

DAY 226

JOY IN SILENCE AND STILLNESS

Scripture: "Be still, and know that I am God." - Psalm 46:10 (NIV)

Devotional: Today, let us explore the theme of finding joy in silence and stillness. In the midst of a noisy and busy world, silence and stillness provide an opportunity for reflection, connection, and peace. Reflect on the joy and serenity you experience when embracing moments of silence and stillness. Take a moment to pray and thank God for the gift of quietude and the joy it brings to your life. Let gratitude for His presence and the joy that comes from stillness and silence fill your heart.

Reflection: In your journal, write about the joy and clarity you experience when embracing moments of silence and stillness. How can you intentionally create space for silence and stillness in your daily routine? How does the act of being still and quiet contribute to your overall sense of inner peace and spiritual connection? How can you use these moments to listen to God's voice and seek His guidance?

Prayer: Loving God, I thank You for the gift of silence and stillness and the joy they bring to my life. Help me to create space for these moments in my daily routine. Show me how to embrace the quietude and find peace in Your presence. Fill my heart with gratitude for the joy that comes from stillness and silence. In Jesus' name, I pray. Amen.

DAY 227

JOY IN WATCHING A SUNRISE

Scripture: "because of the tender mercy of our God. by which the rising sun will come to us from heaven" - Luke 1:78 (NIV)

Devotional: Today, let us focus on finding joy in watching a sunrise. The beauty and symbolism of a new day dawning fill our hearts with hope and anticipation. Reflect on the joy and awe you experience when witnessing the colors and the gradual illumination of the sky. Take a moment to pray and thank God for the gift of each new day and the joy it brings. Let gratitude for His faithfulness and the joy that comes from watching a sunrise fill your heart.

Reflection: In your journal, write about the joy and hope you experience when watching a sunrise. How can you intentionally wake up early to witness the beauty of a new day? How does the act of watching the sunrise inspire you to embrace new beginnings and trust in God's faithfulness? How does finding joy in the simple act of watching a sunrise contribute to your overall sense of hope and gratitude?

Prayer: Gracious God, I thank You for the gift of each new day and the joy that comes from watching a sunrise. Help me to wake up early to witness the beauty of a new day. Show me how to embrace new beginnings and trust in Your faithfulness. Fill my heart with gratitude for Your creation and the joy that comes from watching a sunrise. In Jesus' name, I pray. Amen.

DAY 228

JOY IN CONNECTING WITH LOVED ONES

Scripture: "A friend loves at all times, and a brother is born for a time of adversity." - Proverbs 17:17 (NIV)

Devotional: Today, let us explore the theme of finding joy in connecting with loved ones. Meaningful relationships are a source of joy, support, and companionship in our lives. Reflect on the joy and warmth you experience when you spend quality time with family and friends. Take a moment to pray and thank God for the gift of loved ones and the joy they bring. Let gratitude for His provision and the joy that comes from connecting with loved ones fill your heart.

Reflection: In your journal, write about the joy and fulfillment you experience when you connect with your loved ones. How can you intentionally make time to nurture and deepen your relationships? How does the act of spending quality time with family and friends contribute to your overall sense of belonging and love? How can you use these moments to reflect God's love and bring joy to the lives of those you care about?

Prayer: Loving God, I thank You for the gift of loved ones and the joy they bring to my life. Help me to intentionally make time to nurture and deepen my relationships. Show me how to reflect Your love through my interactions with others. Fill my heart with gratitude for Your provision and the joy that comes from connecting with loved ones. In Jesus' name, I pray. Amen.

DAY 229

JOY IN GIVING

Scripture: "In everything I did, I showed you that by this kind of hard work we must help the weak, remembering the words the Lord Jesus himself said: 'It is more blessed to give than to receive.' " - Acts 20:35 (NIV)

Devotional: Today, let us focus on finding joy in giving. The act of giving allows us to bless others and experience the joy of selflessness. Reflect on the joy and fulfillment you experience when you give generously of your time, resources, or talents. Take a moment to pray and thank God for the gift of giving and the joy it brings to your life. Let gratitude for His provision and the joy that comes from a generous heart fill your heart.

Reflection: In your journal, write about the joy and satisfaction you experience when you give to others. How can you cultivate a heart of generosity and find joy in sharing your blessings with those in need? How does the act of giving contribute to your overall sense of purpose and fulfillment? How can you prioritize giving as a way to reflect God's love and grace to others?

Prayer: Loving Father, I thank You for the gift of giving and the joy it brings to my life. Help me to cultivate a heart of generosity and find joy in sharing my blessings with others. Show me how to prioritize giving as a way to reflect Your love and grace to those in need. Fill my heart with gratitude for Your provision and the joy that comes from a generous heart. In Jesus' name, I pray. Amen.

DAY 230

JOY IN ACTS OF SERVICE

Scripture: "You, my brothers and sisters, were called to be free. But do not use your freedom to indulge the flesh; rather, serve one another humbly in love." - Galatians 5:13 (NIV)

Devotional: Today, let us explore the theme of finding joy in acts of service. Serving others with love and selflessness can bring immense joy and fulfillment to our lives. Reflect on the joy and purpose you experience when serving those in need or helping someone in a meaningful way. Take a moment to pray and thank God for the opportunities to serve and the joy it brings to your life. Let gratitude for His example of servanthood and the joy that comes from acts of service fill your heart.

Reflection: In your journal, write about the joy and fulfillment you experience when serving others. How can you intentionally seek opportunities to serve those in need or assist someone in a meaningful way? How does the act of serving contribute to your overall sense of purpose and empathy? How can you cultivate a heart of service and use your unique gifts to bless others?

Prayer: Gracious God, I thank You for the opportunities to serve and the joy it brings to my life. Help me to intentionally seek opportunities to serve those in need or assist someone in a meaningful way. Show me how to use my unique gifts and abilities to bless others. Fill my heart with gratitude for Your example of servanthood and the joy that comes from acts of service. In Jesus' name, I pray. Amen.

DAY 231

JOY IN SPONTANEOUS ADVENTURES

Scripture: "For I know the plans I have for you," declares the Lord, "plans to prosper you and not to harm you, plans to give you hope and a future." - Jeremiah 29:11 (NIV)

Devotional: Today, let us focus on finding joy in spontaneous adventures. Stepping out of our comfort zones and embracing new experiences can bring a sense of excitement and joy to our lives. Reflect on the joy and anticipation you experience when embarking on a spontaneous adventure or trying something new. Take a moment to pray and thank God for the opportunities to explore and the joy it brings to your life. Let gratitude for His guidance and the joy that comes from stepping into the unknown fill your heart.

Reflection: In your journal, write about the joy and growth you experience when you embrace spontaneous adventures. How can you intentionally create space in your life for new experiences and unexpected opportunities? How does the act of stepping out of your comfort zone contribute to your overall sense of courage and personal development? How can you cultivate a spirit of adventure and trust in God's plans for your life?

Prayer: Heavenly Father, I thank You for the opportunities to embrace spontaneous adventures and the joy they bring to my life. Help me to create space for new experiences and unexpected opportunities. Show me how to step out of my comfort zone and trust in Your guidance. Fill my heart with gratitude for the joy that comes from stepping into the unknown and embracing Your plans for my life. In Jesus' name, I pray. Amen.

DAY 232

JOY IN MUSIC

Scripture: "Sing to the Lord a new song;sing to the Lord, all the earth." - Psalm 96:1 (NIV)

Devotional: Today, let us explore the theme of finding joy in music. Music has the power to uplift our spirits, stir our emotions, and bring us closer to God. Reflect on the joy and inspiration you experience when listening to or making music. Take a moment to pray and thank God for the gift of music and the joy it brings to your life. Let gratitude for His creativity and the joy that comes from melodies and harmonies fill your heart.

Reflection: In your journal, write about the joy and peace you experience when engaging with music. How can you intentionally make time to listen to uplifting and worshipful music that speaks to your heart? How does the act of singing or playing an instrument contribute to your overall sense of connection with God and others? How can you use music as a tool to express your faith and find joy in the melody of life?

Prayer: Loving Father, I thank You for the gift of music and the joy it brings to my life. Help me to make time to listen to uplifting and worshipful music. Show me how to use my voice or play an instrument to express my faith and connect with You. Fill my heart with gratitude for Your creativity and the joy that comes from melodies and harmonies. In Jesus' name, I pray. Amen.

DAY 233

JOY IN ACTS OF FORGIVENESS

Scripture: "Be kind and compassionate to one another, forgiving each other, just as in Christ God forgave you." - Ephesians 4:32 (NIV)

Devotional: Today, let us focus on finding joy in acts of forgiveness. Forgiveness is a transformative act that brings healing, reconciliation, and freedom. Reflect on the joy and peace you experience when you extend forgiveness or receive forgiveness from others. Take a moment to pray and thank God for the gift of forgiveness and the joy it brings to your life. Let gratitude for His grace and the joy that comes from a forgiving heart fill your heart.

Reflection: In your journal, write about the joy and liberation you experience when you extend forgiveness or receive forgiveness. How can you intentionally cultivate a forgiving heart and seek reconciliation in your relationships? How does the act of forgiveness contribute to your overall sense of peace and emotional well-being? How can you use forgiveness as a tool to reflect God's love and bring joy to others?

Prayer: Gracious God, I thank You for the gift of forgiveness and the joy it brings to my life. Help me to cultivate a forgiving heart and seek reconciliation in my relationships. Show me how to extend grace and forgiveness to those who have hurt me. Fill my heart with gratitude for Your grace and the joy that comes from a forgiving heart. In Jesus' name, I pray. Amen.

DAY 234

THE JOY OF PRAYER AND MEDITATION

Scripture: "Do not be anxious about anything, but in every situation, by prayer and petition, with thanksgiving, present your requests to God. And the peace of God, which transcends all understanding, will guard your hearts and your minds in Christ Jesus." - Philippians 4:6-7 (NIV)

Devotional: Today, let's focus on finding joy in prayer and meditation. Take time to seek God's presence in prayer, sharing your thoughts, worries, and hopes with Him. Embrace the peace that comes from meditating on His Word and being still in His presence.

Reflection: In your journal, write about the joy and peace you find in prayer and meditation. How does seeking God's presence and sharing your heart with Him uplift your spirit and bring comfort? How can you cultivate a consistent prayer and meditation practice to deepen your relationship with God? How can you share the joy of communion with God through prayer and meditation with others?

Prayer: Heavenly Father, I thank You for the joy and peace found in prayer and meditation. As I seek Your presence and share my heart with You, help me to find comfort and strength in Your Word. May my prayer and meditation practice deepen my relationship with You and bring joy to my life. In Jesus' name, I pray. Amen.

DAY 235

JOY IN BUILDING MEANINGFUL RELATIONSHIPS

Scripture: "Two are better than one, because they have a good return for their labor" - Ecclesiastes 4:9 (NIV)

Devotional: Today, let us focus on finding joy in building meaningful relationships. We were created for connection, and deep bonds with others bring joy and fulfillment to our lives. Reflect on the joy and warmth you experience when you invest time and effort in building relationships. Take a moment to pray and thank God for the gift of meaningful connections and the joy they bring. Let gratitude for His provision and the joy that comes from authentic relationships fill your heart.

Reflection: In your journal, write about the joy and support you experience when you build meaningful relationships. How can you intentionally invest in the relationships that matter most to you? How does the act of building connections and fostering community contribute to your overall sense of belonging and happiness? How can you use your relationships to reflect God's love and bring joy to others?

Prayer: Loving God, I thank You for the gift of meaningful relationships and the joy they bring to my life. Help me to invest time and effort in building authentic connections. Show me how to nurture the relationships that matter most to me. Fill my heart with gratitude for Your provision and the joy that comes from genuine relationships. In Jesus' name, I pray. Amen.

DAY 236

JOY IN LISTENING TO INSPIRING PODCASTS

Scripture: "So faith comes from hearing, and hearing through the word of Christ." - Romans 10:17 (NIV)

Devotional: Today, let us focus on finding joy in listening to inspiring podcasts. Podcasts provide an opportunity to learn, grow, and be inspired by the wisdom and experiences of others. Reflect on the joy and enrichment you experience when you engage with uplifting and educational podcasts. Take a moment to pray and thank God for the gift of technology and the joy it brings. Let gratitude for His guidance and the joy that comes from listening to inspiring podcasts fill your heart.

Reflection: In your journal, write about the joy and motivation you experience when you listen to inspiring podcasts. How can you intentionally make time to engage with podcasts that align with your interests and values? How does the act of listening to uplifting content contribute to your overall sense of personal growth and spiritual nourishment? How can you use the joy of listening to podcasts to deepen your faith and bring joy to others through sharing meaningful episodes?

Prayer: Heavenly Father, I thank You for the gift of technology and the joy it brings to my life. Help me to intentionally engage with podcasts that uplift and inspire. Show me how to use this medium to grow and deepen my faith. Fill my heart with gratitude for Your guidance and the joy that comes from listening to inspiring podcasts. In Jesus' name, I pray. Amen.

DAY 237

JOY IN ENCOURAGING OTHERS

Scripture: "Therefore encourage one another and build each other up, just as in fact you are doing." - 1 Thessalonians 5:11 (NIV)

Devotional: Today, let us focus on finding joy in encouraging others. Our words and actions have the power to uplift, inspire, and bring joy to those around us. Reflect on the joy and fulfillment you experience when you encourage and build up others. Take a moment to pray and thank God for the opportunities to bring joy and hope to those in need. Let gratitude for His love and the joy that comes from encouraging others fill your heart.

Reflection: In your journal, write about the joy and impact you experience when you encourage and uplift others. How can you intentionally seek opportunities to bring joy and hope to those around you? How does the act of encouraging contribute to your overall sense of purpose and empathy? How can you use your words and actions to reflect God's love and bring joy to others?

Prayer: Heavenly Father, I thank You for the opportunities to encourage others and the joy it brings to my life. Help me to intentionally seek opportunities to bring joy and hope to those in need. Show me how to use my words and actions to reflect Your love and bring joy to others. Fill my heart with gratitude for Your love and the joy that comes from encouraging others. In Jesus' name, I pray. Amen.

DAY 238

JOY IN ACTS OF KINDNESS TO STRANGERS

Scripture: "Do not forget to show hospitality to strangers, for by so doing some people have shown hospitality to angels without knowing it." - Hebrews 13:2 (NIV)

Devotional: Today, let us explore the theme of finding joy in acts of kindness to strangers. The simple act of extending kindness to someone we don't know can bring unexpected joy and blessings. Reflect on the joy and connection you experience when you show hospitality and kindness to strangers. Take a moment to pray and thank God for the opportunities to be a blessing and the joy it brings. Let gratitude for His love and the joy that comes from selfless acts fill your heart.

Reflection: In your journal, write about the joy and fulfillment you experience when you extend kindness to strangers. How can you intentionally seek opportunities to be a blessing to those you encounter in your daily life? How does the act of showing hospitality contribute to your overall sense of compassion and empathy? How can you use acts of kindness to reflect God's love and bring joy to strangers?

Prayer: Gracious God, I thank You for the opportunities to extend kindness to strangers and the joy it brings to my life. Help me to intentionally seek opportunities to be a blessing to those I encounter. Show me how to show hospitality and love to strangers. Fill my heart with gratitude for Your love and the joy that comes from selfless acts. In Jesus' name, I pray. Amen.

DAY 239

JOY IN EMBRACING IMPERFECTION

Scripture: "But he said to me, "My grace is sufficient for you, for my power is made perfect in weakness." Therefore I will boast all the more gladly about my weaknesses, so that Christ's power may rest on me." - 2 Corinthians 12:9 (NIV)

Devotional: Today, let us focus on finding joy in embracing imperfection. We live in a world that often emphasizes perfection, but true joy is found in accepting ourselves and others as we are. Reflect on the joy and freedom you experience when you embrace your imperfections and find beauty in the midst of flaws. Take a moment to pray and thank God for His grace and the joy it brings. Let gratitude for His acceptance and the joy that comes from embracing imperfection fill your heart.

Reflection: In your journal, write about the joy and liberation you experience when you embrace your imperfections and accept yourself as you are. How can you intentionally cultivate a mindset of self-compassion and extend grace to others in their imperfections? How does the act of embracing imperfection contribute to your overall sense of authenticity and self-acceptance? How can you use your imperfections as a means to reflect God's love and bring joy to others?

Prayer: Loving Father, I thank You for Your grace and the joy that comes from embracing imperfection. Help me to cultivate a mindset of self-compassion and extend grace to others in their imperfections. Show me how to find beauty in the midst of flaws and accept myself as I am. Fill my heart with gratitude for Your acceptance and the joy that comes from embracing imperfection. In Jesus' name, I pray. Amen.

DAY 240

JOY IN ACTS OF GENEROSITY

Scripture: "Each of you should give what you have decided in your heart to give, not reluctantly or under compulsion, for God loves a cheerful giver." - 2 Corinthians 9:7 (NIV)

Devotional: Today, let us explore the theme of finding joy in acts of generosity. Giving generously not only blesses others but also fills our hearts with joy and gratitude. Reflect on the joy and satisfaction you experience when you give freely and cheerfully. Take a moment to pray and thank God for the opportunities to be generous and the joy it brings. Let gratitude for His provision and the joy that comes from a giving heart fill your heart.

Reflection: In your journal, write about the joy and fulfillment you experience when you give generously. How can you intentionally cultivate a heart of generosity and find joy in sharing your blessings with others? How does the act of giving contribute to your overall sense of purpose and impact? How can you use acts of generosity to reflect God's love and bring joy to those in need?

Prayer: Heavenly Father, I thank You for the opportunities to be generous and the joy it brings to my life. Help me to cultivate a heart of generosity and find joy in sharing my blessings with others. Show me how to use my resources and gifts to make a positive impact in the lives of those in need. Fill my heart with gratitude for Your provision and the joy that comes from a giving heart. In Jesus' name, I pray. Amen.

DAY 241

JOY IN SHARING A MEAL WITH LOVED ONES

Scripture: "Every day they continued to meet together in the temple courts. They broke bread in their homes and ate together with glad and sincere hearts," - Acts 2:46 (NIV)

Devotional: Today, let us focus on finding joy in sharing a meal with loved ones. The act of gathering around a table, sharing food, and connecting with one another brings joy and strengthens relationships. Reflect on the joy and warmth you experience when you share a meal with those you love. Take a moment to pray and thank God for the gift of food and the joy it brings. Let gratitude for His provision and the joy that comes from shared meals fill your heart.

Reflection: In your journal, write about the joy and connection you experience when you share a meal with loved ones. How can you intentionally create space for shared meals and meaningful conversations? How does the act of breaking bread together contribute to your overall sense of love and unity? How can you use the act of sharing a meal to reflect God's love and bring joy to those around you?

Prayer: Gracious God, I thank You for the gift of food and the joy that comes from sharing a meal with loved ones. Help me to create space for shared meals and meaningful conversations. Show me how to foster love and unity as I break bread with others. Fill my heart with gratitude for Your provision and the joy that comes from shared meals. In Jesus' name, I pray. Amen.

DAY 242

JOY IN EXPRESSING GRATITUDE

Scripture: "give thanks in all circumstances; for this is God's will for you in Christ Jesus." - 1 Thessalonians 5:18 (NIV)

Devotional: Today, let us explore the theme of finding joy in expressing gratitude. Gratitude shifts our focus from what is lacking to what we have, bringing joy and contentment. Reflect on the joy and peace you experience when you cultivate a heart of gratitude. Take a moment to pray and thank God for His blessings and the joy they bring. Let gratitude for His faithfulness and the joy that comes from expressing gratitude fill your heart.

Reflection: In your journal, write about the joy and fulfillment you experience when you express gratitude. How can you intentionally cultivate a mindset of gratitude and find joy in the simple blessings of life? How does the act of giving thanks contribute to your overall sense of joy and well-being? How can you use gratitude as a tool to reflect God's goodness and bring joy to others?

Prayer: Loving Father, I thank You for Your blessings and the joy that comes from expressing gratitude. Help me to cultivate a mindset of gratitude and find joy in the simple blessings of life. Show me how to give thanks in all circumstances and reflect Your goodness to others. Fill my heart with gratitude for Your faithfulness and the joy that comes from expressing gratitude. In Jesus' name, I pray. Amen.

DAY 243

JOY IN WITNESSING ACTS OF KINDNESS

Scripture: "Be kind and compassionate to one another, forgiving each other, just as in Christ God forgave you." - Ephesians 4:32 (NIV)

Devotional: Today, let us explore the theme of finding joy in witnessing acts of kindness. Kindness has the power to uplift, encourage, and bring joy to both the giver and the receiver. Reflect on the joy and inspiration you experience when you witness acts of kindness in your daily life. Take a moment to pray and thank God for the gift of compassion and the joy it brings. Let gratitude for His love and the joy that comes from witnessing acts of kindness fill your heart.

Reflection: In your journal, write about the joy and hope you experience when you witness acts of kindness. How can you intentionally seek opportunities to witness and celebrate acts of compassion and generosity? How does the act of witnessing kindness contribute to your overall sense of faith in humanity and gratitude for God's love? How can you use these moments to reflect God's character and bring joy to others through sharing stories of kindness?

Prayer: Gracious God, I thank You for the gift of kindness and the joy it brings to my life. Help me to intentionally seek opportunities to witness and celebrate acts of compassion and generosity. Show me how to reflect Your love through sharing stories of kindness. Fill my heart with gratitude for Your love and the joy that comes from witnessing acts of kindness. In Jesus' name, I pray. Amen.

DAY 244

JOY IN RECONNECTING WITH NATURE

Scripture: "The heavens declare the glory of God; the skies proclaim the work of his hands."- Psalm 19:1 (NIV)

Devotional: Today, let us explore the theme of finding joy in reconnecting with nature. The beauty and intricacy of the natural world remind us of God's creativity and provision, bringing joy and a sense of awe. Reflect on the joy and peace you experience when you spend time in nature and appreciate its wonders. Take a moment to pray and thank God for His creation and the joy it brings. Let gratitude for His majesty and the joy that comes from reconnecting with nature fill your heart.

Reflection: In your journal, write about the joy and wonder you experience when you reconnect with nature. How can you intentionally make time to be outdoors and appreciate God's creation? How does the act of immersing yourself in nature contribute to your overall sense of peace and spiritual connection? How can you use your appreciation for nature to reflect God's glory and bring joy to others?

Prayer: Gracious God, I thank You for Your creation and the joy that comes from reconnecting with nature. Help me to make time to be outdoors and appreciate the wonders of Your handiwork. Show me how to find peace and spiritual connection through immersion in nature. Fill my heart with gratitude for Your majesty and the joy that comes from reconnecting with nature. In Jesus' name, I pray. Amen.

DAY 245

JOY IN ACTS OF SELF-CARE

Scripture: "Do you not know that your bodies are temples of the Holy Spirit, who is in you, whom you have received from God? You are not your own; you were bought at a price. Therefore honor God with your bodies." - 1 Corinthians 6:19-20 (NIV)

Devotional: Today, let us focus on finding joy in acts of self-care. Taking care of ourselves physically, emotionally, and spiritually is essential for our well-being and brings joy and rejuvenation. Reflect on the joy and renewal you experience when you prioritize self-care. Take a moment to pray and thank God for the gift of your body and the joy it brings. Let gratitude for His grace and the joy that comes from caring for yourself fill your heart.

Reflection: In your journal, write about the joy and restoration you experience when you practice self-care. How can you intentionally make time for activities that nourish your body, mind, and spirit? How does the act of caring for yourself contribute to your overall sense of well-being and personal growth? How can you use self-care as a means to honor God's gift of your body and bring joy to others?

Prayer: Loving Father, I thank You for the gift of my body and the joy that comes from practicing self-care. Help me to make time for activities that nourish my body, mind, and spirit. Show me how to prioritize self-care and honor the gift of my body. Fill my heart with gratitude for Your grace and the joy that comes from caring for myself. In Jesus' name, I pray. Amen.

DAY 246

JOY IN DANCING

Scripture: "Let them praise his name with dancing and make music to him with timbrel and harp." - Psalm 149:3 (NIV)

Devotional: Today, let us focus on finding joy in dancing. Dancing is a form of expression and celebration that can bring joy and liberation to our souls. Reflect on the joy and freedom you experience when you let go and allow your body to move with the rhythm of music. Take a moment to pray and thank God for the gift of movement and the joy it brings. Let gratitude for His creativity and the joy that comes from dancing fill your heart.

Reflection: In your journal, write about the joy and release you experience when you dance. How can you intentionally make time to move your body and embrace the joy of dancing? How does the act of dancing contribute to your overall sense of freedom and self-expression? How can you use dance as a form of worship and bring joy to others through sharing your love for movement?

Prayer: Gracious God, I thank You for the gift of movement and the joy it brings to my life. Help me to make time to dance and express my joy through movement. Show me how to let go and embrace the freedom of dancing. Fill my heart with gratitude for Your creativity and the joy that comes from embracing dance. In Jesus' name, I pray. Amen.

DAY 247

JOY IN ACTS OF CREATIVITY

Scripture: "In the beginning God created the heavens and the earth." - Genesis 1:1 (NIV)

Devotional: Today, let us focus on finding joy in acts of creativity. We are made in the image of a creative God, and engaging in creative pursuits brings joy and a sense of fulfillment. Reflect on the joy and satisfaction you experience when you engage in creative activities. Take a moment to pray and thank God for the gift of creativity and the joy it brings. Let gratitude for His artistic expression and the joy that comes from acts of creativity fill your heart.

Reflection: In your journal, write about the joy and fulfillment you experience when you engage in acts of creativity. How can you intentionally make time for creative pursuits that bring you joy? How does the act of creating contribute to your overall sense of purpose and self-discovery? How can you use your creative gifts to reflect God's beauty and bring joy to others?

Prayer: Gracious God, I thank You for the gift of creativity and the joy that comes from engaging in acts of creativity. Help me to make time for creative pursuits that bring me joy. Show me how to use my creative gifts to reflect Your beauty and bring joy to others. Fill my heart with gratitude for Your artistic expression and the joy that comes from acts of creativity. In Jesus' name, I pray. Amen.

DAY 248

JOY IN FINDING BEAUTY IN EVERYDAY MOMENTS

Scripture: "Finally, brothers and sisters, whatever is true, whatever is noble, whatever is right, whatever is pure, whatever is lovely, whatever is admirable—if anything is excellent or praiseworthy—think about such things." - Philippians 4:8 (NIV)

Devotional: Today, let us explore the theme of finding joy in finding beauty in everyday moments. Life is filled with small miracles and precious moments that bring joy and wonder. Reflect on the joy and gratitude you experience when you pause to appreciate the beauty around you. Take a moment to pray and thank God for the gift of everyday wonders and the joy they bring. Let gratitude for His goodness and the joy that comes from finding beauty in everyday moments fill your heart.

Reflection: In your journal, write about the joy and awe you experience when you find beauty in everyday moments. How can you intentionally cultivate a mindset of appreciation and mindfulness? How does the act of noticing the small miracles contribute to your overall sense of joy and gratitude? How can you use the joy of finding beauty in everyday moments to deepen your connection with God and bring joy to others?

Prayer: Loving Father, I thank You for the gift of everyday wonders and the joy they bring to my life. Help me to cultivate a mindset of appreciation and mindfulness. Show me how to notice the small miracles and find beauty in everyday moments. Fill my heart with gratitude for Your goodness and the joy that comes from finding beauty in the ordinary. In Jesus' name, I pray. Amen.

DAY 249

JOY IN CELEBRATING MILESTONES AND ACHIEVEMENTS

Scripture: "So whether you eat or drink or whatever you do, do it all for the glory of God." - 1 Corinthians 10:31 (NIV)

Devotional: Today, let us focus on finding joy in celebrating milestones and achievements. Recognizing and rejoicing in our accomplishments, both big and small, brings a sense of fulfillment and joy. Reflect on the joy and satisfaction you experience when you celebrate milestones and achievements. Take a moment to pray and thank God for His guidance and the joy it brings. Let gratitude for His provision and the joy that comes from celebrating fill your heart.

Reflection: In your journal, write about the joy and pride you experience when you celebrate milestones and achievements. How can you intentionally make time to acknowledge and rejoice in your accomplishments? How does the act of celebrating contribute to your overall sense of purpose and motivation? How can you use the joy of celebrating milestones and achievements to give glory to God and encourage others?

Prayer: Heavenly Father, I thank You for Your guidance and the joy that comes from celebrating milestones and achievements. Help me to intentionally make time to acknowledge and rejoice in my accomplishments. Show me how to give glory to You in all that I do. Fill my heart with gratitude for Your provision and the joy that comes from celebrating. In Jesus' name, I pray. Amen.

DAY 250

JOY IN ACTS OF COMPASSION

Scripture: "Put on then, as God's chosen ones, holy and beloved, compassionate hearts, kindness, humility, meekness, and patience." - Colossians 3:12 (ESV)

Devotional: Today, let us explore the theme of finding joy in acts of compassion. Showing kindness and empathy to others brings joy and fosters a sense of connection. Reflect on the joy and fulfillment you experience when you extend compassion to those in need. Take a moment to pray and thank God for His love and the joy it brings. Let gratitude for His example of compassion and the joy that comes from acts of compassion fill your heart.

Reflection: In your journal, write about the joy and fulfillment you experience when you show compassion to others. How can you intentionally seek opportunities to extend kindness and empathy? How does the act of showing compassion contribute to your overall sense of love and unity? How can you use acts of compassion to reflect God's love and bring joy to those in need?

Prayer: Gracious God, I thank You for Your love and the joy that comes from acts of compassion. Help me to intentionally seek opportunities to show kindness and empathy. Show me how to extend compassion to those in need. Fill my heart with gratitude for Your example of compassion and the joy that comes from acts of compassion. In Jesus' name, I pray. Amen.

DAY 251

JOY IN SOLITUDE AND REFLECTION

Scripture: "Be still, and know that I am God; I will be exalted among the nations, I will be exalted in the earth." - Psalm 46:10 (NIV)

Devotional: Today, let us explore the theme of finding joy in solitude and reflection. In the midst of our busy lives, taking time to be still and reflect can bring a deep sense of peace and connection with God. Reflect on the joy and serenity you experience when you intentionally create space for solitude and reflection. Take a moment to pray and thank God for the gift of stillness and the joy it brings. Let gratitude for His presence and the joy that comes from quiet moments fill your heart.

Reflection: In your journal, write about the joy and clarity you experience when you embrace solitude and reflection. How can you intentionally make time to be still and connect with God in quiet moments? How does the act of seeking solitude contribute to your overall sense of peace and spiritual growth? How can you use these moments of reflection to deepen your relationship with God and find joy in His presence?

Prayer: Loving Father, I thank You for the gift of solitude and the joy it brings to my life. Help me to intentionally create space for stillness and reflection. Show me how to find peace and spiritual growth in these moments. Fill my heart with gratitude for Your presence and the joy that comes from embracing solitude and reflection. In Jesus' name, I pray. Amen.

DAY 252

JOY IN ENGAGING IN A HOBBY

Scripture: "And whatever you do, whether in word or deed, do it all in the name of the Lord Jesus, giving thanks to God the Father through him." - Colossians 3:17 (NIV)

Devotional: Today, let us focus on finding joy in engaging in a hobby. Hobbies allow us to explore our interests, develop skills, and find joy in activities that bring us fulfillment. Reflect on the joy and satisfaction you experience when you dedicate time to your favorite hobby. Take a moment to pray and thank God for the gift of creativity and the joy it brings. Let gratitude for His provision and the joy that comes from engaging in a hobby fill your heart.

Reflection: In your journal, write about the joy and passion you experience when you engage in your favorite hobby. How can you intentionally make time for your hobby and nurture your talents and interests? How does the act of pursuing a hobby contribute to your overall sense of self-expression and personal growth? How can you use your hobbies to honor God and bring joy to others through sharing your talents?

Prayer: Gracious God, I thank You for the gift of hobbies and the joy they bring to my life. Help me to make time for my favorite activities and develop my talents and interests. Show me how to use my hobbies to honor You and bring joy to others. Fill my heart with gratitude for Your provision and the joy that comes from engaging in a hobby. In Jesus' name, I pray. Amen.

DAY 253

JOY IN WALKING IN NATURE

Scripture: "You make known to me the path of life; you will fill me with joy in your presence, with eternal pleasures at your right hand." - Psalm 16:11 (NIV)

Devotional: Today, let us focus on finding joy in walking in nature. The beauty of God's creation surrounds us, and taking a leisurely walk in nature can bring a sense of peace and wonder. Reflect on the joy and serenity you experience when you immerse yourself in the sights and sounds of the natural world. Take a moment to pray and thank God for the gift of His creation and the joy it brings. Let gratitude for His presence and the joy that comes from walking in nature fill your heart.

Reflection: In your journal, write about the joy and tranquility you experience when you take a walk in nature. How can you intentionally make time to connect with the outdoors and appreciate God's handiwork? How does the act of walking in nature contribute to your overall sense of well-being and spiritual connection? How can you use these moments to seek God's presence and find joy in the simplicity of His creation?

Prayer: Gracious Father, I thank You for the gift of nature and the joy it brings to my life. Help me to make time to walk in nature and appreciate Your beautiful creation. Show me how to find peace and spiritual connection in these moments. Fill my heart with gratitude for Your presence and the joy that comes from immersing myself in Your creation. In Jesus' name, I pray. Amen.

DAY 254

JOY IN JOURNALING

Scripture: "I will recount all of your wonderful deeds. I will be glad and exult in you; I will sing praise to your name, O Most High." - Psalm 9:1-2 (NIV)

Devotional: Today, let us explore the theme of finding joy in journaling. Writing down our thoughts, experiences, and prayers can bring clarity, reflection, and gratitude into our lives. Reflect on the joy and fulfillment you experience when you pour your heart out on paper. Take a moment to pray and thank God for the gift of self-expression and the joy it brings. Let gratitude for His presence and the joy that comes from journaling fill your heart.

Reflection: In your journal, write about the joy and growth you experience when you engage in journaling. How can you intentionally make time to record your thoughts, prayers, and gratitude? How does the act of journaling contribute to your overall sense of self-discovery and spiritual journey? How can you use this practice to recount God's wonderful deeds in your life and find joy in the simplicity of reflecting on His faithfulness?

Prayer: Loving God, I thank You for the gift of journaling and the joy it brings to my life. Help me to make time to express myself and connect with You through writing. Show me how to grow and find joy in this practice. Fill my heart with gratitude for Your presence and the joy that comes from pouring out my heart in journaling. In Jesus' name, I pray. Amen.

DAY 255

JOY IN RANDOM ACTS OF KINDNESS

Scripture: "Each of you should give what you have decided in your heart to give, not reluctantly or under compulsion, for God loves a cheerful giver." - 2 Corinthians 9:7 (NIV)

Devotional: Today, let us focus on finding joy in random acts of kindness. Simple acts of generosity and compassion can brighten someone's day and bring joy to their hearts. Reflect on the joy and fulfillment you experience when you extend kindness to others without expecting anything in return. Take a moment to pray and thank God for the opportunities to be a blessing and the joy it brings. Let gratitude for His love and the joy that comes from acts of kindness fill your heart.

Reflection: In your journal, write about the joy and impact you experience when you perform random acts of kindness. How can you intentionally seek opportunities to bring joy and love to those around you? How does the act of giving contribute to your overall sense of purpose and fulfillment? How can you use acts of kindness to reflect God's love and bring joy to others?

Prayer: Heavenly Father, I thank You for the opportunities to show kindness and the joy it brings to my life. Help me to intentionally seek opportunities to be a blessing to those I encounter. Show me how to extend love and joy through random acts of kindness. Fill my heart with gratitude for Your love and the joy that comes from acts of kindness. In Jesus' name, I pray. Amen.

DAY 256

JOY IN BAKING OR COOKING

Scripture: "Taste and see that the Lord is good; blessed is the one who takes refuge in him." - Psalm 34:8 (NIV)

Devotional: Today, let us explore the theme of finding joy in baking or cooking. The process of creating delicious meals or treats can be both satisfying and joyful. Reflect on the joy and fulfillment you experience when you engage in baking or cooking. Take a moment to pray and thank God for the gift of nourishment and the joy it brings. Let gratitude for His provision and the joy that comes from preparing food fill your heart.

Reflection: In your journal, write about the joy and satisfaction you experience when you bake or cook. How can you intentionally make time to experiment with new recipes or create meals with love? How does the act of preparing food contribute to your overall sense of nourishment and care for others? How can you use your culinary skills to reflect God's goodness and bring joy to those who share in your creations?

Prayer: Gracious God, I thank You for the gift of food and the joy that comes from baking or cooking. Help me to make time to engage in this creative process and nourish myself and others. Show me how to prepare meals with love and reflect Your goodness through food. Fill my heart with gratitude for Your provision and the joy that comes from baking or cooking. In Jesus' name, I pray. Amen.

DAY 257

JOY IN GARDENING

Scripture: "He will be like a tree planted by the water that sends out its roots by the stream. It does not fear when heat comes; its leaves are always green. It has no worries in a year of drought and never fails to bear fruit." - Jeremiah 17:8 (NIV)

Devotional: Today, let us focus on finding joy in gardening. The act of nurturing and tending to plants can bring a sense of peace, growth, and connection with nature. Reflect on the joy and satisfaction you experience when you see the fruits of your labor in a flourishing garden. Take a moment to pray and thank God for the gift of His creation and the joy it brings. Let gratitude for His provision and the joy that comes from gardening fill your heart.

Reflection: In your journal, write about the joy and fulfillment you experience when you engage in gardening. How can you intentionally make time to care for plants and create a green space that brings you joy? How does the act of tending to nature contribute to your overall sense of peace and well-being? How can you use your gardening skills to reflect God's faithfulness and bring joy to others through the beauty of plants?

Prayer: Loving Father, I thank You for the gift of nature and the joy it brings to my life. Help me to make time to tend to plants and create a garden that brings me joy. Show me how to find peace and well-being through gardening. Fill my heart with gratitude for Your provision and the joy that comes from nurturing Your creation. In Jesus' name, I pray. Amen.

DAY 258

JOY IN LISTENING TO CHILDREN'S LAUGHTER

Scripture: "But Jesus said, 'Let the little children come to me and do not hinder them, for to such belongs the kingdom of heaven.'" - Matthew 19:14 (NIV)

Devotional: Today, let us explore the theme of finding joy in listening to children's laughter. The pure and innocent laughter of children can bring joy and remind us of the simplicity of life. Reflect on the joy and warmth you experience when you hear children laughing. Take a moment to pray and thank God for the gift of children and the joy they bring. Let gratitude for His love and the joy that comes from the laughter of children fill your heart.

Reflection: In your journal, write about the joy and happiness you experience when you listen to children's laughter. How can you intentionally create opportunities to be around children and witness their joyful spirits? How does the sound of children's laughter contribute to your overall sense of joy and childlike wonder? How can you use moments with children to reflect God's love and bring joy to their lives?

Prayer: Heavenly Father, I thank You for the gift of children and the joy they bring to this world. Help me to create opportunities to be around children and witness their laughter. Show me how to embrace joy and childlike wonder in my own life. Fill my heart with gratitude for Your love and the joy that comes from the laughter of children. In Jesus' name, I pray. Amen.

DAY 259

JOY IN READING A GOOD BOOK

Scripture: "Your word is a lamp for my feet, a light on my path." - Psalm 119:105 (NIV)

Devotional: Today, let us focus on finding joy in reading a good book. Books have the power to transport us to different worlds, inspire our imagination, and bring joy to our souls. Reflect on the joy and enrichment you experience when you immerse yourself in a captivating story or gain wisdom from insightful words. Take a moment to pray and thank God for the gift of literature and the joy it brings. Let gratitude for His guidance and the joy that comes from reading fill your heart.

Reflection: In your journal, write about the joy and inspiration you experience when you read a good book. How can you intentionally make time for reading and expand your knowledge and understanding? How does the act of reading contribute to your overall sense of joy and personal growth? How can you use the joy of reading to deepen your connection with God and bring joy to others through sharing the gift of literature?

Prayer: Gracious God, I thank You for the gift of literature and the joy it brings to my life. Help me to make time to read and gain wisdom from the words written by others. Show me how to expand my knowledge and understanding through reading. Fill my heart with gratitude for Your guidance and the joy that comes from immersing myself in a good book. In Jesus' name, I pray. Amen.

DAY 260

JOY IN SINGING

Scripture: "Sing to the Lord, praise his name; proclaim his salvation day after day." - Psalm 96:2 (NIV)

Devotional: Today, let us explore the theme of finding joy in singing. Singing allows us to express our hearts, worship God, and experience joy in our souls. Reflect on the joy and freedom you experience when you lift your voice in song. Take a moment to pray and thank God for the gift of music and the joy it brings. Let gratitude for His salvation and the joy that comes from singing fill your heart.

Reflection: In your journal, write about the joy and fulfillment you experience when you sing. How can you intentionally make time to sing praises to God and express your heart through songs? How does the act of singing contribute to your overall sense of joy and spiritual connection? How can you use your voice to reflect God's glory and bring joy to those who hear your songs?

Prayer: Heavenly Father, I thank You for the gift of music and the joy it brings to my life. Help me to make time to sing praises to You and express my heart through songs. Show me how to worship You with all that I am. Fill my heart with gratitude for Your salvation and the joy that comes from singing. In Jesus' name, I pray. Amen.

DAY 261

JOY IN WATCHING WILDLIFE

Scripture: "Look at the birds of the air; they do not sow or reap or store away in barns, and yet your heavenly Father feeds them. Are you not much more valuable than they?" - Matthew 6:26 (NIV)

Devotional: Today, let us explore the theme of finding joy in watching wildlife. Observing the beauty and wonder of God's creatures can bring a sense of awe and appreciation for His creation. Reflect on the joy and fascination you experience when you encounter wildlife in their natural habitats. Take a moment to pray and thank God for the diversity of life and the joy it brings. Let gratitude for His provision and the joy that comes from watching wildlife fill your heart.

Reflection: In your journal, write about the joy and connection you experience when you observe wildlife. How can you intentionally make time to be in nature and witness the wonders of God's creatures? How does the act of watching wildlife contribute to your overall sense of wonder and gratitude for His creation? How can you use these moments to reflect on His provision and find joy in the simplicity of His creatures?

Prayer: Loving Father, I thank You for the gift of wildlife and the joy it brings to my life. Help me to make time to be in nature and witness the wonders of Your creatures. Show me how to find awe and gratitude in these moments. Fill my heart with gratitude for Your provision and the joy that comes from watching wildlife. In Jesus' name, I pray. Amen.

DAY 262

JOY IN WRITING LETTERS

Scripture: "But the fruit of the Spirit is love, joy, peace, forbearance, kindness, goodness, faithfulness." - Galatians 5:22 (NIV)

Devotional: Today, let us explore the theme of finding joy in writing letters. In this digital age, writing and receiving handwritten letters can bring a sense of warmth and connection. Reflect on the joy and nostalgia you experience when you put pen to paper and express your thoughts and emotions in a letter. Take a moment to pray and thank God for the gift of communication and the joy it brings. Let gratitude for His love and the joy that comes from writing letters fill your heart.

Reflection: In your journal, write about the joy and fulfillment you experience when you write letters to others. How can you intentionally make time to communicate through the written word and express your love and care for others? How does the act of writing letters contribute to your overall sense of connection and appreciation for meaningful relationships? How can you use this practice to reflect God's love and bring joy to the lives of those who receive your letters?

Prayer: Gracious God, I thank You for the gift of communication and the joy it brings to my life. Help me to make time to write letters and express my thoughts and emotions to others. Show me how to nurture meaningful relationships through the written word. Fill my heart with gratitude for Your love and the joy that comes from writing letters. In Jesus' name, I pray. Amen.

DAY 263

JOY IN EXPERIENCING THE RAIN

Scripture: "He sends rain on the righteous and the unrighteous." - Matthew 5:45 (NIV)

Devotional: Today, let us focus on finding joy in experiencing the rain. Rain is a natural gift from God, bringing nourishment to the earth and symbolizing renewal and cleansing. Reflect on the joy and refreshment you experience when you feel the rain on your skin and hear the rhythm of its drops. Take a moment to pray and thank God for the gift of rain and the joy it brings. Let gratitude for His provision and the joy that comes from experiencing the rain fill your heart.

Reflection: In your journal, write about the joy and serenity you experience when you embrace the rain. How can you intentionally make time to step outside and immerse yourself in the beauty of a rainy day? How does the act of experiencing the rain contribute to your overall sense of renewal and gratitude for God's provision? How can you use these moments to reflect on His faithfulness and find joy in the simplicity of His creation?

Prayer: Heavenly Father, I thank You for the gift of rain and the joy it brings to my life. Help me to embrace the beauty of a rainy day and experience the refreshment it offers. Show me how to find renewal and gratitude in these moments. Fill my heart with gratitude for Your provision and the joy that comes from experiencing the rain. In Jesus' name, I pray. Amen.

DAY 264

JOY IN HELPING OTHERS

Scripture: "For we are God's handiwork, created in Christ Jesus to do good works, which God prepared in advance for us to do." - Ephesians 2:10 (NIV)

Devotional: Today, let us explore the theme of finding joy in helping others. The act of extending a helping hand and making a positive impact in someone else's life can bring a deep sense of joy and fulfillment. Reflect on the joy and compassion you experience when you lend a helping hand to those in need. Take a moment to pray and thank God for the opportunities to serve and the joy it brings. Let gratitude for His love and the joy that comes from helping others fill your heart.

Reflection: In your journal, write about the joy and satisfaction you experience when you help others. How can you intentionally seek opportunities to make a difference and be a source of kindness and support? How does the act of helping contribute to your overall sense of purpose and fulfillment? How can you use your talents and resources to reflect God's love and bring joy to those around you through acts of service?

Prayer: Gracious God, I thank You for the opportunities to help and the joy it brings to my life. Help me to intentionally seek opportunities to extend a helping hand and make a positive impact in someone else's life. Show me how to be a source of kindness and support. Fill my heart with gratitude for Your love and the joy that comes from helping others. In Jesus' name, I pray. Amen.

DAY 265

JOY IN CELEBRATING SMALL VICTORIES

Scripture: "I can do all this through him who gives me strength." - Philippians 4:13 (NIV)

Devotional: Today, let us focus on finding joy in celebrating small victories. Life is made up of various milestones and accomplishments, big and small, and each one deserves recognition and celebration. Reflect on the joy and satisfaction you experience when you achieve a goal or overcome a challenge. Take a moment to pray and thank God for His strength and the joy it brings. Let gratitude for His guidance and the joy that comes from celebrating fill your heart.

Reflection: In your journal, write about the joy and pride you experience when you celebrate small victories. How can you intentionally make time to acknowledge and appreciate your accomplishments, no matter how small they may seem? How does the act of celebrating contribute to your overall sense of self-confidence and perseverance? How can you use the joy of celebrating small victories to give glory to God and encourage others in their journeys?

Prayer: Heavenly Father, I thank You for Your strength and the joy that comes from celebrating small victories. Help me to intentionally make time to acknowledge and appreciate my accomplishments. Show me how to give glory to You in all that I do. Fill my heart with gratitude for Your guidance and the joy that comes from celebrating. In Jesus' name, I pray. Amen.

Day 266

Humility in Hospitality

Scripture: "Share with the Lord's people who are in need. Practice hospitality." - Romans 12:13 (NIV)

Devotional: Today, let us focus on finding humility in hospitality. Humility calls us to open our hearts and homes to others, welcoming them with love and kindness. Reflect on the joy and blessing that come from embracing humility in extending hospitality. Take a moment to pray and ask God to help you cultivate a humble and welcoming spirit. Let gratitude for His provision and the joy that comes from humble hospitality fill your heart.

Reflection: In your journal, write about the impact of humility in hospitality. How can you intentionally open your heart and home to others, extending love and kindness? How does the act of embracing humility in hospitality contribute to your overall sense of connection, community, and service to others? How can you use your hospitality to reflect God's love and bring joy to others through your humble and welcoming attitude?

Prayer: Gracious God, I thank You for Your provision and the joy that comes from embracing humility in hospitality. Help me to open my heart and home to others, extending love and kindness. Show me how to reflect Your love and bring joy through my humble hospitality. Fill my heart with gratitude for Your grace and the joy that comes from humble service. In Jesus' name, I pray. Amen.

Day 267

Reflection and Thanksgiving

Scripture: "Give thanks in all circumstances; for this is God's will for you in Christ Jesus." - 1 Thessalonians 5:18 (NIV)

Devotional: Today marks the final day of our journey through humility. Take this opportunity to reflect on the themes we've explored, the Scriptures we've studied, and the lessons we've learned. Give thanks to God for His guidance, grace, and faithfulness throughout this journey. Let gratitude fill your heart as you realize the transformative power of embracing humility in all areas of life. Take a moment to pray and offer your heartfelt thanksgiving to God for His love and the joy that comes from humble surrender.

Reflection: In your journal, write about the lessons you've learned and the impact of humility in your life. How has this journey deepened your understanding of humility and its significance in various aspects of life? How have you grown in humility and witnessed its positive effects on your relationships, decisions, and perspective? What are you grateful for as you reflect on this journey? Take this opportunity to express your heartfelt thanksgiving to God for His faithfulness and the joy that comes from humble surrender.

Prayer: Loving Father, I thank You for the transformative journey through humility. Thank You for Your guidance, grace, and faithfulness throughout this process. I am grateful for the lessons learned, the growth experienced, and the joy that comes from humble surrender. I offer my heartfelt thanksgiving to You, knowing that true joy and fulfillment are found in embracing humility and aligning my life with Your will. May Your love continue to shape me, and may I reflect Your humility and bring joy to others. In Jesus' name, I pray. Amen.

DAY 268

HUMILITY IN GRACIOUSNESS

Scripture: "Let your conversation be always full of grace, seasoned with salt, so that you may know how to answer everyone." - Colossians 4:6 (NIV)

Devotional: Today, let us explore the theme of humility in graciousness. Humility calls us to speak with grace, kindness, and wisdom, considering the needs and perspectives of others. Reflect on the impact our graciousness can have on those around us and the joy that comes from embracing humility in our words and actions. Take a moment to pray and ask God to help you cultivate graciousness and humility in all your interactions. Let gratitude for His grace and the joy that comes from humble graciousness fill your heart.

Reflection: In your journal, write about the impact of humility in graciousness. How can you intentionally speak with grace, kindness, and wisdom, considering the needs and perspectives of others? How does the act of embracing humility in graciousness contribute to your overall sense of empathy, understanding, and positive influence? How can you use your graciousness to reflect God's love and bring joy to others through your humble and uplifting attitude?

Prayer: Loving Father, I thank You for Your grace and the joy that comes from embracing humility in graciousness. Help me to speak with grace, kindness, and wisdom, considering the needs and perspectives of others. Show me how to reflect Your love and bring joy through my humble and uplifting words and actions. Fill my heart with gratitude for Your guidance and the joy that comes from humble graciousness. In Jesus' name, I pray. Amen.

DAY 269

HUMILITY IN CONFESSION

Scripture: "Therefore confess your sins to each other and pray for each other so that you may be healed. The prayer of a righteous person is powerful and effective." - James 5:16 (NIV)

Devotional: Today, let us explore the theme of humility in confession. Humility calls us to acknowledge our faults, shortcomings, and sins before God and others. Reflect on the joy and freedom that come from embracing humility in confession. Take a moment to pray and ask God to reveal any areas in your life that need confession and repentance. Let gratitude for His forgiveness and the joy that comes from humble confession fill your heart.

Reflection: In your journal, write about the impact of humility in confession. How can you intentionally approach God and others with a humble and repentant heart, seeking forgiveness and restoration? How does the act of embracing humility in confession contribute to your overall sense of freedom, healing, and reconciliation with God and others? How can you use your confession to reflect God's love and bring joy to others through your humble and honest attitude?

Prayer: Gracious God, I thank You for Your forgiveness and the joy that comes from embracing humility in confession. Reveal any areas in my life that need confession and repentance. Help me to approach You and others with a humble and repentant heart, seeking forgiveness and restoration. Fill my heart with gratitude for Your grace and the joy that comes from humble confession. In Jesus' name, I pray. Amen.

DAY 270

HUMILITY IN GOD'S PRESENCE

Scripture: "But the tax collector stood at a distance. He would not even look up to heaven, but beat his breast and said, 'God, have mercy on me, a sinner.'" - Luke 18:13 (NIV)

Devotional: Today, let us focus on finding humility in God's presence. Humility calls us to recognize our need for His mercy and grace, acknowledging our own brokenness and dependence on Him. Reflect on the joy and reverence that come from embracing humility in God's presence. Take a moment to pray and approach God with a humble and contrite heart. Let gratitude for His mercy and the joy that comes from humble surrender fill your heart.

Reflection: In your journal, write about the impact of humility in God's presence. How can you intentionally approach God with a humble and contrite heart, acknowledging your need for His mercy and grace? How does the act of embracing humility in His presence contribute to your overall sense of awe, surrender, and intimacy with God? How can you use your posture of humility to reflect His love and bring joy to others through your humble and surrendered attitude?

Prayer: Loving Father, I thank You for Your mercy and the joy that comes from embracing humility in Your presence. Help me to approach You with a humble and contrite heart, acknowledging my need for Your grace. Show me how to reflect Your love and bring joy through my humble surrender. Fill my heart with gratitude for Your faithfulness and the joy that comes from humble reverence. In Jesus' name, I pray. Amen.

DAY 271

HUMILITY IN SPEECH

Scripture: "Do not let any unwholesome talk come out of your mouths, but only what is helpful for building others up according to their needs, that it may benefit those who listen." - Ephesians 4:29 (NIV)

Devotional: Today, let us focus on the importance of humility in our speech. Humility calls us to speak with kindness, grace, and wisdom, building others up rather than tearing them down. Reflect on the impact our words have on others and the joy that comes from speaking with humility. Take a moment to pray and ask God to help you use your words to edify and encourage others. Let gratitude for His guidance and the joy that comes from humble speech fill your heart.

Reflection: In your journal, write about the impact of humility in your words. How can you intentionally use your words to build others up, speaking with kindness, grace, and wisdom? How does the act of embracing humility in speech contribute to your overall sense of empathy, compassion, and positive influence? How can you use your speech to reflect God's love and bring joy to others through your humble and uplifting attitude?

Prayer: Heavenly Father, I thank You for Your guidance and the joy that comes from embracing humility in speech. Help me to use my words to build others up, speaking with kindness, grace, and wisdom. Show me how to reflect Your love and bring joy through my humble and uplifting speech. Fill my heart with gratitude for Your grace and the joy that comes from humble words. In Jesus' name, I pray. Amen.

DAY 272

THEME: HUMILITY IN SERVING GOD

Scripture: "Therefore, I urge you, brothers and sisters, in view of God's mercy, to offer your bodies as a living sacrifice, holy and pleasing to God—this is your true and proper worship." - Romans 12:1 (NIV)

Devotional: Today, let us explore the theme of humility in serving God. Humility calls us to offer ourselves as living sacrifices, surrendering our desires and ambitions to follow God's will. Reflect on the joy and purpose that come from embracing humility in serving God wholeheartedly. Take a moment to pray and ask God to help you offer yourself to Him as a humble servant. Let gratitude for His mercy and the joy that comes from humble service fill your heart.

Reflection: In your journal, write about the impact of humility in serving God. How can you intentionally offer yourself as a living sacrifice, surrendering your desires and ambitions to follow His will? How does the act of embracing humility in serving God contribute to your overall sense of purpose, fulfillment, and alignment with His plan? How can you use your service to reflect God's love and bring joy to others through your humble and devoted attitude?

Prayer: Loving Father, I thank You for Your mercy and the joy that comes from embracing humility in serving You. Help me to offer myself as a living sacrifice, surrendering my desires and ambitions to follow Your will. Show me how to reflect Your love and bring joy through my humble service. Fill my heart with gratitude for Your guidance and the joy that comes from humble devotion. In Jesus' name, I pray. Amen.

DAY 273

HUMILITY IN CONFLICT RESOLUTION

Scripture: "Blessed are the peacemakers, for they will be called children of God." - Matthew 5:9 (NIV)

Devotional: Today, let us focus on finding humility in conflict resolution. Humility calls us to seek peace and reconciliation, even in the midst of disagreements or conflicts. Reflect on the importance of humility in fostering understanding, forgiveness, and unity. Take a moment to pray and ask God to help you approach conflicts with humility, seeking resolution and restoration. Let gratitude for His peace and the joy that comes from humble conflict resolution fill your heart.

Reflection: In your journal, write about the impact of humility in conflict resolution. How can you intentionally approach conflicts with humility, seeking understanding and reconciliation? How does the act of embracing humility in conflict resolution contribute to your overall sense of empathy, forgiveness, and unity with others? How can you use your willingness to resolve conflicts to reflect God's love and bring joy to others through your humble and peace-seeking attitude?

Prayer: Gracious God, I thank You for Your peace and the joy that comes from embracing humility in conflict resolution. Help me to approach conflicts with humility, seeking understanding and reconciliation. Show me how to reflect Your love and bring joy through my humble resolution of conflicts. Fill my heart with gratitude for Your grace and the joy that comes from humble peace-seeking. In Jesus' name, I pray. Amen.

DAY 274

HUMILITY IN PATIENCE

Scripture: "Be still before the LORD and wait patiently for him; do not fret when people succeed in their ways, when they carry out their wicked schemes." - Psalm 37:7 (NIV)

Devotional: Today, let us explore the theme of humility in patience. Humility calls us to wait upon the Lord with trust and surrender, even in the face of delays or challenges. Reflect on the peace and wisdom that come from embracing humility in times of waiting. Take a moment to pray and ask God to help you cultivate patience and a humble heart as you wait upon Him. Let gratitude for His faithfulness and the joy that comes from humble patience fill your heart.

Reflection: In your journal, write about the impact of humility in patience. How can you intentionally cultivate patience and trust in God's timing, even when faced with delays or challenges? How does the act of embracing humility in patience contribute to your overall sense of peace, faith, and alignment with God's plan? How can you use your patient waiting to reflect God's love and bring joy to others through your humble and steadfast attitude?

Prayer: Gracious God, I thank You for Your faithfulness and the joy that comes from embracing humility in patience. Help me to cultivate patience and trust in Your timing. Show me how to reflect Your love and bring joy through my humble waiting. Fill my heart with gratitude for Your grace and the joy that comes from humble patience. In Jesus' name, I pray. Amen.

DAY 275

HUMILITY IN ADVERSITY

Scripture: "He has shown you, O mortal, what is good. And what does the LORD require of you? To act justly and to love mercy and to walk humbly with your God." - Micah 6:8 (NIV)

Devotional: Today, let us focus on finding humility in the face of adversity. Humility calls us to walk with God, even in challenging times, trusting in His strength and wisdom. Reflect on the joy and perseverance that come from embracing humility in adversity. Take a moment to pray and ask God to help you trust Him and walk humbly through life's difficulties. Let gratitude for His presence and the joy that comes from humble endurance fill your heart.

Reflection: In your journal, write about the impact of humility in facing adversity. How can you intentionally trust in God's strength and wisdom, even when faced with challenges and difficulties? How does the act of embracing humility in adversity contribute to your overall sense of resilience, faith, and perseverance? How can you use your response to adversity to reflect God's love and bring joy to others through your humble and steadfast attitude?

Prayer: Heavenly Father, I thank You for Your presence and the joy that comes from embracing humility in adversity. Help me to trust in Your strength and wisdom in all circumstances. Show me how to reflect Your love and bring joy through my humble endurance. Fill my heart with gratitude for Your faithfulness and the joy that comes from humble perseverance. In Jesus' name, I pray. Amen.

DAY 276

THE REWARD OF HUMILITY

Scripture: "Humble yourselves before the Lord, and he will lift you up." - James 4:10 (NIV)

Devotional: Today, let us explore the reward of humility. Humility calls us to submit ourselves before the Lord, trusting in His guidance and provision. Reflect on the joy and blessings that come from humbling ourselves before God. Take a moment to pray and ask God to help you embrace humility and experience His elevation in due time. Let gratitude for His faithfulness and the joy that comes from humble surrender fill your heart.

Reflection: In your journal, write about the reward of humility. How can you intentionally humble yourself before the Lord, surrendering your desires and trusting in His plans? How does the act of embracing humility contribute to your overall sense of peace, contentment, and assurance in God's faithfulness? How can you use your humble surrender to reflect God's love and bring joy to others through your obedient and trusting attitude?

Prayer: Gracious God, I thank You for Your faithfulness and the joy that comes from embracing humility before You. Help me to surrender my desires and trust in Your plans. Show me how to reflect Your love and bring joy through my humble surrender. Fill my heart with gratitude for Your provision and the joy that comes from humble obedience. In Jesus' name, I pray. Amen.

DAY 277

HUMILITY IN CHALLENGES

Scripture: "But he said to me, 'My grace is sufficient for you, for my power is made perfect in weakness.' Therefore I will boast all the more gladly about my weaknesses, so that Christ's power may rest on me." - 2 Corinthians 12:9 (NIV)

Devotional: Today, let us focus on finding humility in the midst of challenges. Humility calls us to rely on God's strength and grace when faced with difficulties and weaknesses. Reflect on the power of God's grace working through your challenges and the joy that comes from embracing humility in times of struggle. Take a moment to pray and ask God to help you trust in His power to overcome obstacles. Let gratitude for His presence and the joy that comes from humble reliance fill your heart.

Reflection: In your journal, write about the impact of humility in facing challenges. How can you intentionally surrender your self-reliance and trust in God's power and grace to overcome difficulties? How does the act of embracing humility in challenges contribute to your overall sense of dependence, resilience, and faith in God's provision? How can you use your challenges to reflect God's love and bring joy to others through your humble and victorious attitude?

Prayer: Loving Father, I thank You for Your grace and the joy that comes from embracing humility in challenges. Help me to rely on Your strength and trust in Your power to overcome difficulties. Show me how to reflect Your love and bring joy through my humble dependence on You. Fill my heart with gratitude for Your presence and the joy that comes from humble reliance. In Jesus' name, I pray. Amen.

Day 278

Humility in Influence

Scripture: "Do nothing out of selfish ambition or vain conceit. Rather, in humility value others above yourselves." - Philippians 2:3 (NIV)

Devotional: Today, let us explore the theme of humility in influence. Humility calls us to use our influence for the benefit of others, valuing them above ourselves. Reflect on the responsibility and impact of our influence on those around us and the joy that comes from humble leadership. Take a moment to pray and ask God to help you use your influence to uplift, encourage, and empower others. Let gratitude for His grace and the joy that comes from humble influence fill your heart.

Reflection: In your journal, write about the impact of humility in your influence over others. How can you intentionally use your influence to value and uplift others, rather than seeking personal gain or recognition? How does the act of embracing humility in influence contribute to your overall sense of responsibility, empathy, and servant-hearted leadership? How can you use your influence to reflect God's love and bring joy to others through your humble and empowering attitude?

Prayer: Heavenly Father, I thank You for Your grace and the joy that comes from embracing humility in influence. Help me to use my influence to uplift, encourage, and empower others. Show me how to reflect Your love and bring joy through my humble leadership. Fill my heart with gratitude for Your guidance and the joy that comes from humble influence. In Jesus' name, I pray. Amen.

DAY 279

HUMILITY IN STRENGTH

Scripture: "But he said to me, 'My grace is sufficient for you, for my power is made perfect in weakness.' Therefore I will boast all the more gladly about my weaknesses, so that Christ's power may rest on me." - 2 Corinthians 12:9 (NIV)

Devotional: Today, let us explore the theme of humility in strength. Humility calls us to recognize that our strength comes from God and not from ourselves. Reflect on the power of God's grace and how it works through our weaknesses. Take a moment to pray and ask God to help you rely on His strength in every aspect of your life. Let gratitude for His power and the joy that comes from embracing humility in strength fill your heart.

Reflection: In your journal, write about the impact of humility in finding strength in God. How can you intentionally surrender your self-reliance and trust in God's power and grace? How does the act of embracing humility in strength contribute to your overall sense of dependence, surrender, and alignment with God's purpose? How can you use your strength to reflect God's love and bring joy to others through your humble and empowered attitude?

Prayer: Loving Father, I thank You for Your power and the joy that comes from embracing humility in strength. Help me to rely on Your strength in every aspect of my life. Show me how to reflect Your love and bring joy through my humble dependence on You. Fill my heart with gratitude for Your grace and the joy that comes from humble strength. In Jesus' name, I pray. Amen.

DAY 280

HUMILITY IN SEEKING GOD'S KINGDOM

Scripture: "But seek first his kingdom and his righteousness, and all these things will be given to you as well." - Matthew 6:33 (NIV)

Devotional: Today, let us explore the theme of humility in seeking God's kingdom. Humility calls us to prioritize God's will and His kingdom above our own desires and ambitions. Reflect on the joy and blessings that come from seeking God's kingdom with a humble heart. Take a moment to pray and ask God to align your priorities with His and to help you live for His kingdom. Let gratitude for His guidance and the joy that comes from humble seeking fill your heart.

Reflection: In your journal, write about the impact of humility in seeking God's kingdom. How can you intentionally align your priorities with His and seek His righteousness in all areas of your life? How does the act of embracing humility in seeking God's kingdom contribute to your overall sense of purpose, fulfillment, and alignment with His will? How can you use your pursuit of God's kingdom to reflect His love and bring joy to others through your humble and devoted attitude?

Prayer: Heavenly Father, I thank You for Your guidance and the joy that comes from seeking Your kingdom with humility. Align my priorities with Yours and help me live for Your kingdom. Show me how to reflect Your love and bring joy through my humble pursuit of Your righteousness. Fill my heart with gratitude for Your provision and the joy that comes from humble seeking. In Jesus' name, I pray. Amen.

DAY 281

HUMILITY IN SERVING OTHERS

Scripture: "Do nothing out of selfish ambition or vain conceit. Rather, in humility value others above yourselves." - Philippians 2:3 (NIV)

Devotional: Today, let us focus on finding humility in serving others. Humility is a virtue that calls us to set aside our own desires and pride and to prioritize the needs and well-being of others. Reflect on the joy and fulfillment you experience when you humbly serve those around you. Take a moment to pray and ask God to cultivate a spirit of humility within you. Let gratitude for His example of humble service and the joy that comes from selflessly serving others fill your heart.

Reflection: In your journal, write about the joy and transformation you experience when you serve others with humility. How can you intentionally seek opportunities to put others before yourself and meet their needs? How does the act of humble service contribute to your overall sense of purpose and compassion? How can you use your actions to reflect God's love and bring joy to others through selfless service?

Prayer: Gracious God, I thank You for Your example of humble service and the joy it brings to my life. Help me to cultivate a spirit of humility and to serve others with a selfless heart. Show me how to put the needs of others before my own. Fill my heart with gratitude for Your love and the joy that comes from humble service. In Jesus' name, I pray. Amen.

DAY 282

EMBRACING HUMILITY IN RELATIONSHIPS

Scripture: "Live in harmony with one another. Do not be proud, but be willing to associate with people of low position. Do not be conceited." - Romans 12:16 (NIV)

Devotional: Today, let us explore the theme of embracing humility in relationships. Humility allows us to treat others with respect, kindness, and empathy, regardless of their social status or position. Reflect on the joy and depth of connection you experience when you approach relationships with humility. Take a moment to pray and ask God to humble your heart and guide your interactions with others. Let gratitude for His grace and the joy that comes from embracing humility in relationships fill your heart.

Reflection: In your journal, write about the joy and growth you experience when you embrace humility in your relationships. How can you intentionally practice humility by treating others with respect and empathy? How does the act of embracing humility contribute to your overall sense of unity and harmony in your interactions? How can you use your relationships to reflect God's love and bring joy to others through humble and compassionate interactions?

Prayer: Loving Father, I thank You for the gift of relationships and the joy they bring to my life. Help me to approach my interactions with humility, respect, and kindness. Show me how to value others regardless of their position or status. Fill my heart with gratitude for Your grace and the joy that comes from embracing humility in relationships. In Jesus' name, I pray. Amen.

DAY 283

HUMILITY IN RECEIVING HELP

Scripture: "Humble yourselves, therefore, under God's mighty hand, that he may lift you up in due time." - 1 Peter 5:6 (NIV)

Devotional: Today, let us focus on finding humility in receiving help. Pride can often hinder us from accepting assistance when we need it most. Reflect on the joy and relief you experience when you humbly receive help from others. Take a moment to pray and ask God to humble your heart and allow you to receive His provision through the hands of others. Let gratitude for His care and the joy that comes from humble reception of help fill your heart.

Reflection: In your journal, write about the joy and gratitude you experience when you humbly accept help. How can you intentionally cultivate a humble heart that allows you to receive assistance graciously? How does the act of receiving help contribute to your overall sense of vulnerability and trust in God's provision? How can you use your experiences of receiving help to reflect God's love and bring joy to others through your willingness to extend a helping hand in return?

Prayer: Gracious God, I thank You for Your provision and the joy that comes from receiving help. Help me to cultivate a humble heart that allows me to accept assistance graciously. Show me how to trust in Your provision and recognize Your care through the hands of others. Fill my heart with gratitude for Your love and the joy that comes from humble reception of help. In Jesus' name, I pray. Amen.

DAY 284

HUMILITY IN LEADERSHIP

Scripture: "Whoever wants to become great among you must be your servant." - Matthew 20:26b (NIV)

Devotional: Today, let us explore the theme of humility in leadership. True leadership is not about exerting power and authority but about serving and uplifting others. Reflect on the joy and impact you experience when you lead with humility, putting the needs of others before your own. Take a moment to pray and ask God to shape your leadership style with humility and selflessness. Let gratitude for His guidance and the joy that comes from humble leadership fill your heart.

Reflection: In your journal, write about the joy and transformation you experience when you lead with humility. How can you intentionally cultivate a leadership style that serves and empowers those around you? How does the act of leading with humility contribute to your overall sense of purpose and influence? How can you use your leadership position to reflect God's love and bring joy to others through your servant-hearted approach?

Prayer: Heavenly Father, I thank You for the opportunities to lead and the joy that comes from leading with humility. Help me to cultivate a leadership style that serves and empowers others. Show me how to put the needs of those I lead before my own. Fill my heart with gratitude for Your guidance and the joy that comes from humble leadership. In Jesus' name, I pray. Amen.

DAY 285

HUMILITY IN SUCCESS

Scripture: "Humble yourselves before the Lord, and he will lift you up." - James 4:10 (NIV)

Devotional: Today, let us focus on finding humility in success. Achievements and accomplishments can sometimes lead to pride and self-centeredness. Reflect on the joy and gratitude you experience when you humbly acknowledge that your success is a gift from God. Take a moment to pray and ask God to keep you humble in times of success and to use your achievements for His glory. Let gratitude for His grace and the joy that comes from humble success fill your heart.

Reflection: In your journal, write about the joy and gratitude you experience when you humbly embrace success. How can you intentionally remain humble in the face of achievements and recognition? How does the act of embracing humility in success contribute to your overall sense of gratitude and purpose? How can you use your successes as opportunities to reflect God's love and bring joy to others through your humble and grateful attitude?

Prayer: Gracious God, I thank You for the successes and accomplishments in my life. Help me to remain humble and recognize that my achievements are gifts from You. Show me how to use my successes for Your glory. Fill my heart with gratitude for Your grace and the joy that comes from humble success. In Jesus' name, I pray. Amen.

DAY 286

HUMILITY IN ADVERSITY

Scripture: "Humble yourselves, therefore, under God's mighty hand, that he may lift you up in due time." - 1 Peter 5:6 (NIV)

Devotional: Today, let us explore the theme of humility in adversity. When faced with challenges and trials, it is easy to become discouraged or bitter. Reflect on the joy and strength you experience when you humbly surrender your struggles to God and trust in His provision. Take a moment to pray and ask God to help you embrace humility in the midst of adversity. Let gratitude for His faithfulness and the joy that comes from humble reliance on Him fill your heart.

Reflection: In your journal, write about the joy and resilience you experience when you embrace humility in the face of adversity. How can you intentionally surrender your struggles to God and trust in His guidance? How does the act of embracing humility in adversity contribute to your overall sense of faith and perseverance? How can you use your experiences of overcoming challenges to reflect God's love and bring joy to others through your humble and hopeful attitude?

Prayer: Loving Father, I thank You for Your presence in times of adversity and the joy that comes from humbly relying on You. Help me to surrender my struggles to You and trust in Your provision. Show me how to embrace humility in the face of challenges. Fill my heart with gratitude for Your faithfulness and the joy that comes from humble reliance on You. In Jesus' name, I pray. Amen.

DAY 287

HUMILITY IN SEEKING FORGIVENESS

Scripture: "Bear with each other and forgive one another if any of you has a grievance against someone. Forgive as the Lord forgave you." - Colossians 3:13 (NIV)

Devotional: Today, let us focus on finding humility in seeking forgiveness. None of us are perfect, and we all make mistakes that hurt others. Reflect on the joy and healing you experience when you humbly seek forgiveness and extend forgiveness to others. Take a moment to pray and ask God for the humility to admit your faults and the willingness to forgive those who have wronged you. Let gratitude for His forgiveness and the joy that comes from humble reconciliation fill your heart.

Reflection: In your journal, write about the joy and freedom you experience when you seek forgiveness and extend it to others. How can you intentionally cultivate a humble heart that admits mistakes and seeks reconciliation? How does the act of embracing humility in seeking forgiveness contribute to your overall sense of peace and restoration? How can you use your experiences of forgiveness to reflect God's love and bring joy to others through your humble and compassionate interactions?

Prayer: Gracious God, I thank You for Your forgiveness and the joy that comes from seeking and extending forgiveness. Help me to cultivate a humble heart that admits mistakes and seeks reconciliation. Show me how to forgive as You have forgiven me. Fill my heart with gratitude for Your love and the joy that comes from humble reconciliation. In Jesus' name, I pray. Amen.

DAY 288

HUMILITY IN CONFLICT RESOLUTION

Scripture: "If it is possible, as far as it depends on you, live at peace with everyone." - Romans 12:18 (NIV)

Devotional: Today, let us explore the theme of humility in conflict resolution. Conflict is an inevitable part of human relationships, but how we approach and navigate conflict can make a significant difference. Reflect on the joy and restoration you experience when you humbly seek reconciliation and strive for peace. Take a moment to pray and ask God to grant you humility and wisdom in resolving conflicts. Let gratitude for His guidance and the joy that comes from humble peacemaking fill your heart.

Reflection: In your journal, write about the joy and harmony you experience when you approach conflict with humility. How can you intentionally listen, empathize, and seek understanding in the midst of disagreements? How does the act of embracing humility in conflict resolution contribute to your overall sense of unity and reconciliation? How can you use your experiences of resolving conflicts to reflect God's love and bring joy to others through your humble and compassionate approach?

Prayer: Heavenly Father, I thank You for Your guidance in resolving conflicts and the joy that comes from humble peacemaking. Help me to approach conflicts with humility, grace, and a desire for reconciliation. Show me how to seek unity and understanding. Fill my heart with gratitude for Your love and the joy that comes from humble conflict resolution. In Jesus' name, I pray. Amen.

Day 289

Humility in Using Your Gifts

Scripture: "Each of you should use whatever gift you have received to serve others, as faithful stewards of God's grace in its various forms." - 1 Peter 4:10 (NIV)

Devotional: Today, let us focus on finding humility in using your gifts. Every person has been uniquely gifted by God to contribute to the world in meaningful ways. Reflect on the joy and fulfillment you experience when you humbly use your gifts to serve others. Take a moment to pray and ask God to help you recognize and utilize your gifts with humility. Let gratitude for His grace and the joy that comes from humble service fill your heart.

Reflection: In your journal, write about the joy and impact you experience when you use your gifts to serve others with humility. How can you intentionally identify and develop your gifts to make a positive difference in the lives of those around you? How does the act of embracing humility in using your gifts contribute to your overall sense of purpose and fulfillment? How can you use your unique abilities to reflect God's love and bring joy to others through selfless service?

Prayer: Gracious God, I thank You for the gifts You have bestowed upon me and the joy that comes from using them to serve others. Help me to recognize and develop my gifts with humility and gratitude. Show me how to use my abilities to make a positive impact in the world. Fill my heart with gratitude for Your grace and the joy that comes from humble service. In Jesus' name, I pray. Amen.

DAY 290

HUMILITY IN SEEKING WISDOM

Scripture: "The fear of the Lord is the beginning of wisdom, and knowledge of the Holy One is understanding." - Proverbs 9:10 (NIV)

Devotional: Today, let us explore the theme of humility in seeking wisdom. True wisdom begins with humility—a recognition of our need for guidance and a willingness to learn from God and others. Reflect on the joy and enlightenment you experience when you humbly seek wisdom and understanding. Take a moment to pray and ask God to humble your heart and grant you wisdom. Let gratitude for His guidance and the joy that comes from humble wisdom-seeking fill your heart.

Reflection: In your journal, write about the joy and growth you experience when you seek wisdom with humility. How can you intentionally cultivate a humble heart that is open to learning and seeking guidance? How does the act of embracing humility in seeking wisdom contribute to your overall sense of enlightenment and spiritual maturity? How can you use your wisdom and understanding to reflect God's love and bring joy to others through your humble and wise words and actions?

Prayer: Heavenly Father, I thank You for the gift of wisdom and the joy that comes from seeking it with humility. Help me to cultivate a humble heart that is open to learning and seeking Your guidance. Show me how to grow in wisdom and understanding. Fill my heart with gratitude for Your guidance and the joy that comes from humble wisdom-seeking. In Jesus' name, I pray. Amen.

DAY 291

HUMILITY IN GRACIOUS WORDS

Scripture: "Gracious words are a honeycomb, sweet to the soul and healing to the bones." - Proverbs 16:24 (NIV)

Devotional: Today, let us focus on finding humility in our words. Our words have the power to uplift, encourage, and bring healing to others. Reflect on the joy and impact you experience when you speak with humility and grace. Take a moment to pray and ask God to help you choose your words wisely and use them to reflect His love. Let gratitude for His grace and the joy that comes from humble and gracious words fill your heart.

Reflection: In your journal, write about the joy and transformation you experience when you speak with humility and grace. How can you intentionally choose words that build others up, offer encouragement, and bring healing? How does the act of embracing humility in your speech contribute to your overall sense of compassion and understanding? How can you use your words to reflect God's love and bring joy to others through your humble and gracious communication?

Prayer: Loving Father, I thank You for the gift of words and the joy that comes from speaking with humility and grace. Help me to choose my words wisely and use them to uplift and encourage others. Show me how to reflect Your love through my speech. Fill my heart with gratitude for Your grace and the joy that comes from humble and gracious words. In Jesus' name, I pray. Amen.

DAY 292

HUMILITY IN CELEBRATING THE SUCCESS OF OTHERS

Scripture: "Rejoice with those who rejoice; mourn with those who mourn." - Romans 12:15 (NIV)

Devotional: Today, let us explore the theme of humility in celebrating the success of others. It is easy to let envy or insecurity overshadow the joy of others' achievements. Reflect on the joy and unity you experience when you humbly rejoice with those who succeed. Take a moment to pray and ask God to help you set aside comparisons and genuinely celebrate the accomplishments of others. Let gratitude for His blessings and the joy that comes from humble celebration fill your heart.

Reflection: In your journal, write about the joy and unity you experience when you celebrate the success of others with humility. How can you intentionally set aside envy and comparison and genuinely rejoice with those who achieve greatness? How does the act of embracing humility in celebrating others' success contribute to your overall sense of love and support in your relationships? How can you use your actions to reflect God's love and bring joy to others through your humble and genuine celebration?

Prayer: Gracious God, I thank You for Your blessings and the joy that comes from celebrating the success of others. Help me to set aside envy and comparison and genuinely rejoice with those who achieve greatness. Show me how to support and love others wholeheartedly. Fill my heart with gratitude for Your blessings and the joy that comes from humble celebration. In Jesus' name, I pray. Amen.

DAY 293

HUMILITY IN ADMITTING MISTAKES

Scripture: "Therefore confess your sins to each other and pray for each other so that you may be healed. The prayer of a righteous person is powerful and effective." - James 5:16 (NIV)

Devotional: Today, let us focus on finding humility in admitting mistakes. We all make errors and poor choices, but humility allows us to acknowledge our faults and seek forgiveness and growth. Reflect on the joy and freedom you experience when you humbly admit your mistakes. Take a moment to pray and ask God to help you embrace humility in admitting your shortcomings. Let gratitude for His forgiveness and the joy that comes from humble confession fill your heart.

Reflection: In your journal, write about the joy and freedom you experience when you admit your mistakes with humility. How can you intentionally take responsibility for your actions, seek forgiveness, and grow from your failures? How does the act of embracing humility in admitting mistakes contribute to your overall sense of personal growth and restoration? How can you use your experiences of admitting mistakes to reflect God's love and bring joy to others through your humble and authentic journey?

Prayer: Heavenly Father, I thank You for Your forgiveness and the joy that comes from admitting mistakes with humility. Help me to take responsibility for my actions, seek forgiveness, and grow from my failures. Show me how to reflect Your love through my humble confession. Fill my heart with gratitude for Your forgiveness and the joy that comes from admitting mistakes with humility. In Jesus' name, I pray. Amen.

DAY 294

HUMILITY IN SERVING THE VULNERABLE

Scripture: "Learn to do right; seek justice. Defend the oppressed. Take up the cause of the fatherless; plead the case of the widow." - Isaiah 1:17 (NIV)

Devotional: Today, let us explore the theme of humility in serving the vulnerable. God calls us to stand up for those who are marginalized and oppressed, demonstrating His love and justice. Reflect on the joy and fulfillment you experience when you humbly serve the vulnerable in society. Take a moment to pray and ask God to open your eyes to the needs around you and give you the humility to act. Let gratitude for His compassion and the joy that comes from humble service fill your heart.

Reflection: In your journal, write about the joy and impact you experience when you serve the vulnerable with humility. How can you intentionally seek justice, defend the oppressed, and support those in need? How does the act of embracing humility in serving the vulnerable contribute to your overall sense of purpose and compassion? How can you use your resources, time, and influence to reflect God's love and bring joy to others through your humble and compassionate service?

Prayer: Gracious God, I thank You for Your compassion and the joy that comes from serving the vulnerable. Help me to seek justice, defend the oppressed, and support those in need with humility. Show me how to reflect Your love and compassion in my actions. Fill my heart with gratitude for Your guidance and the joy that comes from humble service. In Jesus' name, I pray. Amen.

DAY 295

HUMILITY IN FINANCIAL STEWARDSHIP

Scripture: "Command those who are rich in this present world not to be arrogant nor to put their hope in wealth, which is so uncertain, but to put their hope in God, who richly provides us with everything for our enjoyment." - 1 Timothy 6:17 (NIV)

Devotional: Today, let us focus on finding humility in financial stewardship. Our possessions and resources are entrusted to us by God, and humility calls us to use them wisely and generously. Reflect on the joy and contentment you experience when you humbly manage your finances with gratitude and trust in God's provision. Take a moment to pray and ask God to help you cultivate a humble heart in your financial decisions. Let gratitude for His abundance and the joy that comes from humble stewardship fill your heart.

Reflection: In your journal, write about the joy and peace you experience when you practice financial stewardship with humility. How can you intentionally manage your resources and finances in a way that reflects gratitude, generosity, and trust in God's provision? How does the act of embracing humility in financial stewardship contribute to your overall sense of contentment and reliance on God? How can you use your resources to reflect God's love and bring joy to others through your humble and wise financial choices?

Prayer: Heavenly Father, I thank You for Your provision and the joy that comes from practicing financial stewardship with humility. Help me to manage my resources and finances in a way that reflects gratitude, generosity, and trust in You. Show me how to use my resources to bring joy and make a positive impact. Fill my heart with gratitude for Your abundance and the joy that comes from humble stewardship. In Jesus' name, I pray. Amen.

DAY 296

HUMILITY IN PARENTING

Scripture: "Start children off on the way they should go, and even when they are old, they will not turn from it." - Proverbs 22:6 (NIV)

Devotional: Today, let us explore the theme of humility in parenting. Raising children is a sacred responsibility that requires humility, grace, and guidance from God. Reflect on the joy and growth you experience when you approach parenting with humility and seek God's wisdom. Take a moment to pray and ask God to help you parent with humility, love, and patience. Let gratitude for His guidance and the joy that comes from humble parenting fill your heart.

Reflection: In your journal, write about the joy and transformation you experience when you parent with humility. How can you intentionally seek God's wisdom and rely on His strength in your parenting journey? How does the act of embracing humility in parenting contribute to your overall sense of love, growth, and connection with your children? How can you use your role as a parent to reflect God's love and bring joy to your children through your humble and compassionate approach?

Prayer: Loving Father, I thank You for the gift of children and the joy that comes from parenting with humility. Help me to seek Your wisdom and guidance as I navigate the challenges and joys of parenting. Show me how to love, guide, and nurture my children with humility and grace. Fill my heart with gratitude for Your guidance and the joy that comes from humble parenting. In Jesus' name, I pray. Amen.

DAY 297

HUMILITY IN PURSUIT OF KNOWLEDGE

Scripture: "The fear of the LORD is the beginning of knowledge, but fools despise wisdom and instruction." - Proverbs 1:7 (NIV)

Devotional: Today, let us focus on finding humility in the pursuit of knowledge. True wisdom begins with humility—a recognition of our need for understanding and a willingness to learn from God and others. Reflect on the joy and enlightenment you experience when you humbly seek knowledge and understanding. Take a moment to pray and ask God to humble your heart and grant you wisdom. Let gratitude for His guidance and the joy that comes from humble pursuit of knowledge fill your heart.

Reflection: In your journal, write about the joy and growth you experience when you pursue knowledge with humility. How can you intentionally cultivate a humble heart that is open to learning and seeking understanding? How does the act of embracing humility in the pursuit of knowledge contribute to your overall sense of enlightenment and personal growth? How can you use your knowledge and understanding to reflect God's love and bring joy to others through your humble and wise words and actions?

Prayer: Heavenly Father, I thank You for the gift of knowledge and the joy that comes from seeking it with humility. Help me to cultivate a humble heart that is open to learning and seeking Your guidance. Show me how to grow in wisdom and understanding. Fill my heart with gratitude for Your guidance and the joy that comes from humble pursuit of knowledge. In Jesus' name, I pray. Amen.

DAY 298

HUMILITY IN SEEKING GUIDANCE

Scripture: "Trust in the LORD with all your heart and lean not on your own understanding; in all your ways submit to him, and he will make your paths straight." - Proverbs 3:5-6 (NIV)

Devotional: Today, let us explore the theme of humility in seeking guidance. In the midst of decisions and uncertainties, humility calls us to rely on God's wisdom and trust His leading. Reflect on the joy and peace you experience when you humbly seek His guidance in all aspects of your life. Take a moment to pray and ask God for the humility to submit to His will and trust His direction. Let gratitude for His faithfulness and the joy that comes from humble guidance-seeking fill your heart.

Reflection: In your journal, write about the joy and peace you experience when you seek God's guidance with humility. How can you intentionally surrender your plans and desires to God, seeking His wisdom and trusting His leading? How does the act of embracing humility in seeking guidance contribute to your overall sense of peace and assurance in His provision? How can you use your experiences of seeking God's guidance to reflect His love and bring joy to others through your humble and obedient journey?

Prayer: Gracious God, I thank You for Your guidance and the joy that comes from seeking it with humility. Help me to surrender my plans and desires to You, seeking Your wisdom and trusting Your leading. Show me how to reflect Your love through my humble submission. Fill my heart with gratitude for Your faithfulness and the joy that comes from humble guidance-seeking. In Jesus' name, I pray. Amen.

DAY 299

HUMILITY IN TIMES OF WAITING

Scripture: "Yet the LORD longs to be gracious to you; therefore he will rise up to show you compassion. For the LORD is a God of justice. Blessed are all who wait for him!" - Isaiah 30:18 (NIV)

Devotional: Today, let us focus on finding humility in times of waiting. Waiting can be challenging and frustrating, but humility calls us to trust in God's timing and remain steadfast in our faith. Reflect on the joy and trust you experience when you humbly wait on God and seek His guidance. Take a moment to pray and ask God to grant you patience and humility as you wait. Let gratitude for His faithfulness and the joy that comes from humble waiting fill your heart.

Reflection: In your journal, write about the joy and trust you experience when you wait on God with humility. How can you intentionally cultivate a patient heart that rests in God's promises and trusts in His timing? How does the act of embracing humility in times of waiting contribute to your overall sense of faith and reliance on God's provision? How can you use your experiences of waiting to reflect God's love and bring joy to others through your humble and hopeful attitude?

Prayer: Heavenly Father, I thank You for Your faithfulness and the joy that comes from waiting on You with humility. Help me to cultivate a patient heart that rests in Your promises and trusts in Your timing. Show me how to reflect Your love and hope in the midst of waiting. Fill my heart with gratitude for Your faithfulness and the joy that comes from humble waiting. In Jesus' name, I pray. Amen.

DAY 300

HUMILITY IN TIMES OF TRIUMPH

Scripture: "But he gives us more grace. That is why Scripture says: 'God opposes the proud but shows favor to the humble.'" - James 4:6 (NIV)

Devotional: Today, let us explore the theme of humility in times of triumph. It is in moments of success and victory that humility becomes even more essential. Reflect on the joy and gratitude you experience when you humbly acknowledge that your accomplishments are gifts from God. Take a moment to pray and ask God to keep you humble in times of triumph and to use your successes for His glory. Let gratitude for His grace and the joy that comes from humble triumph fill your heart.

Reflection: In your journal, write about the joy and gratitude you experience when you embrace humility in times of triumph. How can you intentionally recognize that your achievements are gifts from God and give Him the glory? How does the act of embracing humility in times of triumph contribute to your overall sense of gratitude and reliance on God's grace? How can you use your successes as opportunities to reflect God's love and bring joy to others through your humble and grateful attitude?

Prayer: Gracious God, I thank You for Your grace and the joy that comes from embracing humility in times of triumph. Help me to recognize that my accomplishments are gifts from You and give You the glory. Show me how to use my successes to bring honor to Your name. Fill my heart with gratitude for Your grace and the joy that comes from humble triumph. In Jesus' name, I pray. Amen.

DAY 301

HUMILITY IN CONTENTMENT

Scripture: "I know what it is to be in need, and I know what it is to have plenty. I have learned the secret of being content in any and every situation, whether well fed or hungry, whether living in plenty or in want." - Philippians 4:12 (NIV)

Devotional: Today, let us focus on finding humility in contentment. In a world that constantly promotes the pursuit of more, humility calls us to find satisfaction and gratitude in every circumstance. Reflect on the joy and peace you experience when you humbly embrace contentment. Take a moment to pray and ask God to help you cultivate a heart of gratitude and contentment. Let gratitude for His provision and the joy that comes from humble contentment fill your heart.

Reflection: In your journal, write about the joy and peace you experience when you embrace contentment with humility. How can you intentionally find satisfaction and gratitude in every circumstance, whether in times of plenty or in times of scarcity? How does the act of embracing humility in contentment contribute to your overall sense of peace and trust in God's provision? How can you use your contentment to reflect God's love and bring joy to others through your humble and grateful attitude?

Prayer: Loving Father, I thank You for Your provision and the joy that comes from embracing humility in contentment. Help me to find satisfaction and gratitude in every circumstance. Show me how to trust in Your provision and rest in Your presence. Fill my heart with gratitude for Your goodness and the joy that comes from humble contentment. In Jesus' name, I pray. Amen.

Day 302

Humility in Sharing Your Blessings

Scripture: "Command those who are rich in this present world not to be arrogant nor to put their hope in wealth, which is so uncertain, but to put their hope in God, who richly provides us with everything for our enjoyment. Command them to do good, to be rich in good deeds, and to be generous and willing to share." - 1 Timothy 6:17-18 (NIV)

Devotional: Today, let us explore the theme of humility in sharing your blessings. God has blessed us abundantly, and humility calls us to use our blessings to bless others. Reflect on the joy and fulfillment you experience when you humbly share your resources, time, and love with those in need. Take a moment to pray and ask God to give you a generous and humble heart. Let gratitude for His provision and the joy that comes from humble generosity fill your heart.

Reflection: In your journal, write about the joy and fulfillment you experience when you share your blessings with humility. How can you intentionally use your resources, time, and love to bless others and make a positive impact? How does the act of embracing humility in sharing your blessings contribute to your overall sense of purpose and fulfillment? How can you use your generosity to reflect God's love and bring joy to others through your humble and selfless actions?

Prayer: Gracious God, I thank You for Your provision and the joy that comes from sharing my blessings with humility. Help me to have a generous and humble heart. Show me how to use my resources, time, and love to bless others. Fill my heart with gratitude for Your goodness and the joy that comes from humble generosity. In Jesus' name, I pray. Amen.

DAY 303

HUMILITY IN INTERACTING WITH OTHERS

Scripture: "Clothe yourselves with humility toward one another, because, 'God opposes the proud but shows favor to the humble.'" - 1 Peter 5:5b (NIV)

Devotional: Today, let us focus on finding humility in our interactions with others. Humility allows us to treat others with respect, kindness, and empathy. Reflect on the joy and connection you experience when you approach interactions with humility. Take a moment to pray and ask God to help you cultivate a humble heart and love others genuinely. Let gratitude for His grace and the joy that comes from humble relationships fill your heart.

Reflection: In your journal, write about the joy and connection you experience when you interact with others with humility. How can you intentionally listen, empathize, and show kindness and respect to those around you? How does the act of embracing humility in your interactions contribute to your overall sense of love, unity, and understanding? How can you use your interactions to reflect God's love and bring joy to others through your humble and compassionate approach?

Prayer: Loving Father, I thank You for the gift of relationships and the joy that comes from interacting with others with humility. Help me to cultivate a humble heart that listens, empathizes, and loves genuinely. Show me how to reflect Your love and compassion in my interactions. Fill my heart with gratitude for Your grace and the joy that comes from humble relationships. In Jesus' name, I pray. Amen.

DAY 304

HUMILITY IN CELEBRATING DIVERSITY

Scripture: "There is neither Jew nor Gentile, neither slave nor free, nor is there male and female, for you are all one in Christ Jesus." - Galatians 3:28 (NIV)

Devotional: Today, let us explore the theme of humility in celebrating diversity. In God's kingdom, every person is uniquely created and valuable. Reflect on the joy and unity you experience when you embrace diversity with humility and love. Take a moment to pray and ask God to help you appreciate and celebrate the differences in others. Let gratitude for His creativity and the joy that comes from humble celebration of diversity fill your heart.

Reflection: In your journal, write about the joy and unity you experience when you celebrate diversity with humility. How can you intentionally appreciate and learn from the differences in others, treating them with respect, equality, and love? How does the act of embracing humility in celebrating diversity contribute to your overall sense of unity, justice, and inclusivity? How can you use your actions to reflect God's love and bring joy to others through your humble and accepting attitude?

Prayer: Heavenly Father, I thank You for the beauty of diversity and the joy that comes from celebrating it with humility. Help me to appreciate and learn from the differences in others. Show me how to treat all people with respect, equality, and love. Fill my heart with gratitude for Your creativity and the joy that comes from humble celebration of diversity. In Jesus' name, I pray. Amen.

DAY 305

HUMILITY IN FRIENDSHIP

Scripture: "A friend loves at all times, and a brother is born for a time of adversity." - Proverbs 17:17 (NIV)

Devotional: Today, let us explore the theme of humility in friendship. Humility calls us to love, support, and cherish our friends with a humble and selfless heart. Reflect on the joy and depth that come from embracing humility in our friendships. Take a moment to pray and ask God to help you become a humble and loyal friend, walking alongside others in both good times and adversity. Let gratitude for His gift of friendship and the joy that comes from humble companionship fill your heart.

Reflection: In your journal, write about the impact of humility in friendship. How can you intentionally love, support, and cherish your friends with a humble and selfless heart? How does the act of embracing humility in friendship contribute to your overall sense of connection, trust, and mutual growth? How can you use your friendships to reflect God's love and bring joy to others through your humble and loyal attitude?

Prayer: Gracious God, I thank You for the gift of friendship and the joy that comes from embracing humility in my relationships. Help me to love, support, and cherish my friends with a humble and selfless heart. Show me how to reflect Your love and bring joy through my humble and loyal friendship. Fill my heart with gratitude for the meaningful connections and the joy that comes from humble companionship. In Jesus' name, I pray. Amen.

DAY 306

HUMILITY IN CONFRONTING PRIDE

Scripture: "Pride goes before destruction, a haughty spirit before a fall." - Proverbs 16:18 (NIV)

Devotional: Today, let us explore the theme of humility in confronting pride. Pride hinders our relationships with God and others, but humility allows us to acknowledge our weaknesses and seek God's grace. Reflect on the joy and freedom you experience when you humbly confront and overcome pride. Take a moment to pray and ask God to reveal areas of pride in your life and grant you the humility to surrender them. Let gratitude for His grace and the joy that comes from humble surrender fill your heart.

Reflection: In your journal, write about the joy and freedom you experience when you confront pride with humility. How can you intentionally humble yourself before God and others, acknowledging your weaknesses and seeking His grace? How does the act of embracing humility in confronting pride contribute to your overall sense of freedom and spiritual growth? How can you use your experiences of overcoming pride to reflect God's love and bring joy to others through your humble and authentic journey?

Prayer: Heavenly Father, I thank You for Your grace and the joy that comes from confronting pride with humility. Help me to recognize areas of pride in my life and surrender them to You. Show me how to humble myself before You and others, seeking Your grace and guidance. Fill my heart with gratitude for Your love and the joy that comes from humble surrender. In Jesus' name, I pray. Amen.

DAY 307

HUMILITY IN RECEIVING CORRECTION

Scripture: "Whoever heeds discipline shows the way to life, but whoever ignores correction leads others astray." - Proverbs 10:17 (NIV)

Devotional: Today, let us focus on finding humility in receiving correction. None of us are perfect, and there are times when we need guidance and correction to grow. Reflect on the joy and growth you experience when you humbly receive correction with an open heart. Take a moment to pray and ask God to help you embrace correction and learn from it. Let gratitude for His guidance and the joy that comes from humble growth fill your heart.

Reflection: In your journal, write about the joy and growth you experience when you receive correction with humility. How can you intentionally cultivate a teachable spirit, listening to feedback and seeking personal growth? How does the act of embracing humility in receiving correction contribute to your overall sense of wisdom and maturity? How can you use your experiences of growth to reflect God's love and bring joy to others through your humble and receptive attitude?

Prayer: Gracious God, I thank You for Your guidance and the joy that comes from receiving correction with humility. Help me to cultivate a teachable spirit, listening to feedback and seeking personal growth. Show me how to reflect Your love and wisdom in my responses. Fill my heart with gratitude for Your guidance and the joy that comes from humble growth. In Jesus' name, I pray. Amen.

DAY 308

HUMILITY IN SEEKING HELP

Scripture: "For we do not have a high priest who is unable to empathize with our weaknesses, but we have one who has been tempted in every way, just as we are—yet he did not sin. Let us then approach God's throne of grace with confidence, so that we may receive mercy and find grace to help us in our time of need." - Hebrews 4:15-16 (NIV)

Devotional: Today, let us explore the theme of humility in seeking help. We all face moments of weakness and difficulty, and humility allows us to reach out for support and guidance. Reflect on the joy and comfort you experience when you humbly seek help from God and others. Take a moment to pray and ask God to give you the humility to acknowledge your need for help. Let gratitude for His grace and the joy that comes from humble reliance fill your heart.

Reflection: In your journal, write about the joy and comfort you experience when you seek help with humility. How can you intentionally reach out to God and others, acknowledging your need for support and guidance? How does the act of embracing humility in seeking help contribute to your overall sense of peace and trust in God's provision? How can you use your experiences of receiving help to reflect God's love and bring joy to others through your humble and grateful attitude?

Prayer: Heavenly Father, I thank You for Your grace and the joy that comes from seeking help with humility. Help me to acknowledge my need for support and guidance, reaching out to You and others. Show me how to reflect Your love and compassion in my actions. Fill my heart with gratitude for Your grace and the joy that comes from humble reliance. In Jesus' name, I pray. Amen.

DAY 309

HUMILITY IN PERSONAL ACHIEVEMENTS

Scripture: "Each of you should use whatever gift you have received to serve others, as faithful stewards of God's grace in its various forms." - 1 Peter 4:10 (NIV)

Devotional: Today, let us focus on finding humility in our personal achievements. The abilities and successes we have are gifts from God, and humility calls us to use them to serve others and bring glory to His name. Reflect on the joy and purpose you experience when you humbly use your achievements to make a positive impact. Take a moment to pray and ask God to help you remain humble and focused on serving others. Let gratitude for His gifts and the joy that comes from humble service fill your heart.

Reflection: In your journal, write about the joy and purpose you experience when you use your personal achievements to serve others with humility. How can you intentionally use your abilities, talents, and accomplishments to make a positive impact in the lives of others? How does the act of embracing humility in your achievements contribute to your overall sense of purpose and fulfillment? How can you use your successes to reflect God's love and bring joy to others through your humble and servant-hearted approach?

Prayer: Gracious God, I thank You for the gifts and achievements You have bestowed upon me, and the joy that comes from using them to serve others. Help me to remain humble and focused on bringing glory to Your name. Show me how to reflect Your love and make a positive impact through my abilities and accomplishments. Fill my heart with gratitude for Your gifts and the joy that comes from humble service. In Jesus' name, I pray. Amen.

DAY 310

HUMILITY IN DIFFICULT CONVERSATIONS

Scripture: "My dear brothers and sisters, take note of this: Everyone should be quick to listen, slow to speak and slow to become angry." - James 1:19 (NIV)

Devotional: Today, let us explore the theme of humility in difficult conversations. Interactions that challenge our views or confront sensitive topics require humility, empathy, and grace. Reflect on the joy and growth you experience when you approach difficult conversations with humility. Take a moment to pray and ask God to help you listen attentively, speak with love, and respond with humility. Let gratitude for His guidance and the joy that comes from humble dialogue fill your heart.

Reflection: In your journal, write about the joy and growth you experience when you engage in difficult conversations with humility. How can you intentionally listen attentively, speak with love, and respond with humility and grace? How does the act of embracing humility in difficult conversations contribute to your overall sense of empathy, understanding, and growth? How can you use your dialogue to reflect God's love and bring joy to others through your humble and respectful attitude?

Prayer: Loving Father, I thank You for Your guidance and the joy that comes from engaging in difficult conversations with humility. Help me to listen attentively, speak with love, and respond with humility and grace. Show me how to reflect Your love and wisdom in my dialogue. Fill my heart with gratitude for Your guidance and the joy that comes from humble dialogue. In Jesus' name, I pray. Amen.

DAY 311

HUMILITY IN TIMES OF CRITICISM

Scripture: "Whoever loves discipline loves knowledge, but whoever hates correction is stupid." - Proverbs 12:1 (NIV)

Devotional: Today, let us focus on finding humility in times of criticism. Criticism can be difficult to receive, but humility allows us to learn and grow from it. Reflect on the joy and wisdom you experience when you humbly accept and reflect upon constructive criticism. Take a moment to pray and ask God to help you embrace criticism with humility and use it for personal growth. Let gratitude for His guidance and the joy that comes from humble self-reflection fill your heart.

Reflection: In your journal, write about the joy and wisdom you experience when you embrace criticism with humility. How can you intentionally listen, reflect, and learn from constructive criticism, even when it is challenging to accept? How does the act of embracing humility in times of criticism contribute to your overall sense of self-improvement and maturity? How can you use your experiences of receiving criticism to reflect God's love and bring joy to others through your humble and teachable attitude?

Prayer: Heavenly Father, I thank You for Your guidance and the joy that comes from embracing criticism with humility. Help me to listen, reflect, and learn from constructive feedback. Show me how to use criticism for personal growth and self-improvement. Fill my heart with gratitude for Your guidance and the joy that comes from humble self-reflection. In Jesus' name, I pray. Amen.

DAY 312

HUMILITY IN PRAYER

Scripture: "Humble yourselves, therefore, under God's mighty hand, that he may lift you up in due time. Cast all your anxiety on him because he cares for you." - 1 Peter 5:6-7 (NIV)

Devotional: Today, let us explore the theme of humility in prayer. Prayer is an act of surrender and reliance on God's wisdom and power. Reflect on the joy and peace you experience when you approach prayer with humility. Take a moment to pray and ask God to help you humble yourself before Him, casting your anxieties upon Him. Let gratitude for His care and the joy that comes from humble prayer fill your heart.

Reflection: In your journal, write about the joy and peace you experience when you pray with humility. How can you intentionally humble yourself before God, surrendering your worries and seeking His guidance and comfort? How does the act of embracing humility in prayer contribute to your overall sense of trust and assurance in God's presence? How can you use your prayer life to reflect God's love and bring joy to others through your humble and reliant attitude?

Prayer: Loving Father, I thank You for the gift of prayer and the joy that comes from approaching You with humility. Help me to humble myself before You, surrendering my worries and seeking Your guidance and comfort. Show me how to reflect Your love and bring joy to others through my prayers. Fill my heart with gratitude for Your care and the joy that comes from humble prayer. In Jesus' name, I pray. Amen.

DAY 313

HUMILITY IN SHARING GOD'S WORD

Scripture: "And he said to them, 'Go into all the world and proclaim the gospel to the whole creation.'" - Mark 16:15 (NIV)

Devotional: Today, let us focus on finding humility in sharing God's Word. The message of the Gospel is powerful, and humility calls us to share it with love and compassion. Reflect on the joy and fulfillment you experience when you humbly proclaim God's Word to others. Take a moment to pray and ask God to give you the humility, courage, and wisdom to share His truth. Let gratitude for His salvation and the joy that comes from humble evangelism fill your heart.

Reflection: In your journal, write about the joy and fulfillment you experience when you share God's Word with humility. How can you intentionally proclaim the Gospel with love, grace, and humility, respecting the individual journeys and beliefs of others? How does the act of embracing humility in sharing God's Word contribute to your overall sense of purpose and obedience to God's calling? How can you use your voice to reflect God's love and bring joy to others through your humble and compassionate witness?

Prayer: Heavenly Father, I thank You for the salvation found in Your Word and the joy that comes from sharing it with others. Help me to proclaim the Gospel with humility, love, and compassion. Show me how to respect the individual journeys and beliefs of those I encounter. Fill my heart with gratitude for Your salvation and the joy that comes from humble evangelism. In Jesus' name, I pray. Amen.

Day 314

Humility in Encouraging Others' Gifts

Scripture: "Each of you should use whatever gift you have received to serve others, as faithful stewards of God's grace in its various forms." - 1 Peter 4:10 (NIV)

Devotional: Today, let us focus on finding humility in encouraging others' gifts. Humility calls us to recognize and uplift the unique gifts and talents of those around us. Reflect on the joy and inspiration that come from embracing humility in encouraging others' gifts. Take a moment to pray and ask God to help you become a humble encourager, affirming and empowering others in their God-given abilities. Let gratitude for His grace and the joy that comes from humble encouragement fill your heart.

Reflection: In your journal, write about the impact of humility in encouraging others' gifts. How can you intentionally recognize and uplift the unique gifts and talents of those around you with a humble and affirming heart? How does the act of embracing humility in encouraging others' gifts contribute to your overall sense of community, collaboration, and shared growth? How can you use your encouragement to reflect God's love and bring joy to others through your humble and empowering attitude?

Prayer: Loving Father, I thank You for Your grace and the joy that comes from embracing humility in encouraging others' gifts. Help me to recognize and uplift the unique gifts and talents of those around me with a humble and affirming heart. Show me how to reflect Your love and bring joy through my humble encouragement. Fill my heart with gratitude for Your guidance and the joy that comes from humble empowerment. In Jesus' name, I pray. Amen.

DAY 315

HUMILITY IN FORGIVENESS

Scripture: "Be kind and compassionate to one another, forgiving each other, just as in Christ God forgave you." - Ephesians 4:32 (NIV)

Devotional: Today, let us focus on finding humility in forgiveness. Forgiveness requires humility, grace, and a willingness to let go of resentment. Reflect on the joy and freedom you experience when you humbly forgive others as Christ has forgiven you. Take a moment to pray and ask God to help you cultivate a forgiving heart, releasing any bitterness or grudges. Let gratitude for His forgiveness and the joy that comes from humble reconciliation fill your heart.

Reflection: In your journal, write about the joy and freedom you experience when you forgive others with humility. How can you intentionally cultivate a forgiving heart, extending grace and mercy to those who have wronged you? How does the act of embracing humility in forgiveness contribute to your overall sense of healing, reconciliation, and peace? How can you use your acts of forgiveness to reflect God's love and bring joy to others through your humble and compassionate attitude?

Prayer: Heavenly Father, I thank You for Your forgiveness and the joy that comes from extending it to others. Help me to cultivate a forgiving heart, releasing any bitterness or grudges. Show me how to reflect Your love and bring healing and reconciliation through my acts of forgiveness. Fill my heart with gratitude for Your mercy and the joy that comes from humble reconciliation. In Jesus' name, I pray. Amen.

DAY 316

HUMILITY IN RELATIONSHIPS

Scripture: "Do nothing out of selfish ambition or vain conceit. Rather, in humility value others above yourselves." - Philippians 2:3 (NIV)

Devotional: Today, let us explore the theme of humility in relationships. Humility allows us to value and prioritize the needs of others above our own. Reflect on the joy and connection you experience when you approach relationships with humility. Take a moment to pray and ask God to help you value and love others selflessly. Let gratitude for His grace and the joy that comes from humble relationships fill your heart.

Reflection: In your journal, write about the joy and connection you experience when you value others above yourself with humility. How can you intentionally prioritize the needs, feelings, and well-being of others in your relationships? How does the act of embracing humility in relationships contribute to your overall sense of love, harmony, and empathy? How can you use your interactions to reflect God's love and bring joy to others through your humble and selfless attitude?

Prayer: Loving Father, I thank You for the gift of relationships and the joy that comes from valuing others with humility. Help me to prioritize the needs, feelings, and well-being of those around me. Show me how to reflect Your love and bring joy through my interactions. Fill my heart with gratitude for Your grace and the joy that comes from humble relationships. In Jesus' name, I pray. Amen.

DAY 317

HUMILITY IN TIMES OF SUCCESS

Scripture: "Humble yourselves, therefore, under God's mighty hand, that he may lift you up in due time." - 1 Peter 5:6 (NIV)

Devotional: Today, let us focus on finding humility in times of success. Success can bring recognition and praise, but humility calls us to recognize that our achievements are gifts from God. Reflect on the joy and gratitude you experience when you humbly attribute your successes to God's grace. Take a moment to pray and ask God to help you remain humble and use your successes for His glory. Let gratitude for His faithfulness and the joy that comes from humble success fill your heart.

Reflection: In your journal, write about the joy and gratitude you experience when you attribute your successes to God's grace with humility. How can you intentionally recognize that your achievements are gifts from Him and use them to glorify His name? How does the act of embracing humility in times of success contribute to your overall sense of gratitude, stewardship, and reliance on God's provision? How can you use your successes to reflect God's love and bring joy to others through your humble and grateful attitude?

Prayer: Gracious God, I thank You for Your faithfulness and the joy that comes from humbly acknowledging my successes as gifts from You. Help me to use my accomplishments to bring glory to Your name. Show me how to reflect Your love and make a positive impact through my successes. Fill my heart with gratitude for Your grace and the joy that comes from humble success. In Jesus' name, I pray. Amen.

DAY 318

HUMILITY IN ADVERSITY

Scripture: "But he said to me, 'My grace is sufficient for you, for my power is made perfect in weakness.' Therefore I will boast all the more gladly about my weaknesses, so that Christ's power may rest on me." - 2 Corinthians 12:9 (NIV)

Devotional: Today, let us explore the theme of humility in adversity. In times of difficulty and hardship, humility calls us to rely on God's strength and grace. Reflect on the joy and strength you experience when you humbly surrender your weaknesses to God. Take a moment to pray and ask God to help you find strength and peace in the midst of adversity. Let gratitude for His sustaining grace and the joy that comes from humble reliance fill your heart.

Reflection: In your journal, write about the joy and strength you experience when you surrender your weaknesses to God with humility. How can you intentionally rely on His strength and grace in times of adversity, acknowledging your need for His guidance and provision? How does the act of embracing humility in adversity contribute to your overall sense of trust, resilience, and spiritual growth? How can you use your experiences of relying on God to reflect His love and bring joy to others through your humble and steadfast attitude?

Prayer: Heavenly Father, I thank You for Your sustaining grace and the joy that comes from surrendering my weaknesses to You. Help me to rely on Your strength and guidance in times of adversity. Show me how to reflect Your love and bring comfort to others through my humble reliance on You. Fill my heart with gratitude for Your faithfulness and the joy that comes from humble surrender. In Jesus' name, I pray. Amen.

DAY 319

HUMILITY IN GRATITUDE

Scripture: "Give thanks in all circumstances; for this is God's will for you in Christ Jesus." - 1 Thessalonians 5:18 (NIV)

Devotional: Today, let us focus on finding humility in gratitude. Gratitude is an attitude that humbles us, reminding us of the blessings we have received. Reflect on the joy and contentment you experience when you cultivate a grateful heart. Take a moment to pray and thank God for His goodness and provision in your life. Let gratitude for His faithfulness and the joy that comes from humble gratitude fill your heart.

Reflection: In your journal, write about the joy and contentment you experience when you cultivate gratitude with humility. How can you intentionally count your blessings, expressing thankfulness to God and others for His provision and love? How does the act of embracing humility in gratitude contribute to your overall sense of joy, peace, and perspective? How can you use your grateful heart to reflect God's love and bring joy to others through your humble and appreciative attitude?

Prayer: Gracious God, I thank You for Your goodness and provision in my life. Help me to cultivate a grateful heart, counting my blessings and expressing thankfulness to You and others. Show me how to reflect Your love and bring joy through my humble gratitude. Fill my heart with gratitude for Your faithfulness and the joy that comes from humble appreciation. In Jesus' name, I pray. Amen.

DAY 320

HUMILITY IN WORK

Scripture: "Whatever you do, work at it with all your heart, as working for the Lord, not for human masters." - Colossians 3:23 (NIV)

Devotional: Today, let us focus on finding humility in our work. Humility calls us to approach our work with diligence, integrity, and a servant's heart. Reflect on the joy and purpose that come from embracing humility in our professional lives. Take a moment to pray and ask God to help you work with humility, recognizing that all work is an opportunity to serve Him and others. Let gratitude for His provision and the joy that comes from humble work fill your heart.

Reflection: In your journal, write about the impact of humility in your work. How can you intentionally approach your work with diligence, integrity, and a servant's heart? How does the act of embracing humility in your professional life contribute to your overall sense of purpose, fulfillment, and impact? How can you use your work to reflect God's love and bring joy to others through your humble and dedicated attitude?

Prayer: Heavenly Father, I thank You for the opportunity to work and the joy that comes from embracing humility in my professional life. Help me to approach my work with diligence, integrity, and a servant's heart. Show me how to reflect Your love and bring joy through my humble and dedicated work. Fill my heart with gratitude for Your provision and the joy that comes from humble service. In Jesus' name, I pray. Amen.

DAY 321

HUMILITY IN PARENT-CHILD RELATIONSHIPS

Scripture: "Children, obey your parents in everything, for this pleases the Lord." - Colossians 3:20 (NIV)

Devotional: Today, let us explore the theme of humility in parent-child relationships. Humility calls children to honor and obey their parents with a humble and respectful heart. Reflect on the blessings and growth that come from embracing humility in these relationships. Take a moment to pray and ask God to help you honor and obey your parents with humility, recognizing their love and guidance. Let gratitude for their care and the joy that comes from humble submission fill your heart.

Reflection: In your journal, write about the impact of humility in parent-child relationships. How can you intentionally honor and obey your parents with a humble and respectful heart? How does the act of embracing humility in these relationships contribute to your overall sense of gratitude, growth, and family harmony? How can you use your humility and obedience to reflect God's love and bring joy to your parents through your humble and appreciative attitude?

Prayer: Gracious God, I thank You for the blessing of parent-child relationships and the joy that comes from embracing humility within them. Help me to honor and obey my parents with a humble and respectful heart. Show me how to reflect Your love and bring joy through my humble submission. Fill my heart with gratitude for their care and the joy that comes from humble obedience. In Jesus' name, I pray. Amen.

DAY 322

HUMILITY IN HONORING OTHERS

Scripture: "Do nothing out of selfish ambition or vain conceit. Rather, in humility value others above yourselves." - Philippians 2:3 (NIV)

Devotional: Today, let us explore the theme of humility in honoring others. Humility calls us to value and honor others above ourselves, setting aside selfish ambition and conceit. Reflect on the significance of esteeming others and the joy that comes from humble recognition and respect. Take a moment to pray and ask God to help you see the worth and value in every individual. Let gratitude for His creation and the joy that comes from embracing humility in honoring others fill your heart.

Reflection: In your journal, write about the impact of humility in honoring others. How can you intentionally value and respect the inherent worth and dignity of every person you encounter? How does the act of embracing humility in honoring others contribute to your overall sense of empathy, inclusivity, and unity with others? How can you use your actions and words to reflect God's love and bring joy to others through your humble and honoring attitude?

Prayer: Gracious God, I thank You for Your creation and the joy that comes from embracing humility in honoring others. Help me to see the worth and value in every individual. Show me how to reflect Your love and bring joy through my humble recognition and respect. Fill my heart with gratitude for Your grace and the joy that comes from humble honor. In Jesus' name, I pray. Amen.

DAY 323

HUMILITY IN SERVICE TO OTHERS

Scripture: "For even the Son of Man did not come to be served, but to serve, and to give his life as a ransom for many." - Mark 10:45 (NIV)

Devotional: Today, let us focus on finding humility in service to others. Jesus Himself exemplified humble service, sacrificially giving His life to redeem us. Reflect on the profound example of Christ's humility in serving others and the joy that comes from imitating His servant-hearted attitude. Take a moment to pray and ask God to help you find opportunities to serve and love others selflessly. Let gratitude for His example and the joy that comes from humble service fill your heart.

Reflection: In your journal, write about the joy and fulfillment you experience when you serve others with humility. How can you intentionally seek out opportunities to serve, putting the needs of others before your own? How does the act of embracing humility in serving contribute to your overall sense of purpose, compassion, and unity with others? How can you use your acts of service to reflect God's love and bring joy to others through your humble and selfless attitude?

Prayer: Gracious God, I thank You for the example of Jesus and the joy that comes from serving others with humility. Help me to find opportunities to serve and love others selflessly. Show me how to reflect Your love and bring joy through my humble acts of service. Fill my heart with gratitude for Your grace and the joy that comes from humble service. In Jesus' name, I pray. Amen.

DAY 324

HUMILITY IN RECONCILIATION

Scripture: "If it is possible, as far as it depends on you, live at peace with everyone." - Romans 12:18 (NIV)

Devotional: Today, let us focus on finding humility in reconciliation. Conflict and disagreements can strain relationships, but humility calls us to pursue peace and seek reconciliation. Reflect on the joy and restoration you experience when you humbly work towards reconciling with others. Take a moment to pray and ask God to give you a humble and forgiving heart, willing to extend grace and seek restoration. Let gratitude for His reconciliation and the joy that comes from humble peacemaking fill your heart.

Reflection: In your journal, write about the joy and restoration you experience when you pursue reconciliation with humility. How can you intentionally seek peace, extend forgiveness, and bridge the gaps in your relationships? How does the act of embracing humility in reconciliation contribute to your overall sense of healing, unity, and compassion? How can you use your efforts towards reconciliation to reflect God's love and bring joy to others through your humble and reconciling attitude?

Prayer: Heavenly Father, I thank You for Your reconciliation and the joy that comes from pursuing peace with humility. Help me to seek reconciliation with others, extending forgiveness and bridging gaps in relationships. Show me how to reflect Your love and bring healing through my humble efforts. Fill my heart with gratitude for Your grace and the joy that comes from humble peacemaking. In Jesus' name, I pray. Amen.

DAY 325

HUMILITY IN DECISION-MAKING

Scripture: "Trust in the LORD with all your heart and lean not on your own understanding; in all your ways submit to him, and he will make your paths straight." - Proverbs 3:5-6 (NIV)

Devotional: Today, let us explore the role of humility in decision-making. Humility calls us to recognize our limitations and trust in God's guidance, rather than relying solely on our own understanding. Reflect on the peace and wisdom that comes from humbly submitting to God's will in our decisions. Take a moment to pray and ask God for His wisdom and guidance in your decision-making process. Let gratitude for His provision and the joy that comes from embracing humility in decisions fill your heart.

Reflection: In your journal, write about the impact of humility on your decision-making process. How can you intentionally surrender your own understanding and seek God's guidance in your decisions? How does the act of embracing humility in decision-making contribute to your overall sense of peace, trust, and alignment with God's will? How can you use your decisions to reflect God's love and bring joy to others through your humble and discerning attitude?

Prayer: Gracious God, I thank You for Your wisdom and the joy that comes from embracing humility in decision-making. Guide me in making choices that align with Your will. Show me how to reflect Your love and bring joy through my humble decisions. Fill my heart with gratitude for Your provision and the joy that comes from embracing humility. In Jesus' name, I pray. Amen.

DAY 326

HUMILITY IN RECEIVING PRAISE

Scripture: "Let someone else praise you, and not your own mouth; an outsider, and not your own lips." - Proverbs 27:2 (NIV)

Devotional: Today, let us focus on finding humility in receiving praise. It is natural to desire recognition, but humility calls us to deflect praise and give glory to God. Reflect on the joy and humility you experience when you receive praise with a grateful and humble heart. Take a moment to pray and ask God to help you remain humble in the face of admiration and to use your gifts for His glory. Let gratitude for His blessings and the joy that comes from humble praise fill your heart.

Reflection: In your journal, write about the joy and humility you experience when you receive praise with gratitude. How can you intentionally deflect praise, acknowledging that your abilities and achievements are gifts from God? How does the act of embracing humility in receiving praise contribute to your overall sense of gratitude, humility, and recognition of God's work in your life? How can you use moments of praise to reflect God's love and bring joy to others through your humble and God-centered attitude?

Prayer: Gracious God, I thank You for Your blessings and the joy that comes from receiving praise with humility. Help me to deflect praise and give glory to You. Show me how to reflect Your love and bring joy through my humble recognition of Your work in my life. Fill my heart with gratitude for Your gifts and the joy that comes from humble praise. In Jesus' name, I pray. Amen.

DAY 327

HUMILITY IN EMPATHY

Scripture: "Rejoice with those who rejoice; mourn with those who mourn." - Romans 12:15 (NIV)

Devotional: Today, let us explore the theme of humility in empathy. Empathy calls us to understand and share in the joys and sorrows of others, putting ourselves in their shoes. Reflect on the joy and connection you experience when you humbly empathize with others. Take a moment to pray and ask God to help you cultivate a compassionate and empathetic heart. Let gratitude for His love and the joy that comes from humble empathy fill your heart.

Reflection: In your journal, write about the joy and connection you experience when you empathize with others with humility. How can you intentionally seek to understand and share in the joys and sorrows of those around you? How does the act of embracing humility in empathy contribute to your overall sense of compassion, unity, and service? How can you use your empathy to reflect God's love and bring joy to others through your humble and understanding attitude?

Prayer: Heavenly Father, I thank You for Your love and the joy that comes from humbly empathizing with others. Help me to cultivate a compassionate and understanding heart. Show me how to reflect Your love and bring comfort through my humble empathy. Fill my heart with gratitude for Your grace and the joy that comes from humble connection. In Jesus' name, I pray. Amen.

DAY 328

HUMILITY IN WORDS

Scripture: "Do nothing out of selfish ambition or vain conceit. Rather, in humility value others above yourselves." - Philippians 2:3 (NIV)

Devotional: Today, let us focus on the importance of humility in our words. Humility calls us to speak with kindness, grace, and respect, valuing others above ourselves. Reflect on the impact our words have on others and the joy that comes from speaking with humility. Take a moment to pray and ask God to help you use your words to build up and encourage others. Let gratitude for His grace and the joy that comes from humble speech fill your heart.

Reflection: In your journal, write about the impact of humility in your words. How can you intentionally use your words to edify and encourage others, showing humility in your conversations? How does the act of embracing humility in your speech contribute to your overall sense of empathy, understanding, and unity with others? How can you use your words to reflect God's love and bring joy to others through your humble and uplifting attitude?

Prayer: Loving Father, I thank You for Your grace and the joy that comes from speaking with humility. Help me to use my words to build up and encourage others. Show me how to reflect Your love and bring joy through my humble speech. Fill my heart with gratitude for Your guidance and the joy that comes from humble words. In Jesus' name, I pray. Amen.

DAY 329

THE WISDOM OF HUMILITY

Scripture: "When pride comes, then comes disgrace, but with humility comes wisdom." - Proverbs 11:2 (NIV)

Devotional: Today, let us explore the wisdom of humility. Humility opens our hearts and minds to seek wisdom from God and others, while pride hinders growth and leads to disgrace. Reflect on the contrast between pride and humility and the wisdom that comes with a humble heart. Take a moment to pray and ask God to help you cultivate humility and seek His wisdom. Let gratitude for His guidance and the joy that comes from embracing humility fill your heart.

Reflection: In your journal, write about the wisdom that comes from embracing humility. How does humility allow you to learn from others and seek God's guidance? How can you intentionally cultivate a humble heart, surrendering your pride and embracing wisdom? How does the act of embracing humility in pursuit of wisdom contribute to your overall sense of growth, discernment, and alignment with God's will? How can you use your wisdom to reflect God's love and bring joy to others through your humble and wise attitude?

Prayer: Gracious God, I thank You for Your wisdom and the joy that comes from embracing humility. Help me to cultivate a humble heart and seek Your wisdom in all aspects of life. Show me how to reflect Your love and bring joy through my humble pursuit of wisdom. Fill my heart with gratitude for Your guidance and the joy that comes from embracing humility. In Jesus' name, I pray. Amen.

DAY 330

HUMILITY IN TRUSTING GOD'S PLAN

Scripture: "Trust in the LORD with all your heart and lean not on your own understanding; in all your ways submit to him, and he will make your paths straight." - Proverbs 3:5-6 (NIV)

Devotional: Today, let us focus on finding humility in trusting God's plan. Humility calls us to surrender our own understanding and trust in God's perfect wisdom and guidance. Reflect on the joy and peace you experience when you humbly trust in God's plan. Take a moment to pray and ask God to help you submit to His will and trust His path for your life. Let gratitude for His faithfulness and the joy that comes from humble trust fill your heart.

Reflection: In your journal, write about the joy and peace you experience when you trust God's plan with humility. How can you intentionally surrender your own understanding and submit to God's will in all areas of your life? How does the act of embracing humility in trusting God's plan contribute to your overall sense of peace, assurance, and alignment with His purpose? How can you use your trust in God's plan to reflect His love and bring joy to others through your humble and faithful attitude?

Prayer: Heavenly Father, I thank You for Your faithfulness and the joy that comes from trusting Your plan with humility. Help me to surrender my own understanding and submit to Your will. Show me how to reflect Your love and bring peace through my humble trust in Your guidance. Fill my heart with gratitude for Your provision and the joy that comes from humble trust. In Jesus' name, I pray. Amen.

DAY 331

HUMILITY IN MENTORSHIP

Scripture: "Be shepherds of God's flock that is under your care, watching over them—not because you must, but because you are willing, as God wants you to be; not pursuing dishonest gain, but eager to serve." - 1 Peter 5:2 (NIV)

Devotional: Today, let us explore the theme of humility in mentorship. Humility calls us to guide and mentor others with a selfless and servant-hearted attitude. Reflect on the joy and fulfillment that come from embracing humility in mentoring relationships. Take a moment to pray and ask God to help you become a humble and effective mentor, seeking the growth and success of those you guide. Let gratitude for His guidance and the joy that comes from humble mentorship fill your heart.

Reflection: In your journal, write about the impact of humility in mentorship. How can you intentionally guide and mentor others with a selfless and servant-hearted attitude? How does the act of embracing humility in mentorship contribute to your overall sense of purpose, impact, and investment in the lives of others? How can you use your mentorship to reflect God's love and bring joy to others through your humble and empowering attitude?

Prayer: Heavenly Father, I thank You for Your guidance and the joy that comes from embracing humility in mentorship. Help me to guide and mentor others with a selfless and servant-hearted attitude. Show me how to reflect Your love and bring joy through my humble and empowering mentorship. Fill my heart with gratitude for Your wisdom and the joy that comes from humble investment in others. In Jesus' name, I pray. Amen.

Day 332

Humility in Encouragement

Scripture: "Therefore encourage one another and build each other up, just as in fact you are doing." - 1 Thessalonians 5:11 (NIV)

Devotional: Today, let us focus on finding humility in encouragement. Encouragement is a powerful act of kindness that uplifts and strengthens others. Reflect on the joy and fulfillment you experience when you humbly encourage and build others up. Take a moment to pray and ask God to help you be a source of encouragement and support to those around you. Let gratitude for His love and the joy that comes from humble encouragement fill your heart.

Reflection: In your journal, write about the joy and fulfillment you experience when you encourage others with humility. How can you intentionally seek opportunities to uplift and build others up, offering words of kindness, affirmation, and support? How does the act of embracing humility in encouragement contribute to your overall sense of compassion, empathy, and unity with others? How can you use your encouragement to reflect God's love and bring joy to others through your humble and uplifting attitude?

Prayer: Gracious God, I thank You for Your love and the joy that comes from encouraging others with humility. Help me to be a source of support and encouragement to those around me. Show me how to reflect Your love and bring joy through my humble encouragement. Fill my heart with gratitude for Your grace and the joy that comes from humble encouragement. In Jesus' name, I pray. Amen.

DAY 333

THE HUMILITY OF JESUS

Scripture: "And being found in appearance as a man, he humbled himself by becoming obedient to death— even death on a cross!" - Philippians 2:8 (NIV)

Devotional: Today, let us reflect on the humility of Jesus Christ. Jesus, the Son of God, willingly humbled Himself, even to the point of death on the cross, to fulfill God's plan for salvation. Reflect on the depth of His humility and the profound impact it has on our lives. Take a moment to pray and thank Jesus for His example of humility and obedience. Let gratitude for His sacrifice and the joy that comes from embracing humility fill your heart.

Reflection: In your journal, write about the humility of Jesus and the impact it has on your life. How does His humility inspire you to live a humble life? How can you intentionally imitate His humility in your thoughts, words, and actions? How does the act of embracing humility in light of Jesus' sacrifice contribute to your overall sense of gratitude, surrender, and transformation? How can you use your life to reflect God's love and bring joy to others through your humble and Christ-like attitude?

Prayer: Loving Savior, I thank You for Your humility and the joy that comes from embracing humility in light of Your sacrifice. Help me to imitate Your humility in every aspect of my life. Show me how to reflect Your love and bring joy through my humble and Christ-like attitude. Fill my heart with gratitude for Your grace and the joy that comes from embracing humility. In Jesus' name, I pray. Amen.

DAY 334

THE JOY OF FOSTERING GRATITUDE

Scripture: "Give thanks to the Lord, for he is good; his love endures forever." - Psalm 118:1 (NIV)

Devotional: Today, let's focus on finding joy in fostering gratitude. Embrace the simplicity of cultivating a thankful heart and expressing gratitude to God and others.

Reflection: In your journal, write about the joy and transformation that come from fostering gratitude in your life. How can you be intentional about cultivating a thankful heart, finding joy in the simple blessings and moments of grace? How can you express gratitude to God and others, making thanksgiving a regular part of your prayers and interactions? How can you inspire others to find joy in fostering gratitude and to see God's love and provision in every circumstance?

Prayer: Gracious God, I thank You for the joy and transformation found in fostering gratitude. As I give thanks to You for Your goodness and love, help me to cultivate a grateful heart. May my life be marked by thanksgiving, and may my gratitude be a testimony to Your enduring love. In Jesus' name, I pray. Amen.

DAY 335

THE JOY OF SURRENDERING WORRIES

Scripture: "Cast all your anxiety on him because he cares for you." - 1 Peter 5:7 (NIV)

Devotional: Today, let's find joy in surrendering worries. Embrace the simplicity of laying your anxieties before God, trusting in His care and provision.

Reflection: In your journal, write about the joy and peace that come from surrendering worries to God. How can you be intentional about casting your anxieties on Him and finding solace in His loving care? How can you find joy in releasing the burden of worry, knowing that God is in control and will provide for your needs? How can you inspire others to find joy in surrendering their worries and to experience the peace that comes from trusting in God's unfailing love?

Prayer: Caring God, I thank You for the joy and peace found in surrendering my worries to You. As I cast my anxieties on You and trust in Your care, help me to find solace and rest in Your love. May my heart be free from the burden of worry, and may I inspire others to find joy in surrendering their worries to You. In Jesus' name, I pray. Amen.

DAY 336

THE JOY OF LAMENT AND HEALING

Scripture: "The Lord is close to the brokenhearted and saves those who are crushed in spirit." - Psalm 34:18 (NIV)

Devotional: Today, let's focus on finding joy in lament and healing. Embrace the simplicity of pouring out your heart before God, knowing that He is close to the brokenhearted and brings healing to the wounded soul.

Reflection: In your journal, write about the joy and comfort that come from lamenting before God and finding healing in His presence. How can you be intentional about expressing your grief, pain, and struggles before God, trusting in His love and compassion to mend your heart? How can you find joy in the process of healing, knowing that God brings restoration and wholeness to those who turn to Him in their brokenness? How can you inspire others to find joy in lament and healing, knowing that God's presence is a source of comfort and hope in times of pain?

Prayer: Healing God, I thank You for the joy and comfort found in lamenting before You and finding healing in Your presence. As I pour out my heart and struggles, help me to trust in Your love and compassion to mend my wounds. May the process of healing be a testimony to Your faithfulness and grace, and may I inspire others to find joy in turning to You in their brokenness. In Jesus' name, I pray. Amen.

DAY 337

THE JOY OF CELEBRATING GOD'S CREATION

Scripture: "The heavens declare the glory of God; the skies proclaim the work of his hands." - Psalm 19:1 (NIV)

Devotional: Today, let's find joy in celebrating God's creation. Embrace the simplicity of marveling at the beauty and intricacy of the world around you, recognizing it as a reflection of God's glory.

Reflection: In your journal, write about the joy and wonder that come from celebrating God's creation. How can you be intentional about spending time in nature and appreciating its beauty and splendor? How can you find joy in recognizing the Creator through His creation, seeing His handiwork in every detail of the world around you? How can you inspire others to find joy in celebrating God's creation, knowing that every aspect of nature points to His majesty and power?

Prayer: Creator God, I thank You for the joy and wonder found in celebrating Your creation. As I marvel at the beauty and intricacy of the world around me, help me to recognize Your glory in every detail. May my heart be filled with joy, knowing that all of nature proclaims the work of Your hands. In Jesus' name, I pray. Amen.

DAY 338

THE JOY OF FINDING STRENGTH IN WEAKNESS

Scripture: "But he said to me, 'My grace is sufficient for you, for my power is made perfect in weakness.' Therefore I will boast all the more gladly about my weaknesses, so that Christ's power may rest on me." - 2 Corinthians 12:9 (NIV)

Devotional: Today, let's focus on finding joy in finding strength in weakness. Embrace the simplicity of relying on God's grace and power to carry you through challenging times.

Reflection: In your journal, write about the joy and comfort that come from finding strength in weakness through God's grace. How can you be intentional about relying on His power in times of difficulty and vulnerability? How can you find joy in surrendering your weaknesses to God, knowing that His strength is made perfect in your inadequacies? How can you inspire others to find joy in finding strength in weakness, allowing Christ's power to rest on them and carry them through life's challenges?

Prayer: Mighty God, I thank You for the joy and comfort found in finding strength in my weakness through Your grace. As I rely on Your power in times of difficulty, help me to surrender my weaknesses to You. May Your strength be made perfect in my inadequacies, and may I inspire others to find joy in relying on Your power in their own weaknesses. In Jesus' name, I pray. Amen.

DAY 339

THE JOY OF REFLECTING ON GOD'S FAITHFULNESS

Scripture: "Your love, Lord, reaches to the heavens, your faithfulness to the skies." - Psalm 36:5 (NIV)

Devotional: Today, let's find joy in reflecting on God's faithfulness. Embrace the simplicity of looking back on your journey and recognizing the countless ways God has been faithful and true.

Reflection: In your journal, write about the joy and awe that come from reflecting on God's faithfulness throughout your life. How can you be intentional about remembering and celebrating the ways God has guided and provided for you? How can you find joy in the unchanging nature of God's love and His steadfast presence in every season of life? How can you inspire others to find joy in reflecting on God's faithfulness and to see His handiwork in their own lives?

Prayer: Faithful God, I thank You for the joy and awe found in reflecting on Your faithfulness in my life. As I remember the countless ways You have guided and provided for me, help me to celebrate and appreciate Your unchanging love and presence. May my life be a testament to Your faithfulness, and may I inspire others to find joy in reflecting on Your goodness and grace. In Jesus' name, I pray. Amen.

DAY 340

THE JOY OF RECEIVING UNEXPECTED BLESSINGS

Scripture: "Every good and perfect gift is from above, coming down from the Father of the heavenly lights, who does not change like shifting shadows." - James 1:17 (NIV)

Devotional: Today, let's focus on finding joy in receiving unexpected blessings. Embrace the simplicity of recognizing God's goodness and grace in the surprises He brings into your life.

Reflection: In your journal, write about the joy and gratitude that come from receiving unexpected blessings from God. How can you be intentional about recognizing and celebrating these unexpected gifts in your life? How can you find joy in God's unchanging love and His willingness to bless you in unexpected ways? How can you inspire others to find joy in unexpected blessings and to see them as expressions of God's love and care?

Prayer: Gracious God, I thank You for the joy and gratitude found in receiving unexpected blessings from You. As I recognize Your goodness and grace in the surprises You bring into my life, help me to celebrate and appreciate these unexpected gifts. May my heart be filled with joy, knowing that every good and perfect gift comes from You. In Jesus' name, I pray. Amen.

DAY 341

THE JOY OF CULTIVATING PATIENCE

Scripture: "Be still before the Lord and wait patiently for him." - Psalm 37:7 (NIV)

Devotional: Today, let's find joy in cultivating patience. Embrace the simplicity of waiting on God's timing and learning to trust His plans.

Reflection: In your journal, write about the joy and growth that come from cultivating patience in your life. How can you be intentional about waiting on God's timing and trusting His plans, even when things seem uncertain? How can you find joy in the process of waiting, knowing that God is working behind the scenes for your good? How can you inspire others to find joy in patience and to see waiting as an opportunity for deeper faith and reliance on God?

Prayer: Patient God, I thank You for the joy and growth found in cultivating patience. As I wait on Your timing and trust Your plans, help me to find joy in the process of waiting. May my heart be filled with faith and hope, knowing that You are working all things for my good. In Jesus' name, I pray. Amen.

DAY 342

THE JOY OF LETTING GO OF CONTROL

Scripture: "Trust in the Lord with all your heart and lean not on your own understanding; in all your ways submit to him, and he will make your paths straight." - Proverbs 3:5-6 (NIV)

Devotional: Today, let's find joy in letting go of control. Embrace the simplicity of trusting God completely and submitting to His guidance and plans for your life.

Reflection: In your journal, write about the joy and peace that come from surrendering control to God. How can you be intentional about trusting Him with every aspect of your life and leaning on His wisdom rather than your own understanding? How can you find joy in submitting to God's will and following His lead, knowing that His plans are always good and purposeful? How can you inspire others to find joy in letting go of control and trusting God's guidance, even in uncertain times?

Prayer: Trustworthy God, I thank You for the joy and peace found in letting go of control and trusting You completely. As I submit to Your guidance and plans, help me to find joy in surrendering my will to Yours. May my life be a testament to Your faithfulness and a reflection of the joy that comes from following Your lead. In Jesus' name, I pray. Amen.

DAY 343

THE JOY OF SHARING TESTIMONIES

Scripture: "I will declare your name to my people; in the assembly, I will praise you." - Psalm 22:22 (NIV)

Devotional: Today, let's focus on finding joy in sharing testimonies. Embrace the simplicity of declaring God's faithfulness and goodness in your life, praising Him in the assembly of believers.

Reflection: In your journal, write about the joy and gratitude that come from sharing testimonies of God's work in your life. How can you be intentional about sharing your faith journey and the ways God has transformed and blessed you? How can you find joy in praising God's name and testifying to His love and faithfulness, both within the church and beyond? How can you inspire others to find joy in sharing their testimonies, knowing that every story has the power to impact and encourage others on their own spiritual journey?

Prayer: Faithful God, I thank You for the joy and gratitude found in sharing testimonies of Your work in my life. As I declare Your name and praise You in the assembly, help me to inspire and encourage others on their spiritual journey. May my testimony be a reflection of Your love and faithfulness, and may it bring joy and hope to those who hear it. In Jesus' name, I pray. Amen.

DAY 344

THE JOY OF QUIET MOMENTS

Scripture: "Be still before the Lord and wait patiently for him." - Psalm 37:7 (NIV)

Devotional: Today, let's focus on finding joy in quiet moments. Embrace the simplicity of being still before God, waiting patiently in His presence, and finding solace in the peace that comes from resting in Him.

Reflection: In your journal, write about the joy and tranquility that come from embracing quiet moments with God. How can you be intentional about creating time for stillness and reflection in your daily life? How can you find joy in waiting patiently in God's presence, trusting in His timing and guidance? How can you inspire others to find joy in quiet moments with God, knowing that these moments are opportunities for deeper connection and understanding of His love?

Prayer: Loving Father, I thank You for the joy and tranquility found in quiet moments with You. As I rest in Your presence and wait patiently for Your guidance, help me to find solace in Your peace. May my moments of stillness be a source of renewal and connection with You, and may I inspire others to find joy in quiet moments with You. In Jesus' name, I pray. Amen.

DAY 345

THE JOY OF DREAMING BIG

Scripture: "For I know the plans I have for you," declares the Lord, "plans to prosper you and not to harm you, plans to give you hope and a future." - Jeremiah 29:11 (NIV)

Devotional: Today, let's find joy in dreaming big. Embrace the simplicity of envisioning a future filled with hope and possibility, trusting that God's plans for you are greater than anything you can imagine.

Reflection: In your journal, write about the joy and excitement that come from dreaming big and trusting in God's plans for your future. How can you be intentional about envisioning a future filled with hope and possibility? How can you find joy in taking bold steps towards your dreams, knowing that God is guiding and supporting you every step of the way? How can you inspire others to find joy in dreaming big and to seek God's direction and blessing for their own dreams and aspirations?

Prayer: Faithful God, I thank You for the joy and excitement found in dreaming big and trusting in Your plans for my future. As I envision a future filled with hope and possibility, help me to take bold steps towards my dreams, knowing that You are guiding and supporting me. May my dreams be aligned with Your purpose for my life, and may I inspire others to find joy in dreaming big. In Jesus' name, I pray. Amen.

DAY 346

THE JOY OF HUMILITY

Scripture: "Humble yourselves before the Lord, and he will lift you up." - James 4:10 (NIV)

Devotional: Today, let's focus on finding joy in humility. Embrace the simplicity of recognizing your dependence on God and humbling yourself before Him, knowing that true joy comes from surrendering your will to His.

Reflection: In your journal, write about the joy and peace that come from embracing humility before God. How can you cultivate a humble heart, recognizing your need for God's guidance and grace in every aspect of your life? How can you find joy in surrendering your will to God's and trusting in His plans for your life? How can you inspire others to find joy in humility and to seek God's wisdom and guidance with a humble and open heart?

Prayer: Gracious God, I thank You for the joy and peace found in humility before You. As I recognize my dependence on Your guidance and grace, help me to cultivate a humble heart. May I find joy in surrendering my will to Yours and trusting in Your plans for my life. In Jesus' name, I pray. Amen.

DAY 347

THE JOY OF WELCOMING STRANGERS

Scripture: "Do not forget to show hospitality to strangers, for by so doing some people have shown hospitality to angels without knowing it." - Hebrews 13:2 (NIV)

Devotional: Today, let's find joy in welcoming strangers. Embrace the simplicity of extending hospitality and kindness to those you encounter, recognizing that every stranger is a potential recipient of God's love.

Reflection: In your journal, write about the joy and fulfillment that come from welcoming strangers with hospitality and kindness. How can you be intentional about creating a welcoming and inclusive environment in your community and relationships? How can you find joy in connecting with strangers, knowing that you have the opportunity to reflect God's love and care to them? How can you inspire others to find joy in welcoming strangers and seeing them as fellow recipients of God's grace?

Prayer: Gracious God, I thank You for the joy and fulfillment found in welcoming strangers with hospitality and kindness. As I connect with others, help me to create a welcoming and inclusive environment where Your love is reflected. May every interaction with a stranger be an opportunity to show Your love and grace, and may I inspire others to find joy in welcoming strangers. In Jesus' name, I pray. Amen.

DAY 348

THE JOY OF HUMILITY

Scripture: "Humble yourselves before the Lord, and he will lift you up." - James 4:10 (NIV)

Devotional: Today, let's focus on finding joy in humility. Embrace the simplicity of recognizing your dependence on God and humbling yourself before Him, knowing that true joy comes from surrendering your will to His.

Reflection: In your journal, write about the joy and peace that come from embracing humility before God. How can you cultivate a humble heart, recognizing your need for God's guidance and grace in every aspect of your life? How can you find joy in surrendering your will to God's and trusting in His plans for your life? How can you inspire others to find joy in humility and to seek God's wisdom and guidance with a humble and open heart?

Prayer: Gracious God, I thank You for the joy and peace found in humility before You. As I recognize my dependence on Your guidance and grace, help me to cultivate a humble heart. May I find joy in surrendering my will to Yours and trusting in Your plans for my life. In Jesus' name, I pray. Amen.

DAY 349

THE JOY OF WELCOMING STRANGERS

Scripture: "Do not forget to show hospitality to strangers, for by so doing some people have shown hospitality to angels without knowing it." - Hebrews 13:2 (NIV)

Devotional: Today, let's find joy in welcoming strangers. Embrace the simplicity of extending hospitality and kindness to those you encounter, recognizing that every stranger is a potential recipient of God's love.

Reflection: In your journal, write about the joy and fulfillment that come from welcoming strangers with hospitality and kindness. How can you be intentional about creating a welcoming and inclusive environment in your community and relationships? How can you find joy in connecting with strangers, knowing that you have the opportunity to reflect God's love and care to them? How can you inspire others to find joy in welcoming strangers and seeing them as fellow recipients of God's grace?

Prayer: Gracious God, I thank You for the joy and fulfillment found in welcoming strangers with hospitality and kindness. As I connect with others, help me to create a welcoming and inclusive environment where Your love is reflected. May every interaction with a stranger be an opportunity to show Your love and grace, and may I inspire others to find joy in welcoming strangers. In Jesus' name, I pray. Amen.

DAY 350

THE JOY OF SIMPLE ACTS OF SERVICE

Scripture: "You, my brothers and sisters, were called to be free. But do not use your freedom to indulge the flesh; rather, serve one another humbly in love." - Galatians 5:13 (NIV)

Devotional: Today, let's focus on finding joy in simple acts of service. Embrace the simplicity of serving others humbly and with love, recognizing that every act of kindness has the potential to bring joy to both the giver and the receiver.

Reflection: In your journal, write about the joy and fulfillment that come from serving others with love and humility. How can you be intentional about seeking opportunities to perform acts of service in your daily life? How can you find joy in the selflessness of serving, knowing that you are following Christ's example of love and compassion? How can you inspire others to find joy in simple acts of service and to see them as expressions of God's love in action?

Prayer: Loving Father, I thank You for the joy and fulfillment found in simple acts of service. As I humbly serve others with love, help me to find joy in following Christ's example of selflessness. May every act of service be a reflection of Your love and a source of joy and hope to those I serve. In Jesus' name, I pray. Amen.

DAY 351

THE JOY OF FORGIVING YOURSELF

Scripture: "If we confess our sins, he is faithful and just and will forgive us our sins and purify us from all unrighteousness." - 1 John 1:9 (NIV)

Devotional: Today, let's find joy in forgiving yourself. Embrace the simplicity of accepting God's forgiveness and extending that same grace to yourself.

Reflection: In your journal, write about the joy and freedom that come from forgiving yourself and accepting God's forgiveness. How can you let go of past mistakes and embrace the new beginning God offers through His grace? How can you find joy in God's unconditional love and the assurance of His forgiveness, knowing that you are redeemed and made new in Christ? How can you inspire others to find joy in forgiving themselves and experiencing the freedom of God's grace?

Prayer: Merciful God, I thank You for the joy and freedom found in forgiving myself. As I accept Your forgiveness and let go of past mistakes, help me to embrace the new beginning You offer through Your grace. May my life be a testimony to Your love and redemption, and may I inspire others to find joy in forgiving themselves and experiencing Your transformative grace. In Jesus' name, I pray. Amen.

Day 352

The Joy of Learning from Creation

Scripture: "Ask the animals, and they will teach you, or the birds in the sky, and they will tell you; or speak to the earth, and it will teach you, or let the fish in the sea inform you." - Job 12:7-8 (NIV)

Devotional: Today, let's focus on finding joy in learning from God's creation. Embrace the simplicity of observing nature and its lessons, recognizing the wisdom and glory of the Creator.

Reflection: In your journal, write about the joy and wisdom that come from learning from the natural world around you. How can you be intentional about spending time in nature and observing its wonders? How can you apply the lessons from creation to your own life, drawing inspiration and guidance from God's handiwork? How can you share the joy of learning from creation with others, encouraging them to see God's wisdom and love reflected in His creation?

Prayer: Creator God, I thank You for the joy and wisdom found in learning from Your creation. As I observe nature and its wonders, help me to recognize Your handiwork and find inspiration in Your wisdom. May the lessons from creation guide me in my journey and be a testament to Your glory. In Jesus' name, I pray. Amen.

DAY 353

THE JOY OF EMBRACING DIVERSITY

Scripture: "For just as each of us has one body with many members, and these members do not all have the same function, so in Christ, we, though many, form one body, and each member belongs to all the others." - Romans 12:4-5 (NIV)

Devotional: Today, let's focus on finding joy in embracing diversity. Embrace the simplicity of appreciating the uniqueness of each individual and recognizing the beauty of unity in diversity.

Reflection: In your journal, write about the joy and enrichment that come from embracing diversity in your community and relationships. How can you cultivate a spirit of inclusivity and respect for different cultures, backgrounds, and perspectives? How can you learn from and celebrate the diversity of God's creation, recognizing that every individual is a valuable part of the body of Christ? How can you inspire others to find joy in embracing diversity and to build bridges of understanding and love?

Prayer: God of Unity, I thank You for the joy and enrichment found in embracing diversity. As I appreciate the uniqueness of each individual, help me to cultivate a spirit of inclusivity and respect. May my interactions with others reflect Your love and recognition of the value of every person. In Jesus' name, I pray. Amen.

DAY 354

THE JOY OF SUNRISE AND SUNSET

Scripture: "From the rising of the sun to the place where it sets, the name of the Lord is to be praised." - Psalm 113:3 (NIV)

Devotional: Today, let's find joy in the beauty of sunrise and sunset. Embrace the simplicity of witnessing the beginning and end of each day, marveling at God's creation and the gift of a new day.

Reflection: In your journal, write about the joy and awe you experience when watching sunrise and sunset. How can you be intentional about appreciating the beauty of each day's beginning and end? How can you use these moments to pause and reflect on God's faithfulness and grace? How can you find joy in the daily rhythm of sunrise and sunset, knowing that each day is a gift from God?

Prayer: Creator God, I thank You for the joy and awe found in witnessing sunrise and sunset. As I marvel at the beauty of each day's beginning and end, help me to appreciate the gift of time and the rhythm of life. May my heart be filled with gratitude for each new day, knowing that it is a gift from You. In Jesus' name, I pray. Amen.

DAY 355

THE JOY OF MAKING MEMORIES

Scripture: "The memory of the righteous is a blessing, but the name of the wicked will rot." - Proverbs 10:7 (NIV)

Devotional: Today, let's focus on finding joy in making memories. Embrace the simplicity of cherishing moments spent with loved ones, capturing life's special events, and creating lasting memories to look back on with gratitude.

Reflection: In your journal, write about the joy and significance of making memories with loved ones. How can you be intentional about creating meaningful experiences and capturing moments to cherish in the future? How can you use your memories as a source of gratitude and encouragement during challenging times? How can you inspire others to find joy in making memories and valuing the time spent with those they love?

Prayer: Loving Father, I thank You for the joy and significance found in making memories. As I cherish moments with loved ones and create lasting experiences, help me to appreciate the gift of time and relationships. May the memories I create be a blessing to me and to others, reflecting Your love and faithfulness. In Jesus' name, I pray. Amen.

DAY 356

THE JOY OF REST AND RENEWAL

Scripture: "Come to me, all you who are weary and burdened, and I will give you rest." - Matthew 11:28 (NIV)

Devotional: Today, let's find joy in rest and renewal. Embrace the simplicity of taking time to rest, both physically and spiritually. Allow yourself to step away from the busyness of life and find solace in God's presence, where true rest and renewal are found.

Reflection: In your journal, write about the joy and rejuvenation that come from making time for rest and spiritual renewal. How can you prioritize self-care and Sabbath rest in your daily life to find joy and balance? How can you deepen your relationship with God through moments of solitude and prayer? How can you inspire others to find joy and refreshment in God's presence?

Prayer: Gracious God, I thank You for the joy and rejuvenation found in rest and spiritual renewal. As I take time to be still in Your presence, help me to find solace and peace. May my moments of rest be a reflection of Your grace and a reminder of Your loving care for me. In Jesus' name, I pray. Amen.

DAY 357

THE JOY OF EMBRACING CHANGE

Scripture: "See, I am doing a new thing! Now it springs up; do you not perceive it? I am making a way in the wilderness and streams in the wasteland." - Isaiah 43:19 (NIV)

Devotional: Today, let's focus on finding joy in embracing change. Life is full of transitions and new opportunities. Embrace the simplicity of trusting God's plan and being open to the new things He is doing in your life.

Reflection: In your journal, write about the joy and growth that come from embracing change with faith and courage. How can you practice adaptability and resilience in the face of changes and challenges? How can you see change as an opportunity for God to work in your life and guide you towards new blessings? How can you encourage and support others as they navigate changes and uncertainties?

Prayer: Faithful God, I thank You for the joy and growth found in embracing change. As I navigate transitions and new opportunities, help me to trust Your plan and be open to the new things You are doing in my life. May I find strength and courage in You as I embrace the changes ahead. In Jesus' name, I pray. Amen.

DAY 358

THE JOY OF LENDING A LISTENING EAR

Scripture: "My dear brothers and sisters, take note of this: Everyone should be quick to listen, slow to speak, and slow to become angry." - James 1:19 (NIV)

Devotional: Today, let's focus on finding joy in lending a listening ear. Take time to be fully present and attentive when someone shares their thoughts, struggles, or joys with you. Embrace the simplicity of being there for others and offering them a safe space to be heard and understood.

Reflection: In your journal, write about the joy and connection you experience when you listen to others with empathy and compassion. How can you practice active listening in your daily interactions, both with loved ones and strangers? How can you be a source of comfort and support to those who need someone to listen without judgment? How can you use your gift of listening to bring joy and healing to others?

Prayer: Loving Father, I thank You for the joy and connection found in lending a listening ear. As I practice active listening, help me to be fully present and compassionate towards others. May my willingness to listen and understand reflect Your love and grace. In Jesus' name, I pray. Amen.

DAY 359

THE JOY OF LEARNING FROM CHILDREN

Scripture: "At that time, Jesus said, 'I praise you, Father, Lord of heaven and earth, because you have hidden these things from the wise and learned, and revealed them to little children.'" - Matthew 11:25 (NIV)

Devotional: Today, let's focus on finding joy in learning from children. Children have a unique way of seeing the world and embracing its wonders with curiosity and simplicity. Take time to engage with children, listen to their thoughts, and learn from their innocent perspective.

Reflection: In your journal, write about the joy and wisdom you gain when interacting with children. How can you approach life with childlike wonder and humility, embracing the simple joys and lessons in each day? How can you create opportunities to learn from children and nurture their spiritual growth? How can you share the joy of learning from children with others?

Prayer: Heavenly Father, I thank You for the joy and wisdom found in learning from children. As I interact with them, help me to embrace their innocent perspective and be open to the simple lessons they can teach. May my heart be filled with childlike wonder and humility, and may I nurture the spiritual growth of the young ones around me. In Jesus' name, I pray. Amen.

Day 360

The Joy of Awe and Wonder

Scripture: "When I consider your heavens, the work of your fingers, the moon and the stars, which you have set in place, what is mankind that you are mindful of them, human beings that you care for them?" - Psalm 8:3-4 (NIV)

Devotional: Today, let's find joy in awe and wonder. Take time to observe the beauty of the world around you, from the vastness of the night sky to the intricate details of a flower. Embrace the humility that comes from recognizing God's greatness and the privilege of being part of His creation.

Reflection: In your journal, write about the joy and awe you experience when contemplating the beauty of God's creation. How does the sense of wonder deepen your appreciation for the simplicity and complexity of life? How can you intentionally cultivate a spirit of awe and gratitude in your daily life to find joy in God's presence? How can you share this joy of awe and wonder with others?

Prayer: Creator God, I thank You for the joy and awe found in contemplating Your creation. As I marvel at the beauty of the world around me, help me to embrace humility and gratitude. May the sense of wonder in Your greatness and love inspire me to find joy in Your presence every day. In Jesus' name, I pray. Amen.

DAY 361

THE JOY OF BEING PRESENT

Scripture: "This is the day that the Lord has made; let us rejoice and be glad in it." - Psalm 118:24 (NIV)

Devotional: Today, let's focus on finding joy in being present. Embrace the gift of each moment, whether it's a quiet morning, a busy workday, or time spent with loved ones. Be intentional about being fully present, finding joy in the simplicity of being alive and aware of God's presence in every moment.

Reflection: In your journal, write about the joy and contentment you experience when you are fully present in the moment. How does being mindful of God's presence enrich your daily experiences and interactions? How can you cultivate a practice of mindfulness and gratitude to find joy in each day? How can you inspire others to embrace the joy of being present?

Prayer: Loving Father, I thank You for the joy found in being fully present in each moment. Help me to be mindful of Your presence and find joy in the simplicity of life's everyday experiences. May I rejoice and be glad in the day You have made, reflecting Your love and grace in every interaction. In Jesus' name, I pray. Amen.

DAY 362

THE JOY OF CREATING ART

Scripture: "In the beginning, God created the heavens and the earth."
- Genesis 1:1 (NIV)

Devotional: Today, let's find joy in creating art. Whether it's painting, drawing, writing, or any other form of artistic expression, embrace the creativity that God has placed within you. Use art as a way to celebrate God's creation and find joy in the act of bringing beauty into the world.

Reflection: In your journal, write about the joy and fulfillment you experience when creating art. How does the act of creating reflect the beauty and creativity of God? How can you make time for artistic expression in your daily life to find joy and inspiration? How can you use your art to share God's love and message with others?

Prayer: Creative God, I thank You for the joy and fulfillment found in creating art. As I embrace my creative abilities, help me to use art as a way to celebrate Your creation and share Your love with the world. May my artistic expression be a reflection of Your beauty and creativity. In Jesus' name, I pray. Amen.

DAY 363

THE JOY OF SIMPLE ACTS OF KINDNESS

Scripture: "And do not forget to do good and to share with others, for with such sacrifices God is pleased." - Hebrews 13:16 (NIV)

Devotional: Today, let's find joy in simple acts of kindness. Take time to extend a helping hand, offer a word of encouragement, or perform an act of service for someone in need. Embrace the joy that comes from sharing God's love through acts of kindness.

Reflection: In your journal, write about the joy and fulfillment you experience when showing kindness to others. How can you intentionally seek opportunities to perform simple acts of kindness in your daily life? How can you make kindness a consistent part of your character, reflecting God's love and grace to those around you? How can you inspire others to embrace the joy of spreading kindness?

Prayer: Loving Father, I thank You for the joy that comes from simple acts of kindness. As I extend a helping hand and share Your love with others, may my actions bring glory to Your name. Help me to be a vessel of Your kindness and grace, reflecting Your love in every act of service. In Jesus' name, I pray. Amen.

DAY 364

THE JOY OF OUTDOOR ADVENTURES

Scripture: "The Lord is my rock, my fortress, and my deliverer; my God is my rock, in whom I take refuge, my shield and the horn of my salvation, my stronghold." - Psalm 18:2 (NIV)

Devotional: Today, let's focus on finding joy in outdoor adventures. Take time to explore nature, whether through hiking, camping, or simply taking a leisurely walk in the park. Embrace the beauty of God's creation and find solace in His presence as you immerse yourself in the great outdoors.

Reflection: In your journal, write about the joy and peace you experience during outdoor adventures. How does being in nature uplift your spirit and remind you of God's strength and protection? How can you prioritize spending time outdoors to find joy, rest, and inspiration? How can you use your love for nature to bring awareness to environmental stewardship and God's creation?

Prayer: Creator God, I thank You for the joy and peace found in outdoor adventures. As I immerse myself in the beauty of nature, help me to appreciate Your creation and find solace in Your presence. May my time spent outdoors be a reminder of Your strength and protection, and may I be a steward of Your creation. In Jesus' name, I pray. Amen.

DAY 365

EMBRACING GOD'S PURPOSE THROUGH REST

Scripture: "Come to me, all you who are weary and burdened, and I will give you rest." - Matthew 11:28 (NIV)

Devotional: Today, let us focus on embracing God's purpose through rest. In the midst of busyness and demands, God invites us to find rest and renewal in Him. Reflect on the significance of embracing rest as a means of aligning with His purpose for your life. Take a moment to pray and ask God to help you prioritize rest and seek His peace in times of weariness. Let gratitude for the gift of rest and the joy that comes from surrendering to His rejuvenation fill your heart.

Reflection: In your journal, write about the impact of embracing God's purpose through rest. How can you intentionally prioritize rest and seek His peace in times of weariness and busyness? How does the act of embracing God's purpose through rest contribute to your overall sense of physical, emotional, and spiritual well-being? How can you use your commitment to rest to reflect God's love and bring joy to others through your humble and refreshed attitude?

Prayer: Heavenly Father, I thank You for the gift of rest and the joy that comes from finding renewal in You. Help me to prioritize rest and seek Your peace in times of weariness. Show me how to reflect Your love and bring joy through my commitment to rest. Fill my heart with gratitude for this gift and the joy that comes from embracing Your purpose through rest. In Jesus' name, I pray. Amen.

'ONE GOOD THING' CHALLENGE

When I was struggling most with my internal demons, I was wallowing in a personal negative spiral of darkness and finding every negative aspect of life. One of the best ways I was able to turn my life around was to find 'One Good Thing' each day to turn my outlook on life to the positive. It was a difficult challenge at first as I was trying to do it alone and hiding my shame and depression. The best medicine I experienced was finding 'One Good Thing' each day to find the positive side of life. My journey would have been easier if I would have opened up and had others helping me seek the positive. Positive changes accelerated when I found more people who shared a positive outlook. I challenge you to be a part of a new community of support. Share 'One Good Thing' that happened to you today. Your daily share can be something as simple as a sunset you saw that touched you in a positive way; a blessing you received from a friend or a total stranger; the peaceful breeze on a warm summer night; or something that has special meaning to you. You can find 'One Good Thing' each day. The more you look for it, the more 'Good Things' you will begin to find each day and as a result, will look for opportunities for you to be the Good in the world! Join the challenge, share your experiences and pay it forward on our website www.barefootkicker.com so we will provide a list for others to see and aspire to find their 'Good Thing" each day!

About the Author

Michael Farrell

Michael Farrell, a life thriver, was raised in the suburbs of DC had a rather standard upbringing while dealing with growing social anxiety. His life thrived in his secure social bubble until life changed at 13 years of age with a move to Michigan and a new life. His involvement in sports, scouts, and faith were the path to positive enlightenment and overcoming his anxieties. As a graduate of Adrian College participating in the storied football program and the first Adrian team to participate in the NCAA Division III national playoffs. Mike went on to build a successful career in Materials Management, married and built a family through adoption and became an award-winning advocate for adoptive families.

He authored his Memoir "When Perfection Isn't Perfect" in 2022 and more information can be found on his website www.barefootkicker.com.